Communications
in Computer and Information Science   1081

Commenced Publication in 2007
Founding and Former Series Editors:
Phoebe Chen, Alfredo Cuzzocrea, Xiaoyong Du, Orhun Kara, Ting Liu,
Krishna M. Sivalingam, Dominik Ślęzak, Takashi Washio, Xiaokang Yang,
and Junsong Yuan

Editorial Board Members

More information about this series at http://www.springer.com/series/7899

Rodrigo Pereira dos Santos ·
Cristiano Maciel · José Viterbo (Eds.)

Software Ecosystems, Sustainability and Human Values in the Social Web

8th Workshop of Human-Computer Interaction Aspects
to the Social Web, WAIHCWS 2017
Joinville, Brazil, October 23, 2017
and 9th Workshop, WAIHCWS 2018
Belém, Brazil, October 22, 2018
Revised Selected Papers

 Springer

Editors
Rodrigo Pereira dos Santos (iD)
Federal University of the State
of Rio de Janeiro
Rio de Janeiro, Brazil

Cristiano Maciel (iD)
Federal University of Mato Grosso
Cuiabá, Brazil

José Viterbo (iD)
Fluminense Federal University
Niterói, Brazil

ISSN 1865-0929 ISSN 1865-0937 (electronic)
Communications in Computer and Information Science
ISBN 978-3-030-46129-4 ISBN 978-3-030-46130-0 (eBook)
https://doi.org/10.1007/978-3-030-46130-0

This Springer imprint is published by the registered company Springer Nature Switzerland AG
The registered company address is: Gewerbestrasse 11, 6330 Cham, Switzerland

Preface

This volume contains the extended versions of the selected papers published from two previous editions of the Workshop of Human-Computer Interaction Aspects to the Social Web (WAIHCWS 2017-2018). The event was co-located with the Brazilian Symposium on Human Factors in Computing Systems (IHC), promoted by the Brazilian Computer Society (SBC).

With this book, entitled *Software Ecosystems, Sustainability and Human Values in the Social Web*, WAIHCWS celebrates 10 editions of a successful forum for researchers and practitioners who are interested in opportunities and challenges related to the social web in the context of the human-computer interaction.

The social web, people, and organizations are all interconnected concepts. As such, social web is a key element in allowing different people through diverse applications develop over many platforms and embed them in distinct devices. In the last decade, the Web has faced frequent changes and adapted itself to new ways of interaction promoted by different devices. This is a consequence of emerging technologies that are more accessible and present in the people's mind, transforming the way they relate to each other.

The topics included in this volume cover the following fields connected to the social web: user experience, emotion analysis, interoperability, systems-of-information systems, knowledge-intensive processes, ontology, transportation domain, mobile systems, privacy policies, digital legacy, social networks, recommendation models, scientific events, accessible web, software ecosystems, and sustainability. All the accepted chapters were peer reviewed by three qualified reviewers chosen from our Scientific Committee based on their qualifications and experience.

The editors wish to thank the dedicated Scientific Committee members and the external reviewers for their contributions to this rich material. We also thank Springer for their trust and for publishing the extended proceedings of WAIHCWS 2017–2018.

March 2020

Rodrigo Pereira dos Santos
Cristiano Maciel
José Viterbo

Organization

Scientific Committee

Alfredo Sánchez	LANIA, Mexico
Anna Beatriz Marques	UFC, Brazil
Artur Kronbauer	UNIFACS, Brazil
Awdren Fontão	UFMS, Brazil
Candi Cann	Baylor University, USA
Cesar A. Collazos	Universidad del Cauca, Colombia
Daniel Lucrédio	UFSCar, Brazil
Davi Viana	UFMA, Brazil
Elisa Yumi Nakagawa	USP, Brazil
George Valença	UFRPE, Brazil
Igor Scaliante Wiese	UTFPR, Brazil
Isabela Gasparini	UDESC, Brazil
José Maria David	UFJF, Brazil
Joshua Enslen	United States Military Academy at West Point, USA
Kamila Rodrigues	USP, Brazil
Luciana Zaina	UFSCar, Brazil
Marília S. Mendes	UFC, Brazil
Noor Hasrina Bakar	Universiti Kebangsaan Malaysia, Malaysia
Patrícia C. de Souza	UFMT, Brazil
Rafael Capilla	Universidad Rey Juan Carlos, Spain
Regina Braga	UFJF, Brazil
Tihomir Orehovački	Juraj Dobrila University of Pula, Croatia
Valdemar Graciano Neto	UFG, Brazil
Vinícius Carvalho Pereira	UFMT, Brazil

External Reviewer

Isabel Villanes	UFAM, Brazil

Organizing Committee

Rodrigo Pereira dos Santos	UNIRIO, Brazil
Cristiano Maciel	UFMT, Brazil
José Viterbo	UFF, Brazil

Contents

•

Towards a Conceptual Model to Understand Software Ecosystems Emerging from Systems-of-Information Systems

Valdemar Vicente Graciano Neto[1($\boxtimes$)], Rodrigo Pereira dos Santos[2],
Davi Viana[3], and Renata Araujo[4]

[1] PPGCC - Programa de Pós-Graduação em Ciência da Computação,
Instituto de Informática, UFG - Universidade Federal de Goiás, Goiânia, Brazil
valdemarneto@ufg.br
[2] PPGI – Programa de Pós-Graduação em Informática, UNIRIO – Universidade
Federal do Estado do Rio de Janeiro, Rio de Janeiro, Brazil
rps@uniriotec.br
[3] PPGCC - Programa de Pós-Graduação em Ciência da Computação,
UFMA - Universidade Federal do Maranhão, São Luís, Brazil
davi.viana@lsdi.ufma.br
[4] Grupo de Pesquisa e Inovação em Ciberdemocracia (CIBERDEM),
Universidade Presbiteriana Mackenzie, São Paulo, Brazil
renata.araujo@mackenzie.br

Abstract. Software vendors are currently concerned to the development of software-intensive Information Systems (IS) that interoperate among themselves using web and/or mobile platforms. This phenomenon has risen the concept of System-of-Information Systems (SoIS), which is a set of interoperable and independent IS that exchange data and combine synergistic services to achieve broader business goals. Since new types of sociotechnical relations can be established to increase gains and productivity in this context, considering technical, business and social dimensions, Software Ecosystems (SECO) emerge as a theoretical lens to study SoIS. We claim that the software ecosystem perspective can foster the comprehension about SoIS by exploring the existing relations among constituent ISs within a SoIS as well as the nature of such relations. The main contribution of this work is to offer a conceptual model to support SoIS analysis under a SECO perspective, rising the idea of EcoSoIS. Coding analysis was applied to extract the main concepts of SoIS and SECO from experts and to link these concepts to compose the conceptual model. Smart city was used as an example to illustrate how the model could be instantiated. Once the model enables a conformant representation of the smart city SoIS under a SECO lens, we believe that the model can be used for other SoIS.

Keywords: Systems-of-Information Systems · Systems-of-Systems · Software Ecosystems · Human factors · Information Systems

© Springer Nature Switzerland AG 2020
R. P. d. Santos et al. (Eds.): WAIHCWS 2017/2018, CCIS 1081, pp. 1–20, 2020.
https://doi.org/10.1007/978-3-030-46130-0_1

1 Introduction

Software vendors have been concerned to the development of software-intensive Information Systems (IS), i.e., systems that can automate a set of business processes of their customers [10]. Recently, due to the dynamics of new open and collaborative business scenarios, those IS have demanded to support high levels of interoperability, which consists of the ability of two systems to exchange data and to use this data to perform some action [34]. One remarkable branch of IS software development is the Social Web, where social IS software such as Facebook and Instagram not only support social interaction, but also play the role of platforms for marketing and purchases, besides enable interoperability with several other IS platforms. Therefore, these social IS should be designed to support interoperability, creating more complex business processes, and opening up new business chains [13, 16].

This phenomenon has risen the concept of System-of-Information Systems (SoIS), i.e., a set of interoperable ISs (termed in this context as constituent systems) that exchange data and services to achieve some major business goal [2, 3, 33]. SoIS can be highly dynamic, enabling new constituents to join (or leave) the SoIS to contribute with their specific functionalities and to achieve more complex behaviors. As such, relations among interoperable IS are of utmost importance as novel businesses can be created and sustained, while other businesses can generate more value if those relations are better investigated and understood [6, 7]. New relations can also be established to increase gains and productivity considering technical, business and social dimensions. In turn, an entire business domain can be damaged or eliminated due to harmful business relations among IS. This scenario requires new views on how to understand, describe and analyze the relations among such systems, bringing the vision of ecosystems surrounding them.

The concept of Software Ecosystem (SECO) has helped researchers and practitioners to model and analyze several existing relations among software elements that compose a technological platform, as well as their internal and external actors, such as Apple SECO, SAP SECO or Eclipse SECO [14]. They are important as they enable to predict how to obtain value, return on investment, and how relations between distinct products can be beneficial or harmful for the business progress in IS development [15]. Moreover, SECO is a theoretical lens that enables a joint analysis to interplay social, technical and business dimensions of a system.

We claim that SECO can foster the comprehension about SoIS by exploring the existing relations among IS constituents within a SoIS as well as the nature of such relations. This concern may raise the concept of System-of-Information Systems Ecosystem (EcoSoIS), i.e., a SECO that involves the development and interoperable activity within a set of ISs working together to support business and social goals. This new scenario is worth to be investigated since new IS relations can benefit/harm an organization that delivers products and services, and whose clients can combine those assets to cooperatively work together to achieve a bigger business value [17].

The main contribution of this work is introducing a conceptual model that materializes the interplay between the concepts of IS, SoIS, and SECO that raises the so-called EcoSoIS concept. We aim EcoSoIS to be established as a theoretical lens to support a joint analysis of SoIS under social, technical, and organizational perspectives. We explore the concept of EcoSoIS based on the existing background on IS, SoIS, and SECO, and apply coding analysis on the report of four experts to externalize a conceptual model. Our aim is that the conceptual model can futurely be used to support analysis of SoIS under a SECO perspective, offering a broader and systemic panorama of SoIS to deal with its inherent complexity. Moreover, we explore how SECO perspectives can help us to identify elements that affect SoIS as well as to come up with a research agenda.

This work is organized as follows: Sect. 2 brings a motivational example for illustration purposes; Sect. 3 presents the foundations of IS, SoIS and SECO as the basis for proposing the concept of EcoSoIS in Sect. 4, raising the conceptual model for EcoSoIS, and establishing a research agenda for EcoSoIS; finally, Sect. 5 concludes the paper with final remarks.

2 Motivational Example

To foster the discussion aimed at this work, we provide (i) a motivational example that can illustrate (ii) the envisioned problems, (iii) how the interplay between IS, SoS and SECO can help, and (iv) further needs that justify the contribution brought by this work.

Illustrative Scenario. We motivate the discussion by analysing a smart city, which is remarkably a System-of-Systems (SoS), i.e., it is formed by operationally independent systems managed by different institutions and owners, which turns the architecture to be inherently dynamic, once systems can be turned on or off, join or leave (in geographic terms) the smart city system at any time. Isolated IS that are part of a smart city do not achieve many results working in isolation. This fact demands that different IS that are operational independent and managed by different institutions interoperate, raising a SoIS, as will be explained later in this text. Indeed, an IS for management of public finances and another one for management of power distribution should be interconnected to support more complex behaviors, such as to provide some discount in the property taxes due to a citizen that saves energy. However, this scenario starts to be more interesting when non-trivial aims are analyzed. Figure 1 depicts a situation that potentially involves diverse dimensions of a smart city (social, technical, and business), besides the involved constituent systems of that SoIS. For instance, autonomous cars that join the smart city infrastructure (that include a platform and network) can offer novel services for the population, such as a ride for people when the buses are too crowded. This could be rewarded by a discount given by the fuel station, because the municipal government also gave discount on taxes to the fuel station to reimburse its discount to the driver that improved the quality of city mobility for population. This is a simplistic scenario, but that can be even more complex, tangled and involve many other actors, firms, private and public institutions, and members of society that could offer services for the city.

Problems. Some problems arise from the illustrated scenario, such as: (i) interoperability, since for those systems need to communicate and, to enable that new and not predicted systems join the smart city platform, it should necessarily be an open platform, which characterizes itself (the entire smart city) a SECO; (ii) complexity, since thousands or millions of systems can coexist in a smart city, which can be really hard to deal with and abstractions are necessary; and (iii) interplay between SECO dimensions of a smart city SoIS. A smart city inherently involve several IS and also other types of systems. Providing exchanges of services and reimbursements as illustrated is possible via IS since these systems deal with and process the involved information to provide the intended behavior. However, the illustrated situation is only possible *if* SoIS has SECO characteristics, since a *social* need (need of citizens to arrive in their work damaged by the overcrowded public buses) can be solved in the *technical* perspective (a new system that join the city can support that need and solve the problem) by the establishment of crossed advantages via business alliances between companies (the public sector and private companies) and the citizens as well.

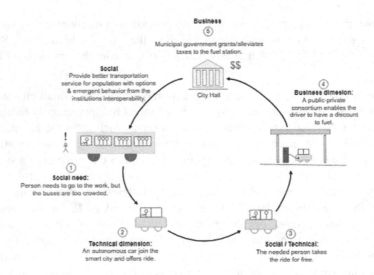

Fig. 1. Illustrative example of three dimensions involved in a Smart city SoIS.

Interplay Between IS, SoS, and SECO. We claim that this type of behavior is only possible to be provided if many IS are joined and able to interoperate in the smart city environment, forming a SoIS (SoS with IS) to establish complex and dynamic business processes, and being open to evolve as a SECO to cohabit the three dimensions.

Gaps and Expected Contributions. There is a need to deal with SoIS under a SECO viewpoint. Hence, the idea of EcoSoIS does not exactly comprise the creation of a new term, but more the externalization of a need to look at SoIS not only from a technical or business perspective, but as a triangulation of the three aspects (social, technical, and business). Some gaps emerge from this scenario, including some challenges that are already recognized in the SoIS context, such as (i) management of inter-organizational and flexible business processes that emerge from the interoperability between independent IS and the inherent dynamic architecture of a smart city [22], (ii) need for formalisms and models to support a precise modeling and analysis of that complex scenario, enabling the visualization of potential interoperability links among constituent systems of a smart city, to enable a better visualization of the interplay that can be established between social, technical, and business perspectives to provide better services for the population, and (iii) need of tools to support the use of the formalisms proposed in the last enunciated gaps. The first step towards contributing to the illustrated problem is to establish the foundations for EcoSoIS, which proposes to look at SoIS from a SECO theoretical lens, since its conception and engineering until the management of the SoIS. To do it, we elaborated a conceptual model shown in this work as the main contribution, which summarizes the main concepts that should be the starting point to engineer sustainable smart cities systems that enable an easy integration of non-predicted systems and creation of value chains between companies, people and public sector to achieve the major objective of a smart city: improvement of life quality for citizens. We argue that this is only possible if a SoIS (as a smart city) is planned and developed under a SECO perspective that enables the interplay between the three SECO dimensions, establishing virtuous circles that can spontaneously emerge. Hence, EcoSoIS is more a name of a paradigm to study SoIS under a SECO perspective. Next sections deepen the foundations to better understand the proposal.

3 Background

This section introduces the main concepts to help us to define the object on which we are exploring in this paper.

3.1 Information Systems

According to the General Systems Theory (GTS) [14], systems are a set of elements dynamically interrelated to perform activities aiming at achieving a specific goal, while consuming energy, materials or data (input) and producing new forms of energy, materials or data (output). The concept of system has been useful to describe and understand the behavior of complex structures in many different knowledge domains [11] - from Biology to Social Sciences, and particularly in IS area.

An *information system* is a set of interrelated components that collect (or retrieve), process, store and distribute information [13]. The use of a mural on an organization wall, where different people share information, can be understood as an IS composed by humans and objects (the mural) where information can be processed, published, retrieved and deleted to cope with the organizational goal of communicating relevant things. Especially in the web and mobile eras, IS research and practice are facing challenges, for example, how to establish and control IS borders and how to govern the software supply network formed over them considering the social web.

Conceptually, IS may also comprise software or other computer technology as one of its elements (computer-based or software-intensive IS). Therefore, the use of an organization's information portal where people report and share news and information using their smartphones with the aim of establishing communication is also an IS. Very often, the term 'information system' is used to specifically refer to a software that processes information for a set of users. These IS are often called as computer-based or *software-intensive IS*. This is correct if we consider that software is composed of interrelated parts (modules, functions etc.) with the aim of processing information. However, one should not restrict his understanding of IS to the software element. Henceforth, we consider software-intensive IS and IS as interchangeable terms.

Back to the GTS [14], systems exist inside other systems (they vary in hierarchy and complexity); they are usually open (they interact with the environment in which they are inserted in and learn with this interaction); their operation depends on their internal structure (the relationship performed by their elements); and they exhibit rules that help them to balance and regulate their operation (they try to avoid variations that will harm their operation or they are able to change and adapt to new balanced situations). Systems behavior can be predictable and descriptive (e.g., computers) or unpredictable, complex and difficult to be described (e.g., social or economic systems).

3.2   Systems-of-Information Systems

Systems can be combined to form what is termed Systems-of-Systems (SoS). SoS are alliances of independent systems (called constituents) that are combined to interoperate and achieve some more complex behavior. Such behavior could not be obtained from these independent systems working separately [1]. SoS share a set of well-defined characteristics [1, 16]: (i) managerial independence of constituents, i.e., constituents are owned and managed by distinct organizations and stakeholders; (ii) operational independence of constituents, as constituents also perform their own activities, even when they are not contributing to the accomplishment of one of the SoS' functionalities; (iii) distribution, i.e., constituents require a network technology to communicate among themselves; (iv) evolutionary development, as SoS evolve due to the evolution of its constituent parts; and (v) emergent behavior, which corresponds to complex functionalities that arise from the interoperability among constituents.

Moreover, SoS should exhibit an opportunist nature, i.e., a system should be able to join other systems to form a SoS that accomplishes a mission, leaving the SoS when the mission finishes. Dynamic architecture has also been considered a remarkable SoS characteristic. In the context of the social web and human aspects research, SoS is still barely investigated, as methods, techniques and tools largely focus on the technical aspects. However, organizational aspects emerge, for example, how developers and users interact with those complex systems in order to accomplish their missions and how the social web environment can aid those stakeholders to communicate and collaborate in order to evolve such systems with new requirements [18].

System-of-Information Systems (SoIS) are a particular type of SoS composed by IS. SoIS are a synergistic alliance of constituent IS concerned to accomplish a set of pre-defined, emerging goals. SoIS have emerged due to the increasing trend of cooperation between distinct companies, combining efforts by offering more complex functionalities as a combination of their own IS [2, 3]. A SoIS is dynamically generated through the alliances among other software-intensive IS products, interoperating to create value to owners and new clients.

Examples of this trend include Virtual Organizations, which comprise several distinct organizations that spontaneously get together over a social web environment, working cooperatively (including their software-intensive ISs) in the context of a specific project, leaving it in the next moment. Movements such as Clean Web[1], in which social network software and information technology are articulated to solve issues related to environmental resources constraints, represent trends in SoIS research and practice [16].

3.3 Software Ecosystems

Software vendors co-evolve their market capabilities around innovation: they work cooperatively and competitively to support and to develop new products, to satisfy customer needs and to innovate continuously [4]. These tight networks of suppliers, distributors, outsourcing companies, developers of related products or services, technology providers, and a plethora of other organizations affect and are affected by the creation and delivery of software vendor's products and services. Aligned to this viewpoint, researchers have coined a new perspective to analyze the software industry, known as Software Ecosystems (SECO) [6, 7].

SECO is an effective way to construct software on top of a common technological platform (e.g., operating system, application, software asset base etc.), by composing applications and technologies developed by multiple actors (i.e., third-party developers, communities and organizations) [16]. Moreover, a SECO comprises a foundation technology or set of components used beyond a single firm which brings multiple parties together for a common business/development purpose or to solve a common problem. In this context, the ecosystem platform can be seen as a broker that supports a social web based on interaction among organizations, developers and users [19, 20, 21].

Pragmatically speaking, we can conjecture that a SECO is formed by a *software platform* and a *community* [23]. Such platform is composed of many *artifacts*, which can be *products* or *services*. In turn, a community is formed by (1) hubs, i.e., main agents in a SECO (e.g., leading organizations that polarize a SECO), and (2) niche players, i.e., all stakeholders who collectively affect a SECO from individual actions onto the platform (e.g., each of them can influence, commit to, contribute to, promote, or extend the platform). Both types of central players in a SECO are associated to a role (e.g., keystone, developers, reseller, end-user etc.).

This common technological platform can originate software products that cooperate and/or compete in the market, or even other relations can be drawn among them. SECO is also characterized by both software production and consumption relations. These relations can be established with third-party developers, communities and/or other organizations to foster components development, supply and evolution in a large ecosystem created over the common technological platform. Examples of SECO

---

[1] http://goo.gl/5oZjss.

include Microsoft SECO, iPhone SECO and Drupal SECO [5]. A SECO can also be part of another SECO, e.g., Microsoft CRM SECO is part of Microsoft SECO.

For example, in iPhone SECO, Apple is the hub (keystone) and external developers, users around the world, smartphone resellers and software/hardware suppliers are the community (niche players). iOS is the platform, which comprises the operating systems but also the API (support for application development), Apple Store (main distribution channel) and Apple Web Portal (for community assistance and transparency), i.e., a plethora of different SECO artifacts and services. In addition, there is a business office responsible for designing, evolving and engaging the community based on the SECO keystone, in which the role of evangelist takes place.

In the social and business perspectives, a SECO provides a complementary organizational view to SoS development, which defines roles, rules of interaction, collaboration and synergistic capabilities for its constituent systems. There exist many similarities between SoS characteristics [9] and SECO technical challenges [15], e.g., how to ensure platform stability, simplicity, security, reliability, and evolution. As such, we can conjecture that SECO and SoIS may also hold intrinsic and synergistic relations that can be explored.

3.4   Modeling Ecosystems in IS

Ecosystems are a very natural and suitable concept to help IS researchers and practitioners in coping with the complexity of contemporary information systems to be built today - connected, adaptive, emergent etc. Recent research starts to figure out how to methodologically guide the process of specifying, building and managing ecosystems, including its underlying technological support [26–28]. They all agree that the first step is to have a conceptual foundation and model as a reference to analyse, design, engineer or managem different types of ecosystems.

Benedict [26] suggested a typology, built upon the results of a literature review, organizing ecosystems in two dimensions: system types (socio-economic, socio-technical or technical systems) and platform focus (non-platform, platform and interorganizational network systems). This typology gave ground to the definition of a conceptual model which focuses three aspects of ecosystem specification: (i) goal modeling (internal organizational/platform goals, external/environment goals and restrictions); (ii) platform modelling (boundary resources, technological architecture, governance measures); and (iii) ecosystem modeling (structural/behavioral modeling of actors/relationships, dynamics, products, business models, technology and interfaces).

Saleh and Abel [27] defined a conceptual model where SoIS are special types of SoS, which, in their turn, are specializations of digital ecosystems - all of them are complex systems. They explicitly distinguish IS from SoIS, interpreting IS as simple systems, meanwhile SoIS as complex systems. Hanelt and Kolbe [28] discusses the need to theorize genuine IS phenomena and the complex nature of the interaction between IS and ecosystems. They conducted a literature review in order to draw the conceptual landscape of ecosystems research following the following dimensions: ecosystems comprehension (ecosystems definition, type of ecosystems, type of ecosystem members, ecosystem layers, ecosystems characteristics), foundation of ecosystems (motivation, theoretical foundation, role of IS, type of IS), and contextual application of ecosystems (industry setting, ecology layer). We discuss this perspective in the next section.

4 Systems-of-Information Systems Ecosystems

Noticeably, SoIS has a strong business nature and constituents' development becomes business-driven [2, 3]. One of the challenges is to cope with the complexity of describing, developing and operating SoIS and the SECO that emerge from it, considering its intrinsic attributes - structure, complexity, openness, need for balance and regulation, and different levels of behavior predictability - and achieving its desired business goals. Moreover, the diversity and amount of stakeholders' relationships mainly supported by a social web environment come up as a critical concern for both organizations and customers.

Due to its nature, a SoIS can hold an entire business, involving suppliers, clients, partners and technological platforms that act as an entire main technology that supports that business. Then, we glimpse that the association among distinct software-intensive IS creates a major/new SECO comprising the emergent behavior resulting from the association of their different business goals into a new and common one - a System-of-Information Systems Ecosystem (EcoSoIS[2]).

Figure 2 illustrates our understanding about EcoSoIS. Interoperability links are established among diverse IS to create novel functionalities and to explore or conceive business opportunities. This happens due to inter-organizational alliances and cooperation. This joint set of IS raises a SoIS at a technical level. We suppose that each organization that composes this 'consortium' owns a different IS platform. However, SoIS only deals with the technical aspects. Other remarkable elements, such as business goals, players, agents, value chains, and production/consumption relations, which are inherent elements in a SECO, are not covered by SoIS technical dimension. As a result, business and social dimensions emerge since the 'ecosystem' nature of the resulting IS involves the interoperable IS that are included in a SoIS context. As shown in Fig. 2, a SECO can emerge or not from an IS that forms a SoIS. For example, ecosystems emerge from IS1 and IS3. However, the EcoSoIS is formed by the relations established with the ecosystems and with the IS themselves.

Rewriting the view presented in Santos et al. [23], EcoSoIS are formed of a *software platform* (the set of interoperable IS that form the underlying SoIS) and a *community*. Such platform is composed of many IS *constituents*, which can offer *products* or *services*, establishing new business links among the involved companies and enabling new functionalities to address new business opportunities. Such community is formed by (1) *hubs*, i.e., main agents in a SECO (e.g., leading organizations that polarize a SECO), and (2) *niche players*, i.e., all stakeholders who collectively affect a SECO from individual actions onto the platform (e.g., each of them can influence, commit to, contribute to, promote, or extend the platform). Both types of central

---

[2] Henceforth, EcoSoIS will be used interchangeably to express singular and plural forms, i.e., "System-of-Information Systems Ecosystems" and "Systems-of-Information Systems Ecosystems".

players in a SECO are associated to a *role* (e.g., keystone, developers, reseller, end-user etc.). Under the perspective presented in Fig. 2, for simplicity, we have a 1:1 relation, i.e., one SECO emerges from one and only one IS. However, we do not discard the possibilities that one SECO can be formed by multiple IS.

This phenomenon creates a SECO that surrounds the SoIS and involves other inner ecosystems that are inserted in that context. Thus, we have envisioned an EcoSoIS (or SoIS SECO), i.e., a SECO the surrounds the inner ecosystems that can be associated with some of the constituent IS that composes a SoIS, besides the value chains, players, business goals and agents that emerge from the interoperability between the various IS that compose a SoIS. Regarding the presence of the 'human element' within the EcoSoIS, an actor appears as a SoIS player (or even a customer) that interacts with the system through its constituents (i.e., SoIS interaction borders) or performs a role in the business process that supports the SoIS mission.

One example for exercising the EcoSoIS perspective lies on the domain of government and electronic democracy [12]. Public institutions have different IS and databases that need to interoperate so as to provide effective services to citizens (e.g., civil identification IS should be integrated with the police department IS and/or the public health system etc.). Additionally, each distinct IS in this context may be maintained within a specific SECO involving vendors, developers, legislation, auditors, citizens etc. Their relationships vary depending on the diversity of business needs, i.e., new procedures or changes in legislation.

Demands for transparency and accountability put a different agent in this ecosystem - the citizen/society, particularly those able to develop their own applications using open data provided by public institutions by force of law. IS developed by individuals or group of individuals are a new SECO in these EcoSoIS, pushing the previous ecosystem to new behavior, results and innovation. Looking at this scene from the perspective of EcoSoIS might help to develop a broader view of this ecosystem arrangements, business potential, emergent behavior, and innovation.

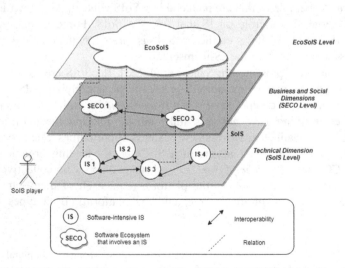

Fig. 2. An illustration of an EcoSoIS.

4.1   Research Opportunities for EcoSoIS

The relations between SoS and SECO have been a recent investigation topic [8, 9]. Association between SoIS and SECO raises a new research branch and opens new perspectives of investigation for a topic in the interdisciplinary research on IS development, human interaction and social web trends. Given that, we list some research challenges (RC) that we envisioned comprising EcoSoIS, as follows:

RC1. Reference Architectures for EcoSoIS. Reference architectures comprise an abstract specification of a family of similar architectures, documenting their similarities, variabilities, and inherent properties [24, 25]. One single IS can occasionally originate a surrounding, vibrant SECO. This can be born due to new commercial partners, business expansion, or market pressure. A single SECO has its own relations, e.g., competition or predation. A reference architecture can be established for this single SECOs, modeling software/business properties and constraints, such as promised/obtained advantages (e.g., access to private organizational databases whose data may be valuable to the business of a third party). However, when we think on EcoSoIS, we not only consider the inherent relations that exist inside a SECO that emerges from one or more IS, but we need to consider all the relations between the interoperable IS of such SoIS, as well as the possible competing ecological relations existing when we consider the entire SECO that emerge from the SoIS. We claim that modeling reference architectures for EcoSoIS is even more complex than for ECOS, and comprises an important challenge.

RC2. Innovation with EcoSoIS. We claim that a single SECO, by itself, does not support innovation in the broad meaning of the word. A SECO that emerges from a single IS can exploit commercial relations, and the variabilities eventually available in the single IS in which such SECO is based on. However, it is not possible, for example, to design novel functionalities as an arrangement of constituents' functionalities, as can be done in the context of a SoIS at runtime. As such, the potential for innovation of a EcoSoIS seems to be more expressive than a single SECO. New businesses can come up from exploring existing relationships within a SoIS. Strategies should be drawn on how to recognize innovation opportunities within an EcoSoIS, as well as how to foster the emergence of innovation opportunities derived from a SoIS creation. Co-innovation is also an important issue to be handled in EcoSoIS, i.e., how to create new functionalities and tools upon the SECO platform aided by the community's members. To support open innovation in EcoSoIS, social web data mining and analysis could support ecosystem maintenance and evolution.

RC3. Conceptual Modeling in EcoSoIS. EcoSoIS is a novel approach to work on and understand business, social, and technical dimensions of SoIS. As such, EcoSoIS implementation demands models, methods, and tools to support its visualization, specification, and engineering. Conceptual models are primary elements for these purposes. These models capture the essential characteristics of the domain being modelled as well as the relevant relations that can be established between the represented concepts. Later, the conceptual model can be adopted either to (i) characterize that domain, enabling to classify a target being analyzed as belonging or not to that class studied; and (ii) to be instantiated, creating a concrete model that represents an instance of the domain being analyzed. The next section displays the methodology we adopted to advance the state-of-the-art on EcoSoIS by externalizing a conceptual model to represent relevant concepts of this emerging topic.

4.2   Towards an EcoSoIS Conceptual Model

SoIS are often large-scale, formed by multiple heterogeneous and independent systems, being also inherently complex. As such, it is difficult to readily understand the impacts of all the interoperability links on the SoS and how to draw complex, emergent behaviors. Moreover, the ecosystem that emerges from a SoIS is also complex, demanding abstraction techniques to deal with such complexity. A conceptual model can help on that need by capturing and abstracting the main concepts of both domains, removing unnecessary details. Therefore, the model can be important when planning and developing an infrastructure for a smart city, for example, to guarantee that that SoIS will enable the spontaneous creation of value chains, as discussed by the motivational example. Moreover, the conceptual model can also support the elaboration of tools to support modeling, simulation and analysis of potential relations that can emerge and systems that can be part of an EcoSoIS.

To elaborate a conceptual model that compiles the important concepts and materializes the idea of EcoSoIS, we followed a qualitative methodology based on the collection of codes. Codes (as keywords, phrases, mnemonics, or numbers) can represent the concepts, aspects or relation regarding some phenomenon. The process of coding became popular as basic technique of the Grounded Theory Methodology [32]. However, we can apply the process of coding for organizing the set of concepts and keywords regarding some research area. In coding process, the researchers apply their knowledge and past research experiences about topic of investigation [31]. Codes and subcodes facilitate the development of taxonomies. Relationship and perspective codes support the development of conceptual models and theories. We applied Atlas.TI tool (https://atlasti.com/) that automatically extract the codes from the texts.

The conception of the model involved four experts (authors of this paper): one expert in SoIS (Expert 1, First Author) and three experts in SECO (Experts 2, 3, and 4). One of the three SECO experts (Expert 2) is also an expert in qualitative methods. The Expert 1 was involved in the conduction of Step 1. Next, Expert 2 independently conducted the Step 2 by extracting the relevant concepts. Step 3 was conducted by Expert 3, and Step 4 was conducted by Expert 2. Expert 1 and Expert 4 acted as peer-reviewers for the obtained model, culminating in the delivered version. The elaborated methodology is composed of four well-defined steps. as follows:

4.2.1   Step 1: Characterization of a Smart City as a SoIS

This step exploits the main characteristics of a SoIS considering an instance of the problem. We chose smart city as an instance of SoIS to investigate how a SECO could emerge. Smart cities are interesting for this scenario since several suppliers play and offer hardware and software platforms to work as the platform of the ecosystem that can potentially emerge. Author 1 was invited to write an excerpt of text that describe what is understood as a SoIS, since this is his area of expertise.

Smart cities have gained attention over the last years. The potential for advances and promotion of life quality and sustainability have motivated investments and research development, creating a new trend of research in many directions, including human computer interaction and software engineering. Smart cities are one of the Grand Challenges for Information Systems Research in Brazil for 2016 to 2026 [31]. The Brazilian Network of Smart and Human Cities[3] has also been created to foster the development of such paradigm in Brazil, as well as the Initiative on Emerging and Sustainable Cities (ICES)[4], which has been created by the Inter-American Development Bank (IDB) for Latin America scale, and allows to explore and compare more than 150 quantitative parameters fed by the public opinion through interactive maps and dashboards to support the development and monitoring of smart cities.

By definition, a SoIS is a class of SoS in which one or more constituents are software-intensive IS [29]. A smart city has several IS involved in its architecture, since the popularity and gains obtained from software-based systems to automate public government and resources management have motivated the development and acquisition of many software-intensive IS. If we consider only a city hall, many IS are used to monitor public security, public health system, and transparency in public administration. A smart city matches the well-defined characteristics that should be covered to consider a system as a SoIS, which are:

Operational Independence of Constituents: A smart city is potentially composed of many independent systems that manages important and individual concerns of a city. They are not interdependent and, in most cases, the interruption in the operation of one or more of them may impact, but not prevent the operation of the other ones. If we think about some constituents, such as smart traffic control system, autonomous cars, emergency and crisis response system, public health support, and education system support, they are individually operated, and interruption of one or more will not prevent the entire city normal routine; so, smart city constituents are operationally independent;

Managerial Independence of Constituents: Canalogously, the aforementioned systems are produced, owned, and managed by independent companies and entities. Hence, they also hold managerial independence;

Distribution: All the constituents of a smart city are distributed and can connect to public internet services to query about meteorological conditions, traffic jams and alternative routes, news about public investments, best prices of fuel vendors, and communication with other systems and vehicles to enable a fluid traffic. Distribution is an inherent property of a smart city;

Evolutionary Development: The entire city and its architecture evolve and change along time due to people who join and leave the city with their autonomous cars and mobile phones. Smart building systems can be upgraded to new versions due to the acquisition of new constituents, and smart hospitals can include smart ambulances to their architecture, turning the development of a smart city inherently evolutionary due to the evolution of their constituents; and

---

[3] http://www.redebrasileira.org/.

[4] http://www.urbandashboard.org/aboutus?lang=EN.

Emergent Behaviors: Smart cities architects and engineers can design intended holistic behaviors to exploit individual capabilities provided by several of the constituents that form a smart city. Such behaviors can provide better quality of life, a fluid traffic, better temperatures inside smart hospitals and buildings by exploiting information provided by meteorological services/smart sensors based on temperatures externally collected and in each room, pavement and common areas; and autonomous cars can regulate speed and smoke production to help in air quality improvement. Then, elaborated behaviors can be achieved by exploring interoperability between the constituents that form a smart city.

4.2.2   Step 2. Application of Coding Analysis

This step comprises the application of coding analysis to select the concepts and relations from the discourse analysis. In this work, we apply the coding process for identifying a conceptual model for EcoSoIS. We consider the following activities: (i) Identification of relevant aspects SoIS and SECO - each aspect can be seen as a code; and (ii) Creation of relationships between the identified aspects - such relationships are important to understand the aspects of SoIS and SECO and how they can integrate to foster the creation of the EcoSoIS conceptual model. This step was conducted by Experts 3 and 4. By applying coding analysis, a set of main excerpts were extracted and originated the concepts to materialize the model and relations, as described in Table 1.

Table 1. Process of extraction of codes from the textual description of EcoSoIS

Excerpt	Concepts and Relations Extracted
"A SoIS is a class of SoS in which one or more constituents are software-intensive IS"	A SoIS is a SoS. A SoS is formed by constituents
SoS share important characteristics: (i) managerial independence, i.e., constituents are owned and managed by distinct organizations and stakeholders, (ii) operational independence, i.e. constituents perform their own activities, even when they are not accomplishing one of the SoS missions, (iii) distribution, i.e. constituents are dispersed requiring connectivity to communicate, (iv) evolutionary development, i.e. SoS evolve due to the evolution of their constituents, environment, and/or missions, and (v) emergent behavior, i.e. complex functionalities emerge from the interoperability among constituents	Emergent Behavior is a property of Systems-of-Systems Evolutionary Development is a property of Systems-of-Systems Distribution is a property of Systems-of-Systems Operational Independence of constituents is a property of Systems-of-Systems Managerial Independence of constituents is a property of Systems-of-Systems
These authors claim that SoIS should (i) be concerned with the flow of information and knowledge among different IS, (ii) address the impact of the interrelationships between different SoIS (SoIS as constituents themselves), (iii) be responsible for generating information from emergent SoIS, and (iv) tackle information interoperability as a key issue	SoIS is associated with Information and Knowledge Flow SoIS is associated with the Impact of the interrelationships SoIS is associated with Information generation SoIS is associated with Interoperability
Functionalities offered by constituents are often referred to as capabilities	Capability is expected by functionality Functionality is a property of constituent

According to what is presented in Fig. 3, a SoIS is a SoS, which has the following properties: managerial and operational independence of constituents, distribution, evolutionary development, and emergent behavior. Besides, SoS (as SoIS) are formed by constituent systems that have independent existence and functionalities, which materialize the expected capabilities to achieve a goal. SoIS is actually a set of inter-operable IS (which are constituents) associated via interoperability. Some characteristics are specifically related to SoIS, such as (i) Information generation, (ii) Information and Knowledge Flow, and (iii) Impact of the interrelationships on the SoIS.

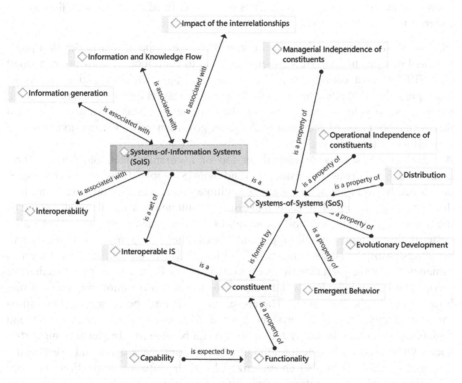

Fig. 3. A conceptual model for SoIS.

4.2.3   Step 3: Preliminary Description of the Emerging SECO and Identification of SECO Elements

In this step, Expert 2 was invited to textually discuss how a SECO could emerge from the same SoIS investigated in Steps 1 and 2, towards an EcoSoIS. By definition, a SECO is a system formed by a common technological platform that comprises applications and technologies developed by multiple actors, either internal or external to the organization that leverage the ecosystem (keystone) [16]. Such platform can refer not only to software development tools (e.g., Eclipse SECO) but also to software-intensive ISs (e.g., SAP SECO). Therefore, both perspectives can be observed in the smart city domain: the first is responsible for supporting the platform architecture maintenance and evolution (e.g., API design, modeling and analysis environments, requirements elicitation tools, model checking etc.); and the second is responsible for supporting the ecosystem management and monitoring (e.g., community knowledge base, IS integration and interoperability, software and systems processes and standards, collaborative work etc.). Regarding the second perspective, if we consider only a city hall, hundreds of IS were/are/will be developed/acquired/reused over time in the public administration. It makes smart city SECO sustainability a grand challenge from several points of view, e.g., Computer Science, Law, Sociology, Business, and Engineering.

Therefore, a smart city can be considered a SoIS from which a SECO can potentially emerge as well, since it also matches the well-defined characteristics that should be covered to consider a system as a SECO, which are:

- IS vendors work cooperatively and competitively to support and to develop products and services to satisfy customer needs and to continuously innovate in a smart city SECO. As a consequence, they create business alliances and networks of interoperability that affect and are affected as their market deliverables are subject to the ecosystem rules - mostly uncontrolled and unpredictable, similar to natural forces in other types of ecosystems. As such, governance is important to ensure the ecosystem sustainability;
- A smart city SECO is developed on top of a common technological platform composed by software-intensive IS (and non-IS) applications and technologies developed by multiple actors, such as multiple companies that provide IS by bidding processes, several fabricants that engineer autonomous cars that will be part of the smart city system, multiple suppliers of hardware and software for IoT-based systems for flood monitoring and emergency response systems, smart buildings/hospitals, and monitoring of public spaces. In this context, the technical dimension is not a guarantee of success anymore: multiple parties play together for a common business and/or social purpose or to solve a common problem - somehow similar to the SoS goals. Therefore, more than a type of service bus infrastructure, a city hall as a keystone should foster community engagement and collaboration so that the ecosystem platform can be seen as a broker that supports a social web based on interaction among organizations, developers and users; and
- A smart city SECO is also characterized by both software production and consumption relations. Therefore, roles, interaction rules, collaboration tactics and synergistic capabilities should be dynamically analyzed and monitored towards supporting the ecosystems diversity. In this case, the technical dimension mainly concerned to the platform architecture should consider stability, simplicity, security, reliability and evolution.

4.2.4 Step 4. Adding SECO Elements to SoIS Model

Elements identified in Step 3 were combined into the model obtained in Step 2. SECO model is merged to the resulting SoIS model to combine both models and form the EcoSoIS model. By performing a similar analysis over the description provided in Sects. 3.1–3.3, other concepts were extracted to be added to the SoIS conceptual model.

According to the model presented in Fig. 4, an EcoSoIS complements a SoIS, which comprises the technical dimension, by adding the business and social concerns. EcoSoIS is a SECO formed by a SoIS. EcoSoIS is associated with a software platform based on the constituent systems that are part of that SoIS. The constituents have independent existence and functionalities. A SoIS inherits the characteristics of a SoS, which include managerial independence, operational independence, distribution, evolutionary development, and emergent behavior. The constituents are interoperable IS associated via interoperability links. EcoSoIS is associated with networks of interoperability, ecosystem sustainability, community engagement and collaboration, and business alliances. By being a SECO, an EcoSoIS involve ecosystem management and monitoring, which include IS integration and interoperability, software and systems processes and stand, community knowledge base, and collaborative work; and platform architecture maintenance evolution, which comprises modeling and analysis environments, API design, requirements elicitation tools, and model checking.

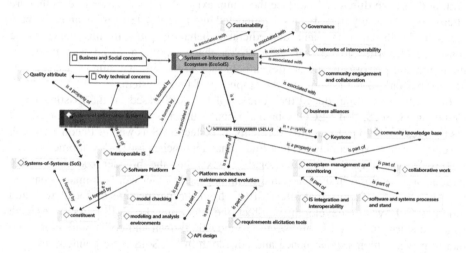

Fig. 4. A conceptual map for EcoSoIS.

4.3   Threats to Validity

Our model was conceived using a qualitative method, which is subject to interpretation and abstraction. Nevertheless, we proceeded with a systematic methodology described and followed, in such a way that the intermediary steps and outcomes are auditable and subject to evaluation. Indeed, we performed a peer-review during the process considering the opinion of experts in the fields being targeted in this research. Hence, we claim for a preliminary validity of our model. Further assessment will be performed soon through a survey with experts. Besides, we also claim that a comparison between the concepts that exist in the literature about both domains (SECO and SoIS) were majorly covered and represented in our model, reinforcing the coverage and consistency of our model.

Possible limitations of our model include characteristics that were not considered and are still relevant, misunderstanding about concepts of one domain that do not have correspondences in another one, and subjectivity of the process followed to extract the concepts. We relieve these threats by proceeding with a survey soon that will validate our model, performing peer-review during the entire process, and also performing cross-validation for each outcome produced.

5   Final Remarks

We are living in a world each day more open and connected, uncovering new opportunities both to business innovation in organizations and to the empowerment of individuals, with more autonomy and satisfaction [13]. This brings challenges to the interdisciplinary research on IS development, human interaction and social web trends, since new types of IS must be approached, such as how to understand, describe, model, build, and manage different IS to face the complexity of building new systems that are not closed artifacts anymore, but a set connected interoperable IS forming an entire new ecosystem, with emerging and unpredictable behavior [30]. In this context, the ecosystem platform can be seen as a broker that supports a social web based on interaction among organizations, developers and users, so that human aspects are strongly relevant to the design and development of those systems.

In this work, we introduced the concept of EcoSoIS based on the existing background on IS, SoIS, and SECO. Our main contribution is to explore how the SECO perspectives can help us to identify elements that affect SoIS as well as to come up with a research agenda. We concluded that traditional approaches for IS development needs to consider not only the organizational contexts but the broader ecosystems that includes organizations, individuals, and technologies. In other words, human, technical and organizational factors that affect SECO from the perspective of social web and computational system development affect the emerging EcoSoISs. As a research agenda, challenges related to architecture, innovation, open and collaborative process, emerging requirements, governance and education in EcoSoIS were pointed out.

As future work, we intend to (i) conduct a survey with experts on the related topics to refine the concept of EcoSoIS, (ii) instantiate the model to real EcoSoIS, (iii) build a tool for modeling and analysis of EcoSoIS on top of our conceptual model, and (iv) analyze how the development environment (tools, objectives, culture etc.) can influence the construction of EcoSoIS, incorporating these concepts on our model.

Acknowledgements. Renata Araujo is supported by CNPq, Brazil, process no 305060/2016-3. We also thank Márcio Imamura by elaborating Fig. 1 that is part of this text.

References

1. Maier, M.W.: Architecting principles for systems-of-systems. In: INCOSE International Symposium, pp. 565–573 (1996)

2. Ciuciu, I., Panetto, H., Debruyne, C., Aubry, A., Bollen, P., Valencia-García, R. (eds.): OTM 2015. LNCS, vol. 9416. Springer, Cham (2015). https://doi.org/10.1007/978-3-319-26138-6
3. Saleh, M., Abel, M.-H.: Information Systems: Towards a System of Information Systems. KMIS 2015 7th International Conference on Knowledge Management and Information Sharing, pp. 193–200. Lisbonne, Portugal (2015)
4. Moore, J.F.: The Death of Competition: Leadership and Strategy in the Age of Business Ecosystems. Harper Business, New York (1996)
5. Santos, R.P., Werner, C., Barbosa, O., Alves, C.: Software ecosystems: trends and impacts on software engineering. In: Proceedings of the 26th Brazilian Symposium on Software Engineering, Natal, Brazil, pp. 206–210 (2012)
6. Jansen, S., Finkelstein, A., Brinkkemper, S.: A sense of community: a research agenda for software ecosystems. In: 2009 ICSE-Companion 31st International Conference on Software Engineering-Companion, pp. 187–190. IEEE (2009)
7. Gawer, A., Cusumano, M.A.: Platform Leadership. Harvard Business School Press, Boston (2002)
8. Junior, H.J., Werner, C.: A systematic mapping on the relations between systems-of-systems and software ecosystems. In: WDES 2015, pp. 65–72 (2015)
9. Santos, R.P., Gonçalves, M.B., Nakagawa, E.Y., Werner, C.M.L.: On the relations between systems-of-systems and software ecosystems. In: Proceedings of the VIII Workshop on Distributed Software Development, Software Ecosystems, and Systems-of-Systems (WDES), Maceió, Brazil, pp. 58–62 (2014)
10. Laudon, K.C., Laudon, J.P.: Management information systems. Pearson Education, London (2016)
11. Bertalanffy, L.V.: General System Theory: Foundations, Development Applications. George Braziller Inc, New York (2015)
12. Araujo, R.M., Cappelli, C., Diirr, B., Engiel, P., Tavares, R.L.: Democracia Eletrônica. In: Mariano Pimentel;Hugo Fuks. (Org.) Sistemas Colaborativos. 1ed. Rio de Janeiro: Campus/SBC, v., p. 110–121 (2011)
13. Tomicic-Pupek, K., Dobrovic, Z., Furjan, M.T.: Strategies for information systems integration. In: Proceedings of the ITI 2012 34th International Conference on Information Technology Interfaces, Cavtat, Dubrovnik, pp. 311–316 (2012)
14. Manikas, K.: Revisiting software ecosystems research: a longitudinal literature study. J. Syst. Softw. 117(2016), 84–103 (2016)
15. Bosch, J.: From software product lines to software ecosystem. In: Proceedings of 13th International Software Product Line Conference (SPLC), San Francisco, USA, pp. 1–10 August 2009
16. Araujo, R.M., Magalhães, A.: Ecossistemas Digitais para o Apoio a Sistemas de Governo Abertos e Colaborativos. In: Simpósio Brasileiro de Sistemas de Informação, 2015, Goiânia. XI Simpósio Brasileiro de Sistemas de Informação. Porto Alegre: Sociedade Brasileira de Computação (2015)
17. Proctor, R., Zandt, T.: Human Factors in Simple and Complex Systems, 2nd edn. CRC Press, Boca Raton (2008)
18. Graciano Neto, V.V., Santos, R.P., Araujo, R.: Sistemas de Sistemas de Informação e Ecossistemas de Software: Conceitos e Aplicações. In: Bruno Zarpelão; Joaquim Uchôa; Heitor Costa; Juliana Greghi. (Org.). Tópicos em Sistemas de Informação: Minicursos SBSI 2017. 1ed.Lavras: UFLA, 2017, v. 1, p. 22–41
19. Lima, T., dos Santos, R.P., Oliveira, J., Werner, C.: The importance of socio-technical resources for software ecosystems management. J. Innov. Digit. Ecosyst. 3(2), 98–113 (2016)

20. Santos, R.P., Viana, D., Maciel, C.: Ecossistemas de Software: Uma Visão sobre Fatores Técnicos, Humanos e Organizacionais. In I. Gasparini, M. Mota (Org.) Livro dos Tutoriais do XV IHC. 15 edn, SBC, v. C, pp. 70–90 (2016)
21. Lima, T., Barbosa, G., Santos, R.P., Werner, C.: Uma Abordagem Socio-técnica para Apoiar Ecossistemas de Software. iSys - Revista Brasileira de Sistemas de Informação **7**(3), 19–37 (2014)
22. Graciano Neto, V.V., Cavalcante, E., El Hachem, J., Santos, D.S.: On the interplay of business process modeling and missions in systems-of-information systems. In: 2017 IEEE/ACM Joint SESoS/WDES, Buenos Aires, pp. 72-73 (2017)
23. Santos, R.P.: ReuseSEEM: an approach to support the definition, modeling, and analysis of software ecosystems. In: 36th ICSE-C, Hyderabad, India, pp. 650–653 (2014)
24. Nakagawa, E.Y., Oquendo, F., Becker, M.: RAModel: A Reference Model for Reference Architectures. In: Joint 2012 ICSA/ECSA, Helsinki, Finland. pp. 297–301 (2012)
25. Graciano Neto, V.V., Garcés, L., Guessi, M., Oliveira, L.B.R., Oquendo, F.: On the equivalence between reference architectures and metamodels. In Proceedings of the 1st International Workshop on Exploring Component-based Techniques for Constructing Reference Architectures (CobRA 2015). Montréal, Canada, pp. 21–24 (2015)
26. Benedict, M.: Modelling Ecosystems in Information Systems – A Typology Approach. In: Proceedings of the 2018 MKWI, Lüneburg, Germany, pp. 453–464 (2018)
27. Saleh, M., Abel, M.: Moving from digital ecosystem to system of information systems. In: Proceedings of the IEEE 20th International Conference on Computer Supported Cooperative Work in Design, pp. 91–96 (2016)
28. Nischak, F., Hanelt, A., Kolbe, L.M.: Unraveling the interaction of information systems and ecosystems – a comprehensive classification of literature. In: International Conference on Information Systems, South Korea, pp 1–21 (2017)
29. Graciano Neto, V.V., Oquendo, F., Nakagawa, E.Y.: Smart systems-of-information systems: Foundations and an assessment model for research development. Grand Challenges in Information Systems for the next 10 years (2016-2026), SBC, pp. 1–12 (2017)
30. Boscarioli, C., Araujo, R.M., Maciel, R.S.P.: I GranDSI-BR – Grand Research Challenges in Information Systems in Brazil 2016–2026. Special Committee on Information Systems (CE-SI). Brazilian Computer Society (SBC) (2017). 184p ISBN: [978-85-7669-384-0]
31. Bohm, A.: Theoretical coding: text analysis in grounded theory. In: Flick, U., Kardorff, E., Steinke, I. (eds.) A Companion to Qualitative Research, pp. 270–275. SAGE Publications, London (2004)
32. Glaser, B.G., Strauss, A.L., Strutzel, E.: The discovery of grounded theory; strategies for qualitative research. Nurs. Res. **17**(4), 364 (1968)
33. Teixeira, P.G., Lopes, V.H.L., Santos, R.P.D., Kassab, M., Neto, V.V.G.: The status quo of systems-of-information systems. In: Proceedings of the 7th International Workshop on Software Engineering for Systems-of-Systems and 13th Workshop on Distributed Software Development, Software Ecosystems and Systems-of-Systems, pp. 34–41. IEEE Press, May 2019
34. ISO/IEC: ISO/IEC 25010 system and software quality models (2010)

KIPO Opportunities for Interoperability Decisions in Systems-of-Information Systems in the Domain of Environmental Management

Juliana Fernandes[1,2(✉)], Fernanda Baião[3(✉)],
and Rodrigo Pereira dos Santos[1(✉)]

[1] Department of Applied Informatics, Federal University of the State
of Rio de Janeiro (UNIRIO), Rio de Janeiro, RJ, Brazil
{juliana.costa, rps}@uniriotec.br
[2] Federal Institute of Piauí (IFPI), Campo Maior, PI, Brazil
[3] Department of Industrial Engineering, Pontifical Catholic University
of Rio de Janeiro (PUC-Rio), Rio de Janeiro, RJ, Brazil
fbaiao@puc-rio.br

Abstract. Considering the increasing exchange of information among systems, the design and development of Information Systems (IS) must guarantee high levels of interaction, communication, and connectivity. To supply the society and organizations demands, IS have been forming an arrangement called Systems-of-Information Systems (SoIS), in which constituents are IS that cooperate with each other to achieve a main goal. Interoperability in this context is a key issue mainly due to the characteristic of managerial and operational independence of these IS. Strategies are necessary to deal with the understanding of the processes involved among IS, people, and organizations that need to interoperate. Since SoIS presents a strong business nature and it has dynamic characteristics, knowledge-intensive processes can emerge around this structure. This study aims to represent interoperability decisions among IS in the environmental management domain through the Knowledge Intensive Process Ontology (KIPO), a meta-model for Knowledge Intensive Process (KIP) modeling. KIPO was chosen due to it capable of making relevant knowledge embedded in a KIP explicit, also, the specialized literature addresses the need for exploring new modeling's in the SoIS domain. As a result, we investigate which processes and interoperability decisions in this context can be modeled with the Knowledge Intensive Process Notation (KIPN), a notation for KIPO. We evaluated the perceived usefulness of KIPN with experts on environmental management and SoIS domain. We concluded that KIPO can be a metamodel alternative of processes in a SoIS. As contribution, we present KIP modeling as an efficient and didactic approach to represent processes that involve interoperability decisions in SoIS.

Keywords: Systems-of-Information Systems · Interoperability · Knowledge Intensive Process Ontology

R. P. d. Santos et al. (Eds.): WAIHCWS 2017/2018, CCIS 1081, pp. 21–41, 2020.
https://doi.org/10.1007/978-3-030-46130-0_2

1 Introduction

The new relationships established by IS[1] converge to a trend of high connectivity with a high interoperability rate [4, 10] in order to deal with today's demands. Thus, a large-scale structure called Systems-of-Information Systems (SoIS) emerges, in which constituents are concentrated in achieving bigger objectives [10, 21]. SoIS constituents are ISs and exhibit a strong business nature. Therefore, Business Process Modeling (BPM) techniques and models can complement such approaches by providing support for requirements specification and an additional point of view for the architectural specification of SoIS [24]. Challenges in the research are discussed for the goal modeling in SoIS [24] since they need to consider a dynamic architecture and total interoperability in their projects [10]. Modeling business processes in the context of SoIS (while considering interoperability between different IS) can aid in the reduction of redundant information in organizational interactions and operational costs, as well as the improvement of scalability of systems and provision of more comprehensive decision-making.

Interoperability in SoIS can involve features such as: (i) intensive interactions between managers and development team; (ii) the need to acquire and represent knowledge about the context and business rules involved in the domain to be inter-operated; (iii) challenges in defining the most appropriate types of solutions to provide interoperability; (iv) different roles and interests involved; and (v) unstructured control flow of activities or processes during decision-making stages. Therefore, these characteristics resemble Knowledge Intensive Process (KIP). KIP represents processes in which there is great need for innovation by an agent involved in this process and may involve the production of unplanned and unscheduled knowledge [6]. As a SoIS addresses the interaction between its constituents, presents a strong business nature and involves dynamic architecture, KIPs may emerge over this structure. BPM and ontologies have been recommended as a component mechanism of strategies to provide interoperability. As such, this work proposes opportunities in KIPO to address important aspects of SoIS in the environmental management domain. During the development of the proposal, related aspects referred to what processes and decisions of this context are subjected to be modeled with Knowledge Intensive Process Notation (KIPN), a notation for KIPO [16]. Due to the nature of business, the dynamics of architecture and the need for interoperability, it was concluded that KIPO can be an alternative processes metamodel in a SoIS.

We evaluated the perceived usefulness of KIPN with experts on environmental management and SoIS domain. The results showed that this approach is efficient and didactic. In addition, as a contribution, we present how the KIP approach can be a way to represent efficiently and didactically processes that include interoperability decisions in SoIS. The modeling is important to better address the organizational interoperability layer that arises when we consider SoIS, also, there are no precedents of a KIP approach for SoIS in the scientific literature [24]. In addition to this introductory section, this work is organized as follows: Sect. 2 provides the basis for the work by

---

[1] For sake of simplicity, herein IS and SoIS will denote both singular and plural forms.

defining SoIS, interoperability in SoIS, KIP and KIPO; Sect. 3 presents the relationship between KIP and SoIS; Sect. 4 describes the case study; Sect. 5 presents an exploratory study carried out in an IS investigated in the case study; Sect. 6 presents the modeling of a SoIS using KIPN; and, finally, Sect. 7 concludes this work.

2 Background

2.1 System-of-Information Systems

In this work, we consider as components of an IS the software intensive IS. We address the trend of high connectivity, in which the purpose of the relationship between IS is relevant [2]. In this perspective, multiple IS have been combined to interoperate, delivering results that add value to customers [3]. This combination of an existing set of IS represents a System-of-Systems (SoS) [2, 7, 14, 21–23, 36]. SoS arose as a result of the need for interoperability among constituents to create more robust applications, offering features that could not be delivered by any of these systems in isolation [22]. SoIS was proposed to address the impact of the flow of information and knowledge between different IS [32, 40]. For a SoS to accomplish a global mission, each constituent is essential, even if it is just an isolated software-based instrument, such as a smart sensor. In a SoIS, the constituents are mostly IS [10].

A set of characteristics for a smart SoIS was discussed, such as: (F1) Independence (decoupling) of constituents, i.e., they are decoupled IS, which have independent existence, operation, and purposes. They offer their capabilities to accomplish a proposal of a SoIS; (F2) Managerial independence of IS, i.e., multiple organizations and stakeholders can hold and contribute with their IS to form a SoIS; (F3) Evolutionary development, i.e., in order to accomplish new requirements, new IS can join and leave the SoIS, with evolving goals, and evolving their own architecture; (F4) Emergent behavior, i.e., such behaviors are results of the interoperability among constituents that produce a global result that cannot be delivered by any one of them in isolation; (F5) Distribution, i.e., a strategy must be established to support communication and data exchange among IS belonging to a SoIS; (F6) Evolutionary (dynamic) architecture, i.e., a smart SoIS must be able to explore capabilities available in a set of IS still in operation, rearranging them to maintain the goal accomplishment in progress; and (F7) Full interoperability, i.e., to comprise the spontaneity of forming a smart SoIS according to needs that emerge in a transparent manner for the user, as well as abstract issues, such as middleware, network, data exchange, and communication support details [38].

The characteristics related to F6 and F7 bring challenges regarding business modeling. In this case, the need for languages that allow the specification of adaptive goals at runtime is recommend [27]. Therefore, based on this need, this work investigated a KIPN approach to process modeling in SoIS.

2.2   Interoperability in Systems-of-Information Systems

According to the IEEE, interoperability is the ability of two or more systems or system components to exchange information and use information that has been exchanged [37]. However, the concept of interoperability is multidimensional and can be understood and approached from several perspectives and directions [15, 17, 19]. Literature argues that many solutions for interoperability are based on the discovery, selection and composition of interoperable services in a specific domain and implemented at project time [20]. Therefore, some challenges in the SoIS context deal with issues related to: modeling, design and simulation of architectures; definition, elaboration and specification of SoIS goals; and designing mechanisms to deal with emerging behavior [12]. Because SoIS exhibits a strong business nature, interoperability needs to be well understood so as to benefit all stakeholders involved in the IS. Table 1 shows commonly discussed layers of interoperability (LI) in a clear fashion [18].

Table 1. Layers of interoperability (LI). Adapted from Kubicek and Cimander [18].

LI	Aim	Objects	Solutions	State of knowledge
Organizational	Automatic linkage of processes among different SI	Processes (workflow)	Architectural models, standardized process elements, e.g., SOA with WSDL, BPML	Conceptual clarity still lacking, vague concepts with large scope of interpretation
Semantic	Processing and interpretations of received data	Information	Common directories, data keys, ontologies	Theoretically developed, but practical implementation problems
Syntactic	Processing of received data	Data	Standardized data exchange formats, e.g., XML, JSON, CSV	Fully developed
Technical	Technically secure data transfer	Signals	Protocol of data transfer	Fully developed

In this case, technical and syntactic LI deal with already established standards; semantic interoperability, while having concepts and methods available, presents practical implementation problems; and organizational interoperability lacks conceptual clarity and is considered to have vague concepts with broad scope of interpretation [18]. Regarding the organizational layer, it is less obvious what should be standardized, who could develop and establish appropriate standards and what is necessary for its operation and maintenance. The semantic and organizational LI still present challenges for the time being [4, 6, 22, 26]. In order to support LI, we mention some interoperability framework initiatives, such as: Government Interoperability Framework (e-GIF)[2]; e-PING[3] [5]; and European Interoperability Framework (EIF)[4]. These frameworks set standards for different systems to integrate. These initiatives support understanding about three LI: technical (the syntactic layer appears as embedded in the technical layer), semantic and organizational. Thus, these three LI can be understood as: (a) organizational interoperability, which deals with why we are interoperating; (b) semantic interoperability, which deals with what we are interoperating; and (c) technical interoperability, which deals with the means we are interoperating with. The interoperability in SoIS should consider the existing business processes among the organizations and the appropriate exchange of information, as well as the understanding of the concepts involved in the flow of knowledge and the skills required for interoperability. As such, semantic interoperability should be well understood in this context. Semantic interoperability is the capacity of organizations from different sectors (e.g., public, private, voluntary) and their IS to: (i) discover necessary information; (ii) explicitly describe the meaning of data that organizations wish to share with one another; and (iii) process information received in a manner consistent with the intended purpose of each information [31]. The discovery of information that includes knowledge of organizational and policy requirements for interoperability among IS can be very relevant in SoIS. The role of ontologies can be explored in this context whereas it is being recommended as an alternative to provide interoperability in different fields of research [9]. Based on KIPO concepts and structures, we seek to understand interoperability decisions among IS of different organizations (managerially and operationally independent) that form a SoIS. Our propose explores interoperability in SoIS to better address the organizational interoperability layer that arises when we consider contexts with different development teams, managers, and IS.

2.3 Knowledge Intensive Process and Knowledge Intensive Process Ontology

KIP are sequences of activities based on the acquisition and intensive use of knowledge, regardless of the type of business or its size [13]. A KIP is characterized by activities that cannot be easily planned, can change rapidly, and are driven by the context of the scenario in which the process is embodied [8]. This sequence of activities aims to create products and services, add value to customers, and is usually represented by a model [29]. BPM is an important field of research that notoriously contributes to fill the gap between the business domain and information technology. Business process modelers strive to create representations that describe how operations are conducted within the organization [16]. Process models are typically represented using visual notations, which comprise a set of graphical symbols and structural rules among them, such as Business Process Modeling Notation (BPMN) [6, 30, 39]. Such symbols and

---

[2] https://www.dit.gov.bt/e-gifnea.

[3] http://eping.governoeletronico.gov.br/.

[4] http://ec.europa.eu/idabc/servlets/Docd552.pdf?id=19529.

rules should ideally be sufficient for expressing important aspects of the business processes, both completely and correctly [16]. Although this notation is widely adopted in both academia and commercial available tools, it strongly focuses on the representation of structured control-flow oriented processes [16]. However, the flow of knowledge on processes and its handover among people have not be well represented by traditional BPM approaches [1]. As the knowledge-intensive activities flow leaves the dynamics of the process barely visible, due to the lack of an explicit approach for modelling KIPs, KIPO was proposed [29]. KIPO explores all elements belonging to the knowledge involved in the process, especially those related to business rules, decision making and collaboration [16]. In addition, it seeks to organize and externalize KIP knowledge related to process motivational factors, social interactions, information flow, innovation and action alternatives [29]. Figure 1 represents the KIPO components and interconnections within its component ontologies. The components that represent the perspectives of the ontologies that comprise KIPO are: Business Process Ontology (BPO), which organizes relevant concepts and relationships to represent common elements of business processes, such as activities, roles, control flows, and data objects; Collaborative Ontology (CO), which organizes relevant concepts and relationships to describe the exchange of knowledge and collaborative activities among process participants; Decision Ontology (DO), which organizes relevant concepts and relationships to explain the "why" and "how" the decision-making was performed by process executors; Business Rules Ontology (BRO), which organizes relevant concepts and relationships to represent constraints or business rules that must be observed while running a KIP; and Knowledge Intensive Process Core Ontology (KIPCO), which organizes KIP-specific concepts and relationships, interconnecting the concepts of the other perspectives [29]. KIPO can be used in any domain to represent the concepts and relationships involved in a KIP and its purpose is to explain the elements of this type of process by defining the concepts related to them [29].

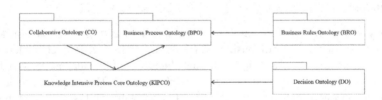

Fig. 1. KIPO components [29].

A visual notation to represent the concepts inherent to KIP defined in the KIPO in a cognitively effective way was proposed [16, 28]. KIPN is composed of six diagrams: (1) KIP Diagram, which depicts a comprehensive overview of the processes and activities using BPMN-based elements [14, 22]. However, the control-flow through the activities is not determined – rather, there is no predefined order of execution for the activities; (2) Socialization Diagram shows the socialization and contingency events that influence the elements produced or handled and decisions made; (3) Decision

Diagram makes it easier to explicit aspects that influence an associated decision-making process in a radial way to the centered icon of the chosen alternative, giving an objective and concise view about the process; (4) Agent Diagram associates the expertise and experience with their corresponding agent to illustrate a competence matrix that maps the skills of those involved in the case; (5) Intention Diagram shows the intrinsic characteristics of agents that mainly influence someone's activities, e.g., desires, feelings and beliefs that motivate an agent to execute an activity to reach a goal; (6) Business-Rules Diagram represents documented business rules that restrict a decision in a KIP [16]. The use of KIPO was realized in two concrete case studies conducted to collect evidence of the perceived usefulness of KIPN. The first one was an academic environment where the process modeled referred to how to "develop master's dissertation", and the other one was performed in a real business environment and where the modeled process dealt with a "data modelling" process [16]. The diagrams proposed by KIPN are built with the aid of the Knowledge Intensive Process Ontology Language (KIPOL), a prototype that facilitates the construction of diagrams through intuitive forms of data entry. Table 2 shows some of the KIPN symbols [16]. In this work, we explore modeling in an environmental management domain such as interoperability decisions. We seek to investigate which decisions of interoperability in SoIS can be modeled with KIPN in order to consider new requirements arising from emergent behaviors, or potential business innovations due to new arrangements of existing capabilities [26].

Table 2. KIPN graphical symbols and descriptions used in this work [16].

Symbol	Description	Symbol	Description
Restriction	Something (a law, a rule, or any known circumstance) that may restrict the decision making.	**Criterion**	Established criteria for analyzing advantages and disadvantages of alternatives.
Advantage	Advantage related to an alternative.	**Disadvantage**	Disadvantage related to an alternative.
Chosen Alternative	Selected alternative to address issues of a decision.	**Decision**	The result of a decision-making process.
Risk	Some possible result that may represent a threaten for a decision.	**Experience**	A previous circumstance or issue known by an agent that may influence a decision.
Question	Some issue considered by the agent when making a decision.	**Speciality**	An academic or professional competence of an Agent that may influence a decision.
	An agent in the process, free from his/her acting role.	**Derivation Rule**	A statement of knowledge derived from other existing knowledge from the domain. As a conclusion, it defines domain concepts with regard to other concepts.
Reaction Rule	A statement specifying an activity that should be carried out on the occurrence of a specific event and condition. It is a reaction business rule.	**Integrity Rule**	A statement that should be kept true regarding the domain concepts and their relationships. It is a structural business rule
Discarded Alternative	Excluded alternatives that were not sufficient to solve the issues of a decision.	**Association**	The association between information and artifacts

3   Systems-of-Information Systems and Knowledge Intensive Process

SoIS are formed by IS which are managed and operated by different organizations that can cooperate to achieve a main goal [10]. As this class of system has a strong business-oriented nature, challenges have emerged regarding how to support SoIS design and development so that the dynamism of architecture and emergent behavior characteristic of this scenario could be contemplated [10]. As such, it is necessary to understand how SoIS can be developed while addressing the phenomena that emerge around an IS when it spontaneously joins another, thus contributing to the achievement of a SoIS' goal [22]. A SoIS is a set of constituents that accomplishes one or more objectives and each objective in this model is structured in two levels: business and system [27]. As SoIS has a strong business nature and BPMN has strong potential to aid the goal modeling, although they state that this notation has been designed for business modeling (and not for goals) [27]. BPMN models continuous process flows while the processes flow in a SoIS context can be dynamic. Different IS in a SoIS can enter or leave the arrangement at any time because each one is independent. Each one can collaborate for SoIS main goal. However, they exist to accomplish their own individual goals [10]. In this case, we decided to explore some KIPN diagrams to show how managers can model non-continuous decision flows, such as interoperability in a SoIS context. The need to propose or extend tools to fill gaps in the SoIS specification is discussed in the specialized literature [27]. Based on this necessity, we sought to integrate the KIP concept for business process models proposed in the literature into the SoIS context [8]. KIP assumes that the scenario determines who should be involved, who is the right person to perform a specific step, and that the set of users involved may not be formally defined and is discovered as the process scenario unfolds [5]. Starting from this notion and comparing it with the main characteristics of a SoIS, it is necessary to understand what kind of KIP can emerge from this scenario, what activities should be performed to meet a broader goal and which IS help to strengthen the business challenges since they are crucial to the fulfillment of the broader goal.

BPMN presents itself as a potential representation in SoIS because it has a business-oriented nature, which comes from the IS domain [26]. The goal specification in SoIS can be seen as a set of goals or objectives to be achieved by performing tasks based on the resources of the constituent IS, i.e., what they can do to: (i) accomplish those goals, and (ii) support interactions among constituent systems that lead to emerging behaviors [25]. The identification and achievement of goals as well as the interoperability decisions among IS usually involve interactions between stakeholders. Therefore, emerging behaviors arising from IS relationships may require new process steps or decision making at runtime based on the context changes that might affect a SoIS. Because of this, the KIP approach was chosen in this study since it can contribute to make explicit the processes which are unpredictable and difficultly captured through conventional models. Thus, KIPO was used in this work with the intention of observing the processes with an outlook of management support and investigating which decisions of interoperability in SoIS should be modeled with KIPN diagrams [16].

4 Interoperability in an Environmental Management Integrated System: An Exploratory Study

In an earlier work, an exploratory study on the interoperability in an IS known as Integrated System of Environmental Management and Water (IS-1) of an Environmental Brazilian agency of State of Piauí was conducted [11]. IS-1 represents case 1 of our research. The analysis was performed based on technical, human and organizational factors (Table 3) intrinsic to software development as discussed by Santos et al. [33]. As such, it has been investigated which Software Ecosystem (SECO)[5] factors are observed, partially observed, or not observed in the IS-1, as well as which of these factors influence their interoperability with other systems.

Table 3. Technical, human and organizational factors affecting a SECO [33].

Factor	Description
F1	Deal with diversity of organizations and relationships within a SECO
F2	Encourage external developers to use a common technological platform
F3	Share content, knowledge, problems, experiences, and abilities
F4	Improve software reuse in the scenario of global software engineering
F5	Reposition organizations to act as network actors and reduce internal workforce
F6	Consider diversity of new functionalities offered to clients
F7	Invest in transparency
F8	Support modular system design
F9	Support organization openness
F10	Define internal characteristics related to SECO health and stability
F11	Define well-established SECO scope/boundaries
F12	Identify capacities and relationships between actors within a SECO
F13	Have a clear definition of the process
F14	Strengthen a communicative character inherent for programming activities
F15	Ensure compliance based on the characteristics of different application domains

The adopted procedures were carried out in two stages, in which the first consisted of: (1) collecting IS-1 documentation (e.g. requirements document, class diagrams, interview with the development team, end-users, and managers); (2) analyzing whether and how each SECO factor occurs in IS-1; (3) tabulating the responses according to the observation of the factors in IS-1; (4) obtaining consensus among each researcher; and (5) conducting a qualitative analysis of the results. Table 4 summarizes the results of the first stage analysis and which SECO factors have been identified in IS-1 (and if there is influence of these factors on the interoperability in this case). By accessing the

---

[5] SECO is defined as an effective way to build software from a common technological platform, composing applications and technologies developed by multiple actors (e.g., third-party developers, communities and organizations) [35]. As SoIS are composed of pre-existing IS, with great potential for innovation and creation of new businesses, each IS of a SoIS can form a SECO around itself [34].

IS-1 documentation and analyzing the use case diagrams, it has been noticed that there is an understanding of the roles each actor plays in IS-1 (F1), including stimulating external developers to use Linux as a platform (F2). When accessing the class diagram, it has been verified that the IS-1 models reflect a modular design (F8), since there is little technical coupling between the constituent elements of its set of functionalities. This feature is a consequence of the traditional Engineering principle from which the system is fragmented into manageable parts for its component-based development [33].

Table 4. Summary of SECO factors observed in IS-1 and if they affect interoperability.

Factor	Researcher 1	Researcher 2	Consensus	Does it affect interoperability?
F1	Yes	Yes	Yes	No
F2	Yes	No	Yes	Yes
F3	Partially	Partially	Partially	Yes
F4	No	No	No	Yes
F5	Partially	Partially	Partially	Yes
F6	No	Yes	No	Yes
F7	No	No	No	Yes
F8	Yes	Yes	Yes	Yes
F9	No	Partially	No	Yes
F10	No	No	No	No
F11	Yes	Yes	Yes	Yes
F12	Partially	Partially	Partially	No
F13	Partially	Partially	Partially	Yes
F14	Partially	Yes	Partially	Yes
F15	Yes	Yes	Yes	No

It has also been observed that there are well-defined market frontiers: although the environmental domain is the main benefited sector, data on rural and urban activities in the State form a basis for economic and social decision-making, as well as support for the definition of public policies (F11). Some concerns were expressed on the use of open-source and cross-platform technologies (e.g., Python, Django, Geoserver, Pycharm, Github). Although there is no formal use of Semiotic Engineering for 'end-user programming', it has been observed that users have an active participation in the promotion of demands, allowing the system to contemplate particular characteristics to those who use it (F15). Factors F3, F5, F12, F13 and F14 were partially observed. It was noted that content sharing is contemplated by IS-1 in accordance with the requirement of transparency in public administration. However, the sharing of knowledge, problems, experiences and skills is not applied due to organizational resistance. The reshuffling of internal actors to act as network actors or even mechanisms to identify relationships between actors have not been observed. Despite the strong focus on integration and/or interoperability, no verification on releases of system versions have been observed. Finally, the communication has been consolidating with the orchestration of products and services among IS. F4, F6, F7, F9 and F10 have not been observed. The lack of external developers has not contributed to global software reuse, although there is reuse of external libraries for geospatial environmental solutions. We also analyzed F1-F15 characteristics in order to directly influence the interoperability. To do so, an interview was conducted by two experts with experience in interoperability. For each SECO factor, each expert analyzed whether it affects interoperability between systems; responses were tabulated; and a consensus was established. After a general analysis of the factors of the first stage of the research, it has been noticed that F2-9, F11, F13 and F14 directly influence interoperability and that, if combined, such factors are able to provide an IS that adds value in a SoIS structure. In order to establish higher levels of interoperability in IS-1, it is necessary to: (a) have a solution reusability project that involves developers and other external actors (F4); (b) include development in app stores to provide new functionality to customers and enrich the structure of SoIS (F6); (c) provide more transparency, offering information on the development process, flaws and interactions between related actors (F7); (d) addressing the critical factor which involves knowledge sharing aspects (F9); and (e) addressing the software production networks formed within a SECO, focusing on its set of participants (F10). The second stage of the research consisted of: (1) studying the e-PING documentation [5], specifically the Organization and Information Exchange segment; (2) analyzing if and how each component of this segment occurs in IS-1; (3) tabulate the responses according to the observation of the components in IS-1; and (4) conducting qualitative analysis of the results. When investigating the interoperability components (IC) of the electronic government standards in the IS-1, it has been noticed that Language for Data Exchange (C1), Data Transformation (C2) and Data Definition for Exchange (C3) have been referred to in IS-1. This is since the development of IS-1 involves the use of XML, JSON and CSV for any need for treatment and transfer of information both internally (in the development team) and externally to meet users' demands and requests from the State agency. It has been observed that the Georeferenced information (C4) and Metadata for georeferenced information (C7) have been partially covered. This is due to the fact that the structuring and integration of the geographic information system module has not been implemented in IS-1. Specification for public transport information (C5) and Specification for real-time public transport information (C6) have not been observed. Table 5 summarizes the findings of the analysis. The second column indicates if each component is adopted (A) by Brazilian government as standard in ePING architecture, i.e., it must be adopted in new IT products/projects; Recommended (R), i.e. component that matches ePING technical policies, although it is not required; and in Studying (S), i.e., the component that was being evaluated by the Brazilian government when the research was performed.

Regarding the e-PING compliance aspect, IS-1 does not deviate from the adopted specifications. Although C4 and C7 have been partially observed, and C5 and C6 have not been contemplated in IS-1, the first two are in the e-PING recommendation group and are not mandatory. From the presented diagnosis, it has been concluded that the present interoperability constituents add value to IS-1. This is due to the fact that it allows advances in the interaction among people, different systems and people through SoIS. However, to achieve advances of such interactions, it is important to find means to adequately model the processes involved in these interrelationships. In the first stage of the exploratory study, during the interview with the IS-1 development team and

Table 5. Summary of the investigated components of e-PING contemplated in IS-1.

Component	e-PING recommendation	Is it contemplated in IS-1?
C1	A	Yes
C2	A	Yes
C3	A	Yes
C4	R	Partially
C5	R	No
C6	S	No
C7	S	Partially

managers, we collected information about other IS that should interoperate with IS-1. The information about other IS is important because, in the SoIS context, these relations involve different organizations and independent IS thus we have no access to documentation from all involved IS in an arrangement. In the stage of this study, we analyze the individual goals from others IS and seek processes that represent the interoperability among these IS.

5 Analysis of Real Case

As the proposal of this work was to apply KIPO to represent SoIS in the environmental management domain, we sought to investigate which processes and decisions of interoperability are possible to be modeled using KIPN in this context. To do so, our research consisted of: (1) studying the documentation and reviewing the interviews conducted in the first stage of the study (discussed in Sect. 2.1); (2) analyzing the specific characteristics of each IS to know if the arrangement formed by them can be considered a SoIS according to the conceptual model in specialized literature [10]; (3) establishing what can be delivered only if all IS are working together; (4) investigating and modelling decisions of interoperability made possible using the KIPN with experts; (5) evaluating the KIPN diagrams; and (6) conducting qualitative analysis of the results. The case study involves some IS of the environmental management at the State and Federal levels in the Brazilian scenario which have the following characteristics: (a) Independence of the constituents – the existence, operation and purposes of each IS are independent, but offer capabilities to contribute to the achievement of an objective in a SoIS; (b) Managerial independence – each IS was developed by different institutions and has its own development team; (c) Evolutionary development – each IS changes according to new requirements, evolution goals and maintains its own architecture; and (d) Distribution – some strategies have been designed to establish communication and data exchange among different IS. However, for this IS set to represent a SoIS, the presence of emergent behavior is required, i.e., a holistic phenomenon which manifests as a result of interoperability among different IS that produce an overall result which cannot be delivered by any of them in isolation. Considering the peculiarities of each of these IS and conjecturing on what they are able to deliver, we consider as: (e) Emerging behavior – the ability to generate biodiversity information of a certain area (municipality or district). This goal allows managers to be aware of the area's environmental support capacity so as to license new activities that impact the environment, e.g., gas emissions, soil degradation, and fire risk. A practical example of this goal of SoIS is the ability to convey to a manager transparent information about the actual environmental impact of a license[6]. While possessing this information, let us suppose that a new enterprise that has an environmental impact (e.g., gas station) wants to operationalize its activities in a certain area. Even if it fulfills all the necessary requirements to obtain an environmental license to operate in the requested area, the responsible agency may choose not to license this activity. Such decision can only be made after having information that the area does not have the capacity of environmental support to accommodate the demand of this activity. This emergent behavior cannot be achieved by an IS in isolation. Each IS has its own particular objectives and operates independently: (case 1) an integrated system of environmental management and water (IS-1) whose objective is to generate electronic licensing and granting processes at the State level (state of Piauí); (case 2) a national system of control of the origin of forest products (IS-2), whose objective is to manage forest activities, forest-based enterprises and related processes subject to the control by agencies of the national environmental system (Federal level); and, finally, (case 3) a rural environmental register system (IS-3), whose objective is to integrate and manage environmental information of rural properties throughout the country to subsidize policies, programs, projects and control activities, as well as monitoring, environmental and economic planning, as well as combating illegal deforestation (Federal level).

6 Modeling Interoperability Decisions in Systems-of-Information Systems Using KIPN

In SoIS, the interoperability of information as well as the flow of information and knowledge among different IS allowed us to identify the need for exploring the application of KIPO in diverse domains [4, 16]. Therefore, this work sought to understand some relationships among agents, business processes and business rules applying KIPN in SoIS in the environmental management domain. KIPN is a graphical notation developed to promote a cognitively effective under-standing of KIP, in addition to covering all characteristics defined by KIPO [16]. KIPN was used in this study to model existing business processes among IS presented in Sect. 5 (i.e., IS-1, IS-2, and IS-3) that form the investigated SoIS. The Knowledge Process Intensive Drawing (KIPDraw[7]) tool was used to support the modeling of the diagrams of this work. KIPDraw facilitates KIP modeling with the use of KIPO and elements of KIPN. The three KIPN diagrams that can be built on KIPDraw are: Decision Map (DM), Agent Matrix (AM), and Business Rules (BR). Therefore, these were the types of diagrams built for this work. A DM was generated in an attempt to understand the "Deploying the electronic process

---

[6] An environmental license is an official document authorizing the implementation of one or several activities that impact the environment.

[7] https://github.com/AliceUniRio/KIPDraw.

opening of Sustainable Forest Management Plan (SFMP) Type" process (P1). An AM was constructed to classify the expertise or experience of agents involved in the "Opening of electronic process of SFMP type" (P2). Finally, a diagram for the BR was constructed to represent the rules involved in process P2 (BR-1). A brief explanation of each diagram and an outline of each representation are shown in the next subsections.

6.1 Decision Map Diagram

The Decision Map Diagram aims at detailing the decision-making process that occurs during the KIP, with its corresponding result [16]. The elements are evidence and facts about issues related to the domain, the proposed alternatives and their criteria, advantages and disadvantages, risks and restrictions, and anything else that adds information to the representation of contributions or socialization activities in the decision making [16]. In Fig. 2, we can notice how to make a decision about deploying a specific process, such as P1. In this example, the State agency (SA) needs to implement the SFMP process. However, it must decide whether the process will be implemented in IS-1 or IS-2. IS-2 is a pre-existing system that belongs to the federal agency. If SA decides to use IS-2, it shall send information from the electronic processes of the SFMP type opened in IS-1 to IS-2. Otherwise, SA should implement the Federal IS-2 and bear the need to maintain another system for opening electronic processes without the guarantee that IS-2 operates with the same flow of activities executed by SA for this type of process. Figure 2 exemplifies the implications of the chosen alternative of "deploying SFMP through IS-1". Thus, its advantage and disadvantage are presented along with their respective decision criteria. In addition, the risks and restrictions of this decision are mapped in the diagram.

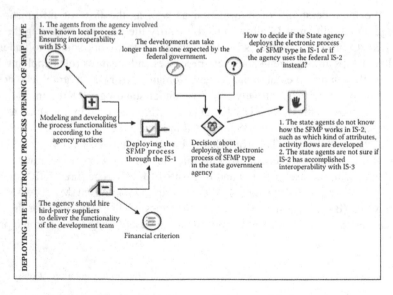

Fig. 2. Decision map diagram modeled.

6.2   Agent Matrix Diagram

The socialization and decision activities ultimately promote new experiences, and even expertise gain to agents [16]. The Agent Diagram was suggested to map the expertise and experience of those agents. In this diagram, it is possible to associate the expertise and experience with their corresponding agent in order to illustrate a competence matrix that maps the skills of those involved [16]. In the Fig. 3, we can notice the expertise and experience of agents involved in process P2. This process is present in IS-1 and IS-2, and we can describe the same agents for the both systems, such as Entrepreneur or Technical manager, Requester, Staff user, Environmental supervisor, Superintendent of the environmental agency, and Citizen. The first column represents a circumstance performed by an Agent that may influence a decision and the professional competence of an Agent that may influence a decision.

6.3   Business-Rules Diagram

The Business Rules Diagram represents documented business rules that restrict a decision in a KIP [16]. This may include organizational rules and procedures, contracts, and laws [16]. For each decision, a business rule diagram must be created to include all the business rules that were considered when analyzing alternatives [16]. These rules are assertive, i.e., formalized data structures in the modeled domain [16].

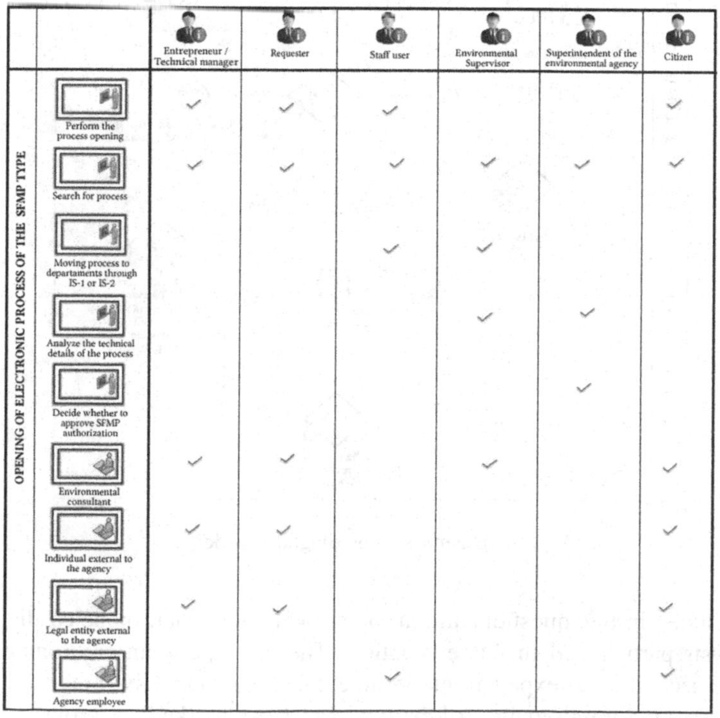

OPENING OF ELECTRONIC PROCESS OF THE SFMP TYPE	Entrepreneur / Technical manager	Requester	Staff user	Environmental Supervisor	Superintendent of the environmental agency	Citizen
Perform the process opening	✓	✓	✓			✓
Search for process	✓	✓	✓	✓	✓	✓
Moving process to departaments through IS-1 or IS-2			✓	✓		
Analyze the technical details of the process				✓	✓	
Decide whether to approve SFMP authorization					✓	
Environmental consultant	✓	✓		✓		✓
Individual external to the agency	✓	✓				✓
Legal entity external to the agency	✓	✓				✓
Agency employee				✓		✓

Fig. 3.   Agent matrix diagram modeled.

A diagram was created with the purpose of modeling the business rules that characterize process P2, as well as making explicit the dependencies among the IS that form the SoIS (Fig. 4). For the execution of P2, some information should be collected. However, this information depends on business rules pre-established by the domain.

7   KIPN Evaluation in Systems-of-Information Systems

A survey was conducted in order to collect evidence of the perceived usefulness of KIPN in a SoIS context. We used a questionnaire for evaluating each KIPN diagram modeled to represent the two environmental process chosen in this study (P1 and P2). The questionnaire has two sections: the first one refers to subject characterization while the second refers to the evaluation of each KIPN diagram. The evaluation was based on choosing a Likert-scale score (from strongly disagree to strongly agree) for each modeled process.

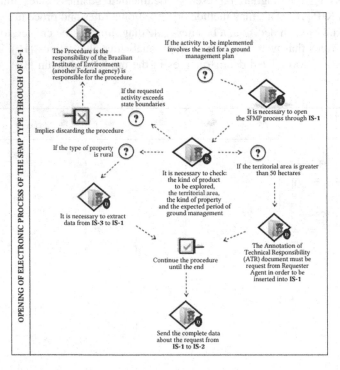

Fig. 4. Business-rules diagram modeled.

We included in this questionnaire an open field about each modeled diagram and three analysts participated in this evaluation. The first one is an environmental consultant, the second is an expert in environmental management systems, and the third has expertise in SoIS domain. All participants have worked as project managers.

These different experiences were important to evaluate if the use of our approach could be efficient and didactic for representing interoperability decisions in SoIS. The evaluation focused on the perception of usefulness regarding the interoperability of information and the flow of information and knowledge among different IS.

7.1 Decision Map Diagram Modeled for Deploying the Electronic Process Opening of Sustainable Forest Management Plan Process

When analyzing if KIPN clarified the decision-making process that involves the deployment of the electronic SFMP process at the State agency, one of the participants answered 'agree' and two participants answered 'strongly agree' with the first statement. In this case, they believe that the decision map diagram can be useful to understand interoperability decisions regarding independent IS. It also facilitates the understanding of how the whole decision-making process took place. The environmental consultant has highlighted it:

"The use of graphical elements in this question, as well as in the others, facilitates the understanding of how the whole decision-making process took place, i.e., make the interpretation of the process faster and more practical."

The expert participant in SoIS domain also commented:

"KIPN Notation can imply an extensive and confusing diagram to represent decisions that involve more information than the example in question."

7.2 Business Rules Diagram Modeled for Opening of Electronic Process of Sustainable Forest Management Plan Type

Regarding the business rules diagram, one participant indicated 'neutral, one participant indicated 'agree', and one participant indicated 'strongly agree' with the statement: *Was KPN helpful in understanding the business rules that characterize the "opening of electronic process of sustainable forest management plan type"?*. About such diagram the expert participant in SoIS domain commented:

"KIPN notation may imply an extensive and confusing diagram to represent decisions involving a greater amount of information than the example in question."

7.3 Agent Matrix Diagram Modeled for Opening of Electronic Process of Sustainable Forest Management Plan Type

Regarding the agents matrix diagram, three participants answered that they 'strongly agree' with the statement: *Was KIPN helpful in understanding the specialties and experiences of all the agents involved in the "opening of electronic process of sustainable forest management plan type"?*. About such diagram the expert participant in SoIS domain commented:

"Seems it can be replaced by a table."

7.4   Benefits, Difficulties and Opportunities of KIPO for Systems-of-Information Systems

Current research points out the need for establishing strategies for designing SoIS [12], seeking to orchestrate the involved IS to ensure that the broader goal of this system arrangement is reached. In the SoIS context, different interests can rise due to the existence of a plethora of stakeholders around the different IS and multiple organizations, each one with different goals. As such, its nature is business-driven.

Although BPMN is widely accepted and used to model business processes, this study sought to bring the KIP approach, through the KIPO metamodel, to assist in processes involving interoperability around IS in SoIS. The main motivation stemmed from some needs pointed out by the academic community researching about SoIS, such as: (i) reuse and/or adapt BPM tools to flexible business processes [26]; and (ii) broaden or search for strategies based on ontology and semantic representation that can help in the discovery of IS that are potentially necessary to solve some SoIS goals [38]. As benefits that can be observed with the use of KIPO through KIPN symbols, we can highlight the possibility of representing restrictions and criteria for interoperability decision making, advantages, disadvantages, risks, and important issues that emerge when implementing a new IS. In addition, it provides tools to map experience and expertise of the agents involved in certain processes.

Limitations and difficulties are also identified in the research, since not all diagrams have been modeled, such as KIP Diagram, Socialization Diagram and Intention Diagram. Because the KIPO metamodel is not yet widely available, there is a lack of examples of the use of KIPN with more diversified and comprehensive modeling, as well as models from other domains. However, this opens up perspectives for evaluating and proposing other scenarios in SoIS that help in the understanding of, for example, emerging behaviors arising from IS interoperability. The evaluation was performed with a small number of participants. However, the profile was diverse and corresponded to the domains investigated in this study (environmental management and SoIS).

8   Conclusion

This work has characterized SoIS interoperability and sought opportunities in the KIPO metamodel to represent interoperability decisions SoIS in a case in the environmental management domain. As a result, we attempted to build decisions process that can be modeled with KIPN diagrams among selected systems of the environmental management domain (IS-1, IS-2, and IS-3). Three out of six diagrams provided by KIPN were used for the SoIS case modeling. The Decision Map, Agent Matrix, and Business Rules diagrams were chosen as they can be created based on the KIPDraw tool.

The Decision Map diagram was modeled in an attempt to depict the decisions involved in the "Deploying the electronic process opening of SFMP type" (Fig. 2); the Agent Matrix (Fig. 3) was modeled to represent the expertise and experiences of the agents involved in the process; and, finally, the Business Rules diagram was modeled in an attempt to describe rules and interoperation among systems that involve the

"SFMP process opening process" (Fig. 4). The evaluation was performed with three participants. The first one is an environmental consultant, the second is an expert in environmental management systems, and the third has expertise in SoIS domain. We concluded that KIPO may be an alternative to represent some processes that need to interoperate between systems in the context of SoIS. However, it is necessary to model other procedures and rules and use other diagrams (such as the Socialization Diagram) in which it is possible to perceive the knowledge flow of agents. In addition, it is important to evaluate the concepts represented in the diagrams with other experts that are part of the SoIS context investigated in this work to ratify if the processes involved in KIPN modeling are well-documented and allow analyzes of strengths, weaknesses and reengineering for interoperability.

As a contribution, we preliminarily addressed concepts of KIP and sought to relate them to the context of SoIS based on the need for exploring approaches that deal with requirements that come from emergent behaviors that arise from the SoIS arrangement. As such, we present KIP modeling as an efficient and didactic approach to represent processes that involve interoperability decisions in SoIS. The modeling is important to better address the organizational interoperability layer that arises when we consider SoIS. In addition, we provide a possibility to discuss KIP approach for SoIS.

Acknowledgments. This work was supported by FAPERJ.

References

1. Bahrs, J., Müller, C.: Modelling and analysis of knowledge intensive business processes. In: Althoff, K.-D., Dengel, A., Bergmann, R., Nick, M., Roth-Berghofer, T. (eds.) WM 2005. LNCS (LNAI), vol. 3782, pp. 243–247. Springer, Heidelberg (2005). https://doi.org/10.1007/11590019_28
2. Boardman, J., Sauser, B.: System of systems - the meaning of of. In: IEEE/SMC International Conference on System of Systems Engineering, Los Angeles, CA, pp. 118–123 (2006)
3. Boehm, B.: A view of 20th and 21st century software engineering, p. 12. In: Proceedings of the 28th International Conference on Software Engineering (ICSE '06). Association for Computing Machinery, New York, NY, USA, pp. 12–29 (2006). https://doi.org/10.1145/1134285.1134288
4. Boscarioli, C., Araujo, R.M, Maciel, R.S.P.: I GranDSI-BR – Grand research challenges in information systems in Brazil 2016–2026. Special Committee on Information Systems (CE-SI). Brazilian Computer Society (SBC) (2017). ISBN [978-85-7669-384-0]. 184 p.
5. Brazilian Federal Government: Electronic Government Interoperability Standards. Doc. Ref. (2017). http://eping.governoeletronico.gov.br
6. Caire, P., et al.: Visual notation design 2.0: towards user comprehensible requirements engineering notations. In: 21st IEEE International Requirements Engineering Conference (RE), Rio de Janeiro, pp. 115–124 (2013)
7. Carlock, P.G., Fenton, R.E.: System of Systems (SoS) enterprise systems engineering for information-intensive organizations. Syst. Eng. **4**, 242–261 (2001). https://doi.org/10.1002/sys.1021
8. Di Ciccio, C., Marrella, A., Russo, A.: Knowledge-intensive processes: an overview of contemporary approaches. In: 1st International Workshop on Knowledge-intensive Business Processes, pp. 33–47 (2012)

9. Farinelli, F., Almeida, M.B., Elkin, P.L., Smith, B.: Interoperability among prenatal EHRs: a formal ontology approach. In: AMIA (2016). https://doi.org/10.13140/RG.2.2.16743.34729

10. Fernandes, J., Ferreira, F., Cordeiro, F., Graciano Neto, V.V., Santos, R.: A conceptual model for systems-of-information systems. In: IEEE 20th International Conference on Information Reuse and Integration for Data Science (IRI), Los Angeles, CA, USA, pp. 364–371 (2019)

11. Fernandes, J., Santos, R.: Exploratory study on interoperability in the SIGA ecosystem: an analysis of the dimensions of ePing. In: IX Workshop of Human-Computer Interaction Aspects to the Social Web, pp. 95–104 (2017). (in Portuguese)

12. Neto, V.V.G., Oquendo, F., Nakagawa, E.Y.: Systems-of-Systems: challenges for information systems research in the next 10 years. In: İ Grand Research Challenges in Information Systems in Brazil, Special Committee on Information Systems (CE-SI). Brazilian Computer Society, pp. 1–3 (2016)

13. Hagen, C.R., Ratz, D., Povalej, R.: Towards self-organizing knowledge intensive processes. J. Univ. Knowl. Manage. 2, 148–169 (2005)

14. Jamshidi, M.: System of systems engineering - new challenges for the 21st century. IEEE Aerosp. Electron. Syst. Mag. 23(5), 4–19 (2008). https://doi.org/10.1109/maes.2008.4523909

15. Javanbakht, M., et al.: A new method for decision making and planning in enterprises. In: 3rd International Conference on Information and Communication Technologies: From Theory to Applications, Damascus, pp. 1–5 (2008)

16. Netto, J.M., Barboza, T., Baião, F.A., Santoro, F.M.: KiPN: a visual notation for knowledge-intensive processes. Int. J. Bus. Process Integr. Manage. 9(3), 197–219 (2019)

17. Kajan, E.: Electronic Business Interoperability: Concepts, Opportunities and Challenges, 1st edn. IGI Global, Hershey (2011)

18. Kubicek, H., Cimander, R.: Three dimensions of organizational interoperability. Eur. J. ePract. 6, 1–12 (2009)

19. Kuziemsky, C.E., Weber-Jahnke, J.H.: An eBusiness-based framework for eHealth interoperability. J. Emerg. Technol. Web Intell. 1(2), 129–136 (2009). https://doi.org/10.4304/jetwi.1.2.129-136

20. Maciel, R.S.P., David, J.M.N., Claro, D.B.: Full interoperability : challenges and opportunities for future information systems. In: İ Grand Research Challenges in Information Systems in Brazil, Special Committee on Information Systems (CE-SI). Brazilian Computer Society (SBC), pp. 107–118 (2017)

21. Maier, M., Rechtin, E.: The art of systems architecting, 2nd edn. CRC Press, Inc., Boca Raton (2000)

22. Maier, M.W.: Architecting principles for systems-of-systems. Syst. Eng. J. Int. Counc. Syst. Eng. 1(4), 267–284 (1998)

23. Mittal, S., Zeigler, B.P., Martín, J.L.R., Sahin, F., Jamshidi, M.: Modeling and simulation for systems of systems engineering. In: Jamshidi, M. (ed.) System of Systems Engineering (2008). https://doi.org/10.1002/9780470403501.ch5

24. Teixeira, P.G., Lopes, V.H., Kassab, M., Santos, R., Graciano Neto, V.V.: The status quo of systems-of-information systems. In: 7th International Workshop on Software Engineering for Systems-of-Systems and 13th Workshop on Distributed Software Development, Software Ecosystems and Systems-of-Systems (SESoS-WDES '19). IEEE Press, pp. 34–41 (2019). https://doi.org/10.1109/SESoS/WDES.2019.00013

25. Neiva, F.W., David, J.M.N., Braga, R., Campos, F.: Towards pragmatic interoperability to support collaboration: a systematic review and mapping of the literature. Inf. Softw. Technol. 72, 137–150 (2016)

26. Graciano Neto, V.V., Cavalcante, E., El Hachem, J., Santos, D.S.: On the interplay of business process modeling and missions in systems-of-information systems. In: IEEE/ACM Joint 5th International Workshop on Software Engineering for Systems-of-Systems and 11th Workshop on Distributed Software Development, Software Ecosystems and Systems-of-Systems (JSOS), Buenos Aires, pp. 72–73 (2017)
27. Graciano Neto, V.V., et al.: A study on goals specification for systems-of-information systems: design principles and a conceptual model. In: XIV SBSI, p. 21 (2018)
28. Netto, J.M., França, J.B., Baião, F.A., Santoro, F.M.: A notation for knowledge-intensive processes. In: Proceedings of the 2013 IEEE 17th International Conference on Computer Supported Cooperative Work in Design (CSCWD), pp. 190–195. IEEE (2013)
29. dos Santos França, J.B., Netto, J.M., do ES Carvalho, J., Santoro, F.M., Baião, F.A., Pimentel, M.: KIPO: the knowledge-intensive process ontology. Softw. Syst. Model. **14**(3), 1127–1157 (2015)
30. Business Process Model and Notation (BPMN) 2.0. www.omg.org/spec/BPMN/2.0
31. Ojo, A., Janowski, T., Estevez, E.: Semantic interoperability architecture for electronic government. In: 10th Annual International Conference on Digital Government Research: Social Networks: Making Connections between Citizens, Data and Government. Digital Government Society of North America, pp. 63–72 (2009)
32. Saleh, M., Abel, M.-H.: Information systems: towards a system of information systems. In: 7th International Joint Conference on Knowledge Discovery, Knowledge Engineering and Knowledge Management - Volume 3: KMIS (IC3K 2015), pp. 193–200 (2015). ISBN 978-989-758-158-8. https://doi.org/10.5220/0005596101930200
33. Santos, R.P., Viana, D., Maciel, C.: Ecossistemas de Software: Uma Visão sobre Fatores Técnicos, Humanos e Organizacionais. In: Gasparini, I., Mota, M. (Org.) Livro dos Tutoriais do XV IHC, 15th edn., vol. C, pp. 70–90. SBC, Porto Alegre (2016). (in Portuguese)
34. Santos, R., Werner, C.: A proposal for software ecosystem engineering. In: International Workshop on Software Ecosystems (IWSECO/ICSOB), Brussels, Belgium, pp. 40–51 (2011)
35. Santos, R., Werner, C., Barbosa, O., Alves, C.: Software ecosystems: trends and impacts on software engineering. In: 26th Brazilian Symposium on Software Engineering, pp. 206–210 (2012)
36. Simpson, J.J., Dagli, C.H.: System of systems: power and paradox. In: IEEE International Conference on System of Systems Engineering (SoSE '08), pp. 1–5 (2008)
37. The Institute of Electrical and Electronics Engineers: IEEE Standard Glossary of Software Engineering Terminology (1990)
38. Neto, V.V.G., Oquendo, F., Nakagawa, E.Y.: Smart systems-of-information systems: foundations and an assessment model for research development. In: I Grand Research Challenges in Information Systems in Brazil, Special Committee on Information Systems (CE-SI). Brazilian Computer Society, pp 13–24. SBC (2017)
39. Wand, Y., Weber, R.: Research commentary: information systems and conceptual modeling - a research agenda. Inf. Syst. Res. **13**(4), 363–376 (2002)
40. Yahia, E., Yang, J., Aubry, A., Panetto, H.: On the use of description logic for semantic interoperability of enterprise systems. In: Meersman, R., Herrero, P., Dillon, T. (eds.) OTM 2009. LNCS, vol. 5872, pp. 205–215. Springer, Heidelberg (2009). https://doi.org/10.1007/978-3-642-05290-3_31

Exploring Sustainability in Real Cases of Emerging Small-to-Medium Enterprises Ecosystems

Pillar Benedetti Vasconcellos Luz[1(⊠)], Juliana Fernandes[1,2(⊠)],
George Valença[3(⊠)], and Rodrigo Pereira dos Santos[1(⊠)]

[1] Department of Applied Informatics, Federal University of the State
of Rio de Janeiro (UNIRIO), Rio de Janeiro, RJ, Brazil
{pillar.luz, juliana.costa, rps}@uniriotec.br
[2] Federal Institute of Piauí (IFPI), Campo Maior, PI, Brazil
[3] Department of Computer Science,
Federal Rural University of Pernambuco (UFRPE), Recife, PE, Brazil
george.valenca@ufrpe.br

Abstract. The effort and costs required to maintain complex software systems in the modern, global industry are often high, involving continuous refactoring to ensure longevity in the face of changing requirements. As such, it is challenging to treat systems sustainability as a quality requirement. This fact has been particularly challenging with the emergence of software ecosystems (SECO). A SECO is a set of actors that interact with a marketplace distributed between software and services and supported by a common technological platform. In this work, three real cases of SECO were modeled by applying a framework for systems sustainability to better understand the influence of such requirement. We also used a set of ecosystem factors that facilitate the understanding of the existing relationships in each SECO. The produced models were submitted to expert reviews based on a questionnaire and semi-structured interviews to understand and validate the analysis. Results indicate the difficulty in treating sustainability as a requirement due to lack of research on the topic, but highlight the importance of analyzing this requirement to assist in the SECO evolution.

Keywords: Software ecosystems · Sustainability · Small-to-medium enterprises

1 Introduction

A software ecosystem (SECO) is often defined as a set of actors working as a unit and interacting with a shared market for software and services, centered on a common technological platform [1]. SECO supports social web since it plays a central role enabling interactions through a platform towards its sustainability. The effort and costs required to maintain complex software systems in SECO are often high, involving continuous refactoring to ensure longevity in the face of changing requirements. According to Capilla et al. [2], the longevity of a system affects its sustainability, i.e.

R. P. d. Santos et al. (Eds.): WAIHCWS 2017/2018, CCIS 1081, pp. 42–59, 2020.
https://doi.org/10.1007/978-3-030-46130-0_3

meeting current needs without compromising the ability of future generations to meet their own needs. However, there is a lack of understanding on how to treat sustainability as a software system requirement, especially when it comes to a SECO. In this scenario, sustainability must become a requirement to analyze ecosystem health since it neither is addressed in a pragmatic way nor is considered when planning a new SECO. Few research initiatives addressed this requirement, such as the framework for assessing the sustainability dimensions proposed by Lago et al. [3], the only framework found for this purpose based on a systematic mapping study on the field [4].

In this work, we present the analysis of real SECO cases based on the use of this framework for systems sustainability. We also describe the relevance of sustainability in SECO context based on a set of 15 technical, human, and organizational factors compiled by Santos et al. [5]. To assess the resulting models, we performed two expert reviews, which relied on questionnaires and semi-structured interviews.

This paper is organized as follows: Sect. 2 presents the background. In Sect. 3, we describe the system sustainability framework from Lago et al. [3] and its application in our real cases. Section 4 presents an analysis on how SECO factors from Santos et al. [5] were observed in the real cases. Section 5 discusses the evaluation and interviews conducted with the experts, and summarize some key insights. Finally, in Sect. 6, we conclude the paper with the main contributions and limitations due to the lack of research addressing this topic [6], as well as pointing out future work.

2 Background

2.1 Software Ecosystems

Bosch and Bosch-Sijtsema [7] state that a SECO consists of a set of software solutions that automate activities and transactions of actors associated with a social or business ecosystem. In Fig. 1, we present the most common elements that form a SECO together with their relationships based on the work of Santos [8]. In a SECO, a platform is often provided to support the creation of products and services. These solutions can be included, modified or extended as software artifacts. An ecosystem also has a community of hubs (e.g. leading agents) and niche players (i.e. all stakeholders who affect the ecosystem through individual actions, such as contributing to the platform). Both participants play specific roles in this community, e.g. end-user or developer.

In this context, the relationships between a common technological platform and its actors can be analyzed from a set of technical, human and organizational factors that affect an ecosystem [5], as shown in Table 1. According to Santos et al. [5], the first factor (F1) deals with the management of diversity of organizations and relationships in a SECO, whose concern is the identification and understanding of the roles that each actor must play within an ecosystem. The next factor (F2) brings to the light possible contribution of external developers acting on a central platform and what actions must be taken into consideration when ensuring SECO performance. In turn, the third factor (F3) focuses on the sharing of content, knowledge, problems, experiences, and skills. The promotion of reusability is decisive in the fourth factor (F4), which deals with improvements in software reuse in the scenario of global software engineering, since a SECO appears as a promising approach in this case.

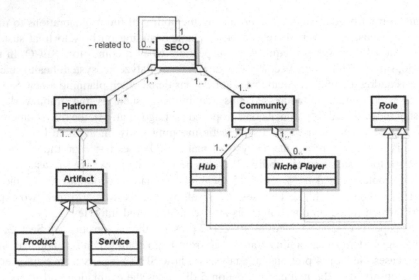

Fig. 1. SECO elements and their relationships [8].

Table 1. Technical, human and organizational factors affecting a SECO [5].

Factor	Description
F1	Deal with diversity of organizations and relationships within a SECO
F2	Encourage external developers to use a common technological platform
F3	Share content, knowledge, problems, experiences, and abilities
F4	Improve software reuse in the scenario of global software engineering
F5	Reposition organizations to act as network actors and reduce internal workforce
F6	Consider diversity of new functionalities offered to clients
F7	Invest in transparency
F8	Support modular system design
F9	Support organization openness
F10	Define internal characteristics related to SECO health and stability
F11	Define well-established SECO scope/boundaries
F12	Identify capacities and relationships between actors within a SECO
F13	Have a clear definition of the processes
F14	Strengthen a communicative character inherent for programming activities
F15	Ensure compliance based on the characteristics of different application domains

According to Bosch and Bosch-Sijtsema [7], organizations want to reposition themselves to act as network actors and reduce their internal workforce, as the fifth factor (F5) highlights. An example of this effort involves the sixth factor (F6), which focuses on new features available to customers, i.e. what can be observed in app stores. To ensure that there is transparency, a SECO must provide information related to the platform development, such as the chosen programming language, as highlighted by the seventh factor (F7). This factor is aligned with the eighth factor – modular system design (F8) – that applies an engineering principle: decompose a system into manageable parts to develop it from its modules.

When dealing with the organization opening in the ninth factor (F9), we refer to a critical factor for knowledge sharing. The definition of internal characteristics related to SECO health and stability is pointed out in the tenth factor (F10) and targets SECO participants and everything that involves them, e.g. size, roles, connectivity etc. SECO should have well defined boundaries (market, technology, infrastructure, or company), as referred in the eleventh factor (F11). The twelfth factor (F12) highlights the importance of taking care of any inconsistencies caused by evolutions and thereby reinforces the identification of capacities and relationships among SECO actors.

SECO evolution requires a clear definition of processes as stated by the thirteenth factor (F13). Since new external actors are involved in the development process and need to work with 'traditional' actors, strengthening the communicative character inherent to programming has a great level of importance, as represented in the fourteenth factor (F14). Finally, fifteenth factor (F15) claims that management should be done in a centralized way but recognizing that the community keeps the SECO providing demands and solutions for the platform [8].

2.2 System Sustainability Framework

Since sustainability refers to the ability to support and preserve the function of a system over a period, the longevity of a platform is directly related to sustainability [9]. According to Lago et al. [3], sustainability can only be achieved when four dimensions are considered: economic, social, environmental, and technical. In Fig. 2, we present the system sustainability framework proposed by Lago et al. [3] whose structure is extended from ISO/IEC 42030 – Architecture Assessment. This framework specifies relevant elements that characterize sustainability in a software system, assisting in the visual identification of its dimensions, as well as facilitating the understanding of the influence among its elements.

The goal of the framework is to identify to what extent the sustainability components influence each other. To evaluate sustainability of an ecosystem, we must consider a set of quality requirements, as well as criteria for evaluation. Since these criteria can influence system requirements and all sustainability dimensions, they should be aligned with the concerns of all stakeholders. With that said, it is clear that the whole framework should be considered when collecting data for assessing sustainability in ecosystems.

Considering the sustainability dimensions, social sustainability aims to ensure that future generations have access to social resources. It supports communities in any domain, activity or process that directly or indirectly creates social benefits. Environmental sustainability is concerned with ecological requirements, e.g. energy efficiency and ecological awareness. Technical sustainability focuses on embracing frequent changes and updates in the technological world, without harming its longevity. Finally, economic sustainability aims to define strategies to save capital and generate value.

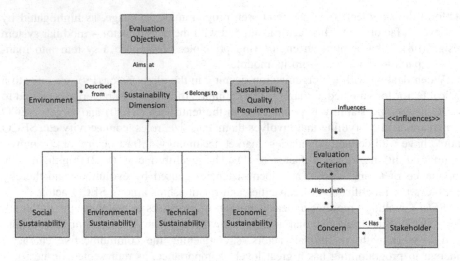

Fig. 2. Structure of the system sustainability framework proposed by Lago et al. [3].

3 Framing Sustainability

This section presents the application of the system sustainability framework proposed by Lago et al. [3] in the context of three SECO cases. We highlight it is possible to apply this framework to a SECO software platform as we would apply to software systems, since software is the common element. The difference lies in the borders, as a SECO is open for external developers and a software system might not be. The resulting sustainability model presents four different sustainability dimensions (small boxes). It also shows their parameters and evaluation methods. Based on these requirements, we interrelate the parameters through positive/negative relationships («influences»), where a positive influence means a parameter can leverage another one. In Fig. 3, we present the structure of the model. In particular, parameters and evaluations are not, in essence, positive or negative; they are metrics.

Social Dimension	Environmental Dimension	Technical Dimension	Economic Dimension
Sustainability Quality Requirements	**Sustainability Quality Requirements**	**Sustainability Quality Requirements**	**Sustainability Quality Requirements**
+ *Parameter*	+ *Parameter*	+ *Parameter*	+ *Parameter*
- *Evaluation*	- *Evaluation*	- *Evaluation*	- *Evaluation*

Fig. 3. System sustainability framework elements.

3.1   Small-to-Medium Enterprises SECO

A recent trend of small-to-medium enterprises (SME) is their close collaboration to create new products and reach new market niches. In this context, sustainability emerges as an important requirement of an ecosystem formed by companies (actors), mainly thinking of its longevity and survival. In Fig. 4, we show an instance of the system sustainability framework to the case of an emerging SME SECO.

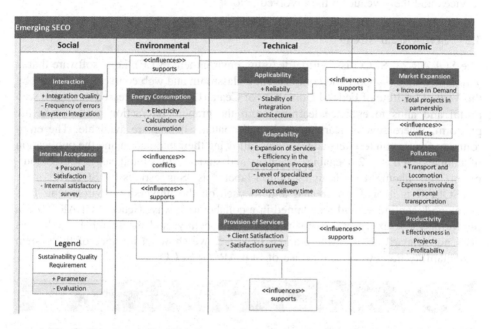

Fig. 4. System sustainability framework applied to the emerging SME SECO.

By applying the framework, we could analyze specific requirements, their parameters and how they should be evaluated. When looking at the social dimension, we perceive the lack of interactions among companies affecting the quality of products and services, which prevents a smooth operation of projects together and affects market expansion. Internal satisfaction of each ecosystem actor could be measured throughout the change period as well as the frequency defined by the organization in order to allow SECO improvements. On the environmental dimension, once SECO companies perform joint meetings, they may affect the environment with pollution and diesel oil consumption. In addition, as demand increases, electricity consumption also increases, as it requires more and/or a longer working environment.

In technical terms, the efficiency and reliability of the delivered products will be measured according to the existing delivery time standards aiming to achieve the ecosystem/products stability (e.g. an application developed by a service provider). There should be a technical adaptation, which could lead to expansion of services if the expertise level is high. According to these aspects and considering the scenario presented by Valença et al. [10], it is possible to evaluate the services provided through a customer satisfaction survey research. This survey with stakeholders will be a direct result of the economic dimension, since profitability depends on the effectiveness of the projects.

Another impact of this dimension refers to employees' expenses with urban movements (what we called "Pollution" requirement) for project meetings with the contracting companies or with partners in the ecosystem. An increasing demand may lead to expansion (and possible dominance) of the SECO, raising the number of services and the revenue to the involved actors.

3.2 SOLAR 2.0 SECO

The SOLAR 2.0 SECO is a virtual learning environment (VLE), i.e. a software that is available online (support and complement a classroom and web courses), developed by the Virtual Institute of Federal University of Ceará (UFC). It is accessed through a web portal and aims to enhance learning from the graphic interaction provided in the platform, where several learning tools and content sharing are available. The environment focuses on teachers and students, allowing their interaction and the publication of courses. SOLAR 2.0 enables teachers and students to submit suggestions, complaints and 'like/unlike' through a button labeled as "Suggestions for SOLAR".

SOLAR is a platform created and focused on the university environment. It is developed, configured and maintained in a collaborative way. Hence, SOLAR 2.0 is a platform whose expenses are not necessarily monetary, and the search for solutions does not primarily look at the market. In Fig. 5, we show an instance of the system sustainability framework to the case of SOLAR 2.0 SECO.

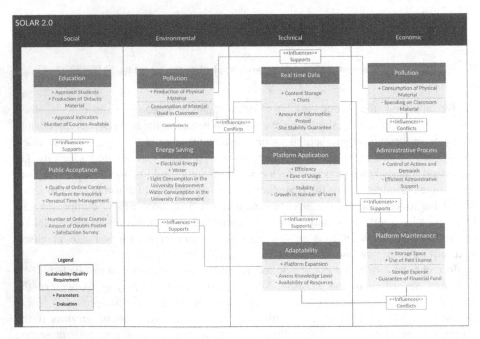

Fig. 5. System sustainability framework applied to the SOLAR 2.0 SECO.

In the social dimension, several requirement indicators are related to students and professors. Both requirements have material and approval as evaluation specifications. It shows the importance of commitment from all sides and their relevance for the SECO to stay alive – without students and/or professors, there is no ecosystem to sustain. The influence of a good and stable platform as well as the management of time when looking at the students harnessing are also part of this dimension.

The technical dimension is possibly the one of greater complexity in the identification of parameters and definition of evaluation methods. It helps to evaluate a possible expansion for being supported by other operating systems (iOS and Windows Phone). Developers know this fact and consider the limitation of having a platform available only via web, for Android users. Hence, they see a probable loss of students with direct access to the platform. This adaptability would lead to greater acceptance of the public. The factors of real-time data sharing are also raised, such as the available chat and the storage and immediate availability of a forum-posted data or a student-uploaded file for task delivery, for example. These factors conflict with the energy savings mentioned in the environmental dimension, as the use of machines increases. In addition, having an efficient (stable) and easy-to-use platform, user adaptability becomes more practical, indirectly influencing the growing number of users.

In the economic dimension, an actor depends on the common technological platform, whose expenditures cannot be properly sized in a monetary way [11]. If a software license ceases to be free, there will be an expense to keep the platform working as intended. In addition, depending on the total of users accessing the platform, there may be a need to store more data and offer more support (and there will be a cost). These elements can affect the users' behavior and acceptance, since it will hamper the platform expansion [12]. Expenditures for administrative controls conflict with the pollution indicators because there is a need to control the demands; e.g. control may require a quantity of available physical material, even at lesser proportions than that used by a teacher at each class. Finally, it is estimated the need for operational support to organize and maintain demands and actions that the platform requires from its community. For the employee allocation, there may be extra costs for a given sector.

3.3 Projudi SECO

Projudi system, whose purpose is to support the activities of the Judiciary in the State of Paraná and in other 18 Brazilian States, is formed by interconnected systems. Besides, it is influenced by internal and external actors, whose interactions aim at performing transactions and assisting in social contexts [7]. The 'informatization' of legal systems, such as Projudi, goes through a process known as a virtual judicial process (or virtual/electronic process), which aims to manage and control judicial process procedures electronically. It also facilitates the processes' dynamics, since it would allow the immediate access to them, regardless of the physical location of the user. In Fig. 6, we show an instance of the system sustainability framework to the case of Projudi SECO. This study is important to clearly visualize what can be understood from each dimension in this case.

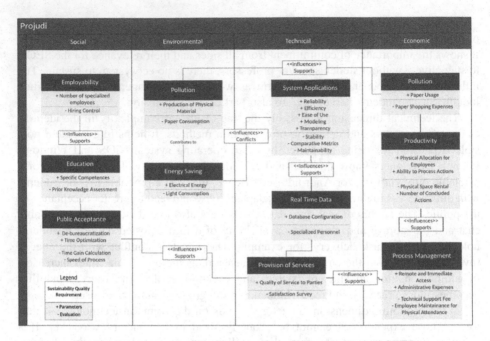

Fig. 6. System sustainability framework applied to the Projudi SECO.

In social terms, employability will increase, since the number of specialized employees should raise – this type of hiring depends on the demand. As far as public acceptance is concerned, there will be less use of physical transport for resolution of legal proceedings. This situation fosters de-bureaucratization in the legal sphere and optimizes the time of internal actors. Besides, there should be a remote and qualified service (i.e. a positive service delivery leads to greater public acceptance). This can even be an influencing factor, increasing the amount of users.

There will be an impact in the educational field, as it requires the use of virtual means as well as to charge specialized judges, lawyers and other actors. However, not all actors who will act in this platform have prior knowledge on technology. Previously, actors did not need to master the notion of interrelated works and working in real time, which can lead to primary difficulties for some users (seen in the technical dimension). For this reason, education and employability are influential: where there is a need for knowledge, there must be someone available to transferring it (i.e. teaching).

Looking at the environment, we know that spending on electricity, while decreasing in printing levels and control of physical documentation, will cause an increase in the use of computers. However, it is possible to evaluate the production of physical material, which possibly will decrease, since the deliveries of documentation can be done through the system, with no need of printing services and then contributing to decrease the consumption of electricity.

In the technical dimension, reliability, efficiency, ease of use (we can consider these three as a group to be evaluated), modeling and transparency may lead to stability, given a growing number of users and a strong demand for maintenance. This point ends up conflicting with the energy savings quoted in the environmental dimension: the greater the need for support and maintenance, the more active machines will have turned to this service. Quality personnel should also be available to ensure the operation of databases and their interconnections. Despite the existence of the platform, user services may not end. Besides physical support, the ecosystem must provide virtual support, which can be analyzed through user searches. Moreover, interconnections between systems for information exchange are needed. Only a certain level of interoperability enables them.

In the economic dimension, based on the calculation of paper reams as an evaluation method in the framework, it is possible to verify if there is any improvement over the paper purchase expense. This direct influences the amount of waste that can be produced by the exacerbated use of reams. Moreover, in terms of productivity, by improving the method of work, income grows without necessarily hiring new employees. For the economic sphere, this means savings. However, once new processes become easier, the amount of work increases, and there is a new access platform for the SECO actors.

Those who are assigned to work by providing support, even if virtual, will need to be allocated at a table with the right material to work with. This need directly influences the administration of processes, which deals with the management of employees assigned to the user service. It is known that there may be extra expenses (as provided by law), if the available space is not sufficient. In addition, the demand for employees that will act in the support influences the service delivery: without sufficient and qualified support, a satisfaction survey would bring negative results.

Analyzing the first instance of the built model, it is verified that the current way of work brings several changes, and most of them bring benefits in terms of the sustainability of the related ecosystem [7]. It allows us to not only point a possible and considerable change in the work process and in the functioning of the Judiciary activities, but also show that there are critical concerns, especially when talking about technical content. One of the main challenges of this system is its integrity, ensuring that the attached documents are not violated or pass through undue areas (security/privacy).

4   Analysis of SECO Factors

4.1   Emerging SME SECO

We observed the diversity of organizations and relationships (F1) among the factors that could affect relationships in an emerging SME SECO. In addition, clients receive different functionalities (F6), which is one of the goals for such SECO to become grow. We can also observe attention to programming aspects (F14), since developers from different companies must be aligned to deliver new solutions integrated with each other.

Several SECO factors were partially observed. It is the case of sharing content, knowledge, problems, experiences, and skills (F3), which already appear in an emerging SME SECO. In addition, there is an idea of improving software reuse in the global software engineering (F4) scenario and repositioning organizations that focus on reducing the internal workforce as well, acting as network actors (F5).

We also perceived a need for transparency (F7), despite the lack of guidance on how to address it. SECO scopes and frontiers are still unclear (F11), as well as the identification of capacity and relationships among actors in such ecosystem (F12), which hamper the definition of clear software processes (F13). Finally, we could not fully identify the application domains with their respective characteristics (F15).

The SECO factors that could not be observed in this case include the encouragement of external developers to use the platform (F2), modular system design (F8), and definition of internal characteristics that are related to SECO health and stability (F10). This may be due to the emergent nature of the SECO, possibly neglecting some aspects of its environment (i.e. defining characteristics involving health and stability), or requiring a stable, open platform for external developers.

4.2 SOLAR 2.0 SECO

Using the list of technical, human and organizational factors to analyze the second case, it was possible to verify that SOLAR 2.0 SECO was able to stimulate external developers to use the common technological platform (F2). In addition, there is sharing of content, knowledge, problems, experiences and skills (F3), since SOLAR 2.0 is a platform for learning. Whether one is a student or a teacher, there are several innovative features that are presented in the platform (F6). It is also separated into modules (F8) and the ecosystem has well defined scopes and boundaries (F11), knowing exactly where it will act and what it wants to achieve. There is no problem in the understanding of the relationship between SECO actors (F12) and maintaining communication as a pillar between external and internal developers. Although being a platform with source code information open to the public, management is centralized (F15) and its managers make the decisions based on what is best for the user community.

Among the factors partially observed in this case, the internal force reduction process is still underway (F5), since the platform continues to rely on internal workforce (from the university environment). Considering transparency (F7), SOLAR 2.0 has no option other than to charge users for a registration, as no people without authentication is allowed to have access to the platform. This SECO also does not have its clearly structured processes (F13), and it is not possible for any common user to know exactly what he/she is dealing with.

The unobserved factors (F1, F4, F9, and F10) refer to the reusability in software engineering, diversity in SECO relations, organization openness and the way in which this SECO internally defines characteristics related to its health and stability. These factors do not exist within the SOLAR 2.0 SECO since, in the first instance, it was started from a UFC project and there is no intention of opening the organization. In addition, no study was conducted to analyze health and stability of this ecosystem.

4.3   Projudi SECO

When looking at the list of human, technical and organizational factors, it is known that Projudi SECO actors are well defined (F1) and has a well-defined view of the role and relationship of each other. In addition, there is clearly a repositioning of organizations to act as network actors (F5), thereby reducing the internal workforce, where everyone has a primary role and can act properly within the ecosystem. Customers have the responsibility of acting in several new functions (F6), such as tracking the process through virtual means. This platform is decomposed into manageable parts and developed into modules (F8). All actors in this SECO are aware of their capabilities and the relationship between them (F12) and, even knowing that it is the community that maintains the ecosystem, the application management is centralized (F15).

There are factors partially observed in Projudi SECO, as the case of F3, F11 and F13. F3 was partially observed because there is content sharing, but not sharing of experiences, knowledge etc. F11 points to well-defined boundaries and scopes; Projudi platform is still in the process of expansion, i.e. stakeholders do not know exactly its borders and how far it can go. Finally, its processes are still not 100% clear (F13), since there is integration with other platforms and this can often confuse users.

Factors F2, F4, F7, F9, F10 and F14 could not be analyzed within Projudi SECO because they were not observed. Because it is a legal platform, its environment must be protected and cannot be completely open and fully transparent due to its nature as well. Moreover, precisely because it is not an open platform, there is no incentive for external developers to use the central platform; such developers do not exist in this SECO.

5   Evaluation of Results

To evaluate our findings, we conducted two expert reviews. Initially, we applied a questionnaire with experts in each selected SECO. The instrument involved three questions to verify whether results were in accordance with the existing reality of a given ecosystem (Table 2). We also used the definition of the Goal-Question-Metric (GQM) approach [13] to establish the goal of the analysis, as shown in Table 3. Next, we performed interviews with the same experts in order to make some aspects clearer.

Table 2. Interview questions.

Q1	Is the presented analysis consistent with the SECO case? Are the mentioned points aligned with the reality of such SECO? If not, what would be the proper form of explanation?
Q2	Does the system sustainability framework applied to SECO elements (parameters and evaluation methods) refer to social, environmental, technical and economic dimensions? Do such elements have consistent evaluation methods? Are the relations of influence between the elements pointed out in a right way?
Q3	Suggestions and recommendations

Table 3. GQM method.

Analyze	System sustainability framework and SECO factors
With the objective of	Evaluate
With respect to	Modeling and analysis of the studied SECO
From the point of view of	Researchers
In the context of	Real SECO cases

We used a consent form to state the purpose of the study as well as the participants' responsibilities and rights. In addition, we reinforced data confidentiality. The participants had access to selected parts of the real case analysis and to a questionnaire that had to be fulfilled after reading and understanding the material. Qualitative information on the execution of the study was collected, as well as suggestions of improvements based on the evaluation experience.

The instruments used to perform the study were prepared in MS Word 2016. We selected the participants by convenience, considering his/her extensive knowledge regarding each analyzed SECO: this fact was confirmed in the light of scientific papers published on the SECO theme by each participant. The main goal of the evaluation was to understand whether the system sustainability framework in conjunction with SECO factors contribute to model and analyze sustainability as a SECO requirement.

5.1 Emerging SME SECO Results

On December 21st, 2017, the emerging SME SECO participant received an e-consent form containing a brief explanation of the work and the confidentiality agreement. After acceptance and return of the signed document (December 27th, 2017), a document containing the selected emerging SME SECO model and analysis based on the framework was sent out (again by e-mail).

At that moment, the answers were given by the expert according to his/her understanding from what has been presented. The questionnaire was available for seven days. The result was received by e-mail on January 9th, 2018, with comments, but the questionnaire itself was not answered. After asking the participant to review the model on February 9th, 2018, the questionnaire was received. This result is presented in detail below, after reading, understanding and analyzing the received data.

Most of the answers were regarding the changes that could be helpful. Since it is an emerging SME SECO, there is some integration that is not common when studying other SECO environment, considered the traditional ones. There was a question about having the same parameters at two different dimensions: *"why is 'pollution' in two dimensions? Should not it be only environmental?"* – It made sense, but not in that way. Considering that this emerging SME SECO does not require much physical contact, it is not correct to consider it when thinking about environment. On the other hand, thinking about a financial situation, any moves to join teams would need an effort from both parts and it would affect the economic side.

There was also a suggestion pointed in Q2: the participant informed that the integrations between parameters are not clear and the use of plus (+) and minus (−) can create some confusion. In order to better understand the issues identified in the study, another expert review was conducted as a semi-structured interview. This interview was scheduled via e-mail and made effective via Skype on April 25th, 2018. Five questions were asked, all based on the result of the evaluation, as shown in Table 4. The responses were recorded during the interview.

Table 4. Questions used in the interview for emerging SME SECO.

Q1	In general, do you believe that the system sustainability framework instantiation applies to the case of this SECO? If not, why?
Q2	Was it clear that two different methods were used to conduct the study? In this case, a framework for modeling/analysis and an analysis of SECO factors. If not, why?
Q3	Is the "integration architecture stability" setting related to the evaluation inserted within the applicability (technical dimension) requirement?
Q4	What name do you think we should give to this SECO? (considering that "Emerging SECO" was not a good choice)
Q5	Clarification and acknowledgments

Regarding the first question, the participant explained that *"some items are not feasible to explore (we will not necessarily have data)"* and *"it is not necessarily useful to evaluate some pointed issues for the environment being evaluated"*. This refers directly to the fact that there are blind spots on the environmental dimension: it is mostly speculation due to the frequent changes and adaptations this SECO has. According to the participant, *"there was not much relationship between SECO factors and ecosystem modeling"*. This is correct: both methods are different and have different purposes but can be complementary for analyzing a SECO.

A valuable thing was to collect more information on the SECO platform, as observed in the answer for the third question: *"since it does not have a pre-established platform, it is integration"*. Such fragment explains why it is harder to determine some dimensions (e.g. environmental) and how the relation between requirements can change over time. Regarding the fourth question, the participant got confused on the SECO name: *"if the name 'emergent' goes to this case study, it is correct"*. Finally, the opportunity of applying the framework allowed us to use the signs plus (+) and minus (−), as they both were used by the original system sustainability framework [3].

5.2 SOLAR 2.0 SECO Results

On November 10th, 2017, the SOLAR 2.0 SECO participant received the consent form by e-mail containing a brief explanation of the work and the confidentiality agreement. After accepting and returning this form (signed on the 13th of the same month), the document with model and analysis of SOLAR 2.0 SECO was sent to the participant, including explanations of the theoretical basis, model and evaluation of SECO factors. We received the answer by e-mail on November 17th, 2017.

The evident dependence of SOLAR 2.0 SECO on the acceptance and number of users (in social terms) affects the allocation of funds from the Federal Government for the development and maintenance of its platform (in economic terms) – a specific fact highlighted in the excerpt from the participant: "*SOLAR SECO is very dependent on the UAB (Brazilian Open University) students, the majority of users. This aspect is sensitive because it depends on Federal Government funds, and this aspect affects all logistics, infrastructure and financially in the several poles of the distance education*".

Although the coherence of the model was confirmed according to part of the evaluation, the participant said that "*in general, I consider coherent with SOLAR SECO 2.0. (...) the points cited (in my view) are well related to the reality of SECO, more specific and hitherto unknown points were raised. For example, the existence of several poles in different cities in the State of Ceará and the way students' allocation is worked affect the ecosystem*". As such, there is a need to make available material and resources, thus affecting energy expenditure and pollution – pointed in the environmental dimension shown in Fig. 5.

In addition, by moving to the technical dimension, it is possible to relate the SECO platform to other systems that use data from it: "*(...) relationship with other support systems (managerial, logistic, financial etc.) of SOLAR 2.0 for other purposes*". The participant also highlights the material that comes from the discussion forums available on the platform, adding to what was said about the real-time chat.

According to the citation: "*(...) I missed many types of professionals involved in both use (students, tutors, coordinators etc.) and development (programmers, testers, designers, managers etc.) of SOLAR 2.0*". The professionals involved in the use of SOLAR 2.0 (e.g. tutors, coordinators) as well as the development team were not directly mentioned. Both were considered as members of a single team whose expenses would be included in the funds provided by the Federal Government.

Once again, in order to better understand the issues identified in the study, another expert review was conducted as a semi-structured interview. This interview was scheduled via e-mail and made effective via Skype. Five questions were asked, considering the result of the evaluation (Table 5).

Table 5. Questions used in the interview for SOLAR 2.0 SECO.

Q1	When and how do new students enter UAB? Are there significant and immediate changes to student leaving/entering?
Q2	When you talk about support systems (managerial, logistical, financial etc.), how is one system connected to another? Do they communicate with each other?
Q3	Does the Federal Government's budget vary according to the number of students? If so, how long does it take to assemble the planning (with logistics, infrastructure and availability of the poles)?
Q4	After some time passed from the presentation of this research, are there any suggestions and/or recommendations you would like to make?
Q5	Clarification and acknowledgments

When answering the first question, the participant said that there is an annual entrance exam and there is no formal data about the evasion (but it is a huge number). It was also said that the number of poles depends on the Ministry of Education (if it releases financial grant over time). There was no knowledge about the logistics. Regarding the third question, it was pointed that the systems were built as needed and they do not relate to each other (but some of them extract information from the same data source). As a final suggestion, the participant asked us to explain a bit about the influences that are set in the SOLAR 2.0 model, and we did it after the interview.

5.3   Projudi SECO Results

On November 10th, 2017, the Projudi SECO participant received the consent form by e-mail containing a brief explanation of the work and the confidentiality agreement. After accepting and returning this form (signed on the 23th of the same month), the document with model and analysis of Projudi SECO was sent to the participant, including theoretical basis, model and evaluation of SECO factors. We received the answer by e-mail on November 29th, 2017.

In the Projudi SECO's assessment, although the analysis is apparently coherent, the participant emphasized that the real case has its own characteristics: *"it appears to be in agreement, but given the fact that this SECO is predominantly public, there are some particular characteristics"*. Considering the sustainability dimensions, a question arose when the participant observed the social one, according to his/her citation: *"(...) I do not know if the hiring process supports the education. Most of the contracting acts are by public bidding, so I wonder if it is not education that supports the hiring, or if education is present in SECO"*.

In addition, the participant also pointed to the possibility of hierarchical partnerships (or not), within the business niche. In the technical dimension, it was observed the lack of integrations: *"in the technical question I wonder if the framework should not have something that contemplates the integration issues, because this is very strong in Projudi SECO"*. In the economic dimension, there was again an opinion on the existence of a requirement: *"The items of Economic Pollution appear to be so small by the size of SECO"*. Two of the three questions in the questionnaire related to the current Projudi SECO case were not answered. The Projudi SECO interview took place on January 30th, 2018. Table 6 lists the questions asked for the participant.

Table 6. Questions used in the interview for Projudi SECO.

Q1	Was there any specific reason related to the submitted text that prompted you to request more time for this evaluation? If so, which one?
Q2	By citing pollution in the economic dimension of SECO, what makes you think it is something small? Would you have any suggestions for this dimension?
Q3	Would the integrations cited in the technical dimension be related to hierarchical partnerships?
Q4	After some time passed from the presentation of this research, are there any suggestions and/or recommendations you would like to make?
Q5	Clarification and acknowledgments

Regarding the time spent to return the answers, the participant said that it was not expected to be something "*that big*", so it required more time to look at it. It was pointed that the lack of information about specific situations for this case could make it hard to analyze the ecosystem. Moreover, to the second question: "*Projudi came to meet a demand (processes on physical paper are a problem, excess of work to control these processes) (...) today it is easier to control deadlines and query processes, as well as the security of a digitalized process*". For the third question, the expert said that it depends on how each process goes, but it can be scaled in hierarchical levels.

6 Conclusions

Our analysis revealed the concept of sustainability in different types of SECO. We instantiated the system sustainability framework, and assessed our results with experts from each studied ecosystem. We noticed the relevance and importance of different sustainability dimensions. Moreover, the topic still lacks modeling and analysis tools focused on the software industry needs. Three cases were studied with the use of that framework to better understand the influence of this requirement in this context. The generated models were evaluated through expert reviews based on questionnaires and semi-structured interviews with the purpose of verifying the analysis performed by the researchers. The results show that the technical and (especially) social dimensions of sustainability present a set of factors that may affect the longevity of platforms and/or ecosystems, including the ones who are emerging (in case of SME SECO). Although it was possible to notice the relevance of analyzing sustainability in a SECO, it was not easy to do so. However, such difficulty was expected since there is not much research papers regarding this matter.

Despite the supported offered by Brazilian Government, the three studied ecosystems have different purposes. Notably, we were able to highlight more technical and social factors, as well as their relations. Even when introducing a new SECO in a scientific work, researches do not usually look deeply into economic and environmental matters. If we consider immediate impact, SOLAR 2.0 and Projudi are willing to make a difference on the environment they act. They change how education and jurisdiction works and how the efforts are allocated. We emphasize that the analysis of the real emerging SME SECO case contains less information on the environmental dimension if compared to both others (SOLAR 2.0 SECO and Projudi SECO).

As contributions, we highlight the application of the system sustainability framework in the context of real SECO cases as well as the identification of factors that affect the ecosystem longevity, demonstrating the importance of treating 'sustainability' in this scenario. While there is a concern for sustainability, little is known about what is needed to effectively be sustainable in Information Systems and Software Engineering areas.

Despite the difficulty in finding specific data to all three cases, it was possible to extract information based on the interviews. We also noticed a lack of understanding on how to treat sustainability as a requirement of a platform and/or SECO in general. Therefore, we intend to develop a tool to model and analyze a SECO case to explore elements of the 'sustainability' requirement. Hence, another possible future work is to conduct additional case studies to evaluate the effectiveness of this tool in relation to the impacts generated by each sustainability dimension.

Acknowledgments. This study was financed in part by the Coordenação de Aperfeiçoamento de Pessoal de Nível Superior - Brasil (CAPES) - Finance Code 001.

References

1. Jansen, S., Finkelstein, A., and Brinkkemper, S.: A Sense of community: a research agenda for software ecosystems. In: Proceedings of the 31st International Conference on Software Engineering (ICSE 2009), New and Emerging Research Track, Vancouver, Canada, pp. 187–190 (2009)
2. Capilla, R., Nakagawa, Y.E., Zdun, U., Carrillo, C.: Toward architecture knowledge sustainability: extending system longevity. IEEE Softw. **34**(2), 108–111 (2017)
3. Lago, P., Koçak, A.S., Crnkovic, I., Penzenstadler, B.: Framing sustainability as a property of software quality. Commun. ACM **58**(10), 70–78 (2015)
4. Vegendla, A., Duc, A.N., Gao, S., Sindre, G.: A systematic mapping study on requirements engineering in software ccosystems. J. Inf. Technol. Res. (JITR) **11**(1), 21 (2018)
5. Santos, R., Viana, D., Maciel, C.: Ecossistemas de Software: Uma Visão sobre Fatores Técnicos, Humanos e Organizacionais. In: Gasparini, I., Mota, M. (Org.) Livro dos Tutoriais do XV IHC, Portuguese, vol. C, pp. 70–90 (2016)
6. Barbosa, O., Santos, R., Alves, C., Werner C., Jansen, S.: A systematic mapping study on software ecosystems from a three-dimensional perspective. In: Jansen, S., Brinkkemper, S., Cusumano, M.A. (Org.) Software Ecosystems. Analyzing and Managing Business Networks in the Software Industry. 1ed. Cheltenham UK, Northampton USA: Edward Elgar Publishing, 1, pp. 59–81 (2013)
7. Bosch, J., Bosch-Sijtsema, P.: From integration to composition: On the impact of software product lines, global development and ecosystems. J. Syst. Softw. **83**(1), 67–76 (2010)
8. Santos, R.: Managing and monitoring software ecosystem to support demand and solution analysis. PhD thesis, COPPE/UFRJ, Rio de Janeiro, Brazil (2016)
9. Hilty, M.L., Arnfalk, P., Erdmann, L., Goodmand, J., Lehmann, M., Wägera, A.P.: The relevance of information and communication technologies for environmental sustainability: a prospective simulation study. Environ. Model Softw. **21**(11), 1618–1629 (2006)
10. Valença, G., Alves, C., Heimann, V., Jansen, S., Brinkkemper, S.: Competition and collaboration in requirements engineering: a case study of an emerging software ecosystem. In: Proceedings of the IEEE 22nd International Requirements Engineering Conference (RE 2014), Karlskrona, Sweden, pp. 384–393 (2014)
11. Coutinho, E.F., Viana, D., Santos, R.: An exploratory study on the need for modeling software ecosystems: the case of SOLAR SECO. In: Proceedings of the 9th International Workshop on Modelling in Software Engineering (MiSE 2017), Buenos Aires, Argentina, pp. 47–53 (2017)
12. Lago, P., Penzenstadler, B.: Editorial: reality check for software engineering for sustainability – pragmatism required. J. Softw. Evol. Proc. **29**(2), 1–4 (2017)
13. Basili, R.V.: Software modeling and measurement: the Goal/Question/Metric paradigm. Technical report: software modeling and measurement: The Goal/Question/Metric paradigm. University of Maryland at College Park College Park, MD, USA (1992)

Analysis of Terms of Use and Privacy Policies in Social Networks to Treat Users' Death

Gabriel Trocha Viana[1]([✉]), Cristiano Maciel[1]([✉]),
Patricia Cristiane de Souza[1]([✉]), and Ney Alves de Arruda[2]([✉])

[1] Laboratório de Ambientes Virtuais Interativos, Instituto de Computação,
Universidade Federal de Mato Grosso (UFMT), Cuiabá, MT, Brazil
gabitvl00@gmail.com, crismac@gmail.com,
patricia@ic.ufmt.br
[2] Faculdade de Direito, Universidade Federal de Mato Grosso (UFMT),
Cuiabá, MT, Brazil
neyarruda@gmail.com

Abstract. Social networks are now the main means of communication between people. Users access them many times throughout the day and have their data stored in these systems. If people are born and evolve in social networks, their passing away should be addressed by these systems as well. Terms of use and privacy policies are documents that determine the relationship between users and digital service companies. This paper reports the results from a qualitative analysis on how such documents address issues of post-mortem digital legacy in the following social web platforms: Facebook, Pinterest, Instagram, Foursquare/Swarm, LinkedIn, WhatsApp, and YouTube. In our comparative analysis, we highlight the different solutions adopted by these social networks, considering the Brazilian Laws.

Keywords: Digital legacy · Social networks · Social web · Terms of use · Privacy policies

1 Introduction

We live in a globalized world, with constant transformations in our society, in which many people depend on the way we communicate, supported by the development of new technology. With the advent of e-mails, for example, we stopped sending letters and faxes. Included in this list of changes, there are social networks, which are already considered the main vehicle intermediating communication between people. These networks promoted many changes in daily communication between individuals, intermediating the sharing of images, videos, feeling, events, tastes, aversions, dates, status, and several notifications about important life events.

The manner in which people interact with one another has always been the subject of studies belonging to several fields of science. With the resounding establishment of the internet as a mediator of human relations, experiences and opinions are then passed on and exposed to vast groups of connected people. This coexistence occurs especially

© Springer Nature Switzerland AG 2020
R. P. d. Santos et al. (Eds.): WAIHCWS 2017/2018, CCIS 1081, pp. 60–78, 2020.
https://doi.org/10.1007/978-3-030-46130-0_4

through social networks, whose terms of use and privacy policies [21] establish how people will interact with each other.

Movements by online users are collected and stored through digital service providers. As the volume of data circulating across the platforms increases, a few legal management methods are used to safeguard users and providers, such as the terms of use that can cover most of the functions and behavior of a social network [42].

The term of use is what can be called a service agreement between the owner of the social network and the user. In general, this document describes the terms of the relationship between the product/service and the user, rules of operation, and user rights and responsibilities. However, these are not always clear and harmonious to all the possibilities and particularities of human relations. Such documents need to be clear and specific in order to guide users about their digital properties, and that is not always the case. After a user passes away, a lot of data is lost or misused due to misinterpretation of the terms of the social network or user oversight when alive. If people "are born and evolve" into these communities, it should be expected that main social networks address the death of their users.

Although this is relatively a recent topic, some academic investigations are already available, as discussed by Maciel [22], Maciel and Pereira [23, 24], Brubaker et al. [7, 45], Maciel et al. [20, 25], Prates et al. [33, 34] and de Toledo el al. [46], who discuss and present solutions to address digital legacy through software engineering, including the context of social networks. Studies by Gach [48], say that "post-mortem profile deletion is a difficult experience because it is drastically different from any offline post-mortem disposal practice". Meireles and Batalha [27] proposed a software model that addresses digital legacy, while also analyzing several tools and their terms of use. However, from the legal viewpoint, especially in the case of Brazil, more discussion is necessary.

Therefore, understanding how some social networks address the death of the user and performing an analysis of the documents that govern these networks in Brazil is the main contribution of this work. For this purpose, the authors selected the following social networks: Facebook, Pinterest, Instagram, Foursquare/Swarm, LinkedIn, WhatsApp and YouTube.

It should also be noted that the death of users has been treated differently in social networks. Death can be observed to be a profitable business in capitalist societies, and there is already a whole death industry that provides for funeral services until the destination of the physical body. In the digital world, such an industry has already been discussed [29] and deserves attention.

To this end, Sect. 2 discusses the concepts and techniques that guide the functioning of a social network, as well as the legal aspects regarding the existence of these contractual documents between companies and users, adopting an interdisciplinary view. In Sect. 3, the regulations of each social network are analyzed and the different solutions presented are analyzed, such as: the possibility to exclude the account or to register an "heir", or legacy contact, to manage it after the owner's death; the operation of the registry of heirs and the care in the treatment of the digital goods, protecting privacy rights in case of death.

Different results were found for each web application and all of them were correlated in the attempt to ascertain the possibilities of the heir and their attributions, or deleting of the account in case death is detected, as well as the way a system is able to detect the death of a user accepting their volatility regarding the sharing and exposure of their information. The discussion regarding the results obtained is presented in Sect. 4. Finally, it should be noted that not all applications treat the digital legacy in synchrony with the recommendations present in the literature related to the theme.

2 Founding Concepts

In order to discuss this theme, two issues need to be explored: the legal repercussions of death and existing regulations; and terms of use and privacy policies.

2.1 Death and the Law

Death can be discussed through different lenses. Regarding legislation, this is a subject containing different approaches, covering, among others, issues related to inheritance law, image protection or respect for mortal remains. For Nalini [28], "Death and the law intertwine. Death can be found in every branch of the leafy and increasingly tangled legal tree." According to the author, "If, according to the law, the human saga ends with death … it is only the starting point. Not the end, but only the beginning. The beginning of a new right".

For Ascensão [30], as "there are no absolute notions in the law. As is the case with life. The law has to accept the relativity of life; as well as the very simple truth, all too often ignored, which is that, in the individual point of view, every life means that death is approaching. That is the tragedy of human life – at least as long as we do not know how to incorporate the reality of death".

Nalini [28] adds that "the law focuses on human life in design, impending, in development and after the earthly experience has ceased". At this point, and considering the presence of death in digital environments, new concerns arise, associated with the treatment of post-mortem digital assets. To understand matters from the legal point of view, Brazilian legislation is discussed.

Assets and property rights are addressed in Articles 79 to 97 of the Brazilian Civil Code [6]. This legal code is the main document incorporating property rights in Brazil and it is the foundation for the provision of services. Article 607 states that a service contract is terminated if one of the parties passes away, and this is a relevant research question when comparing the law to documents governing social networks.

Legal provisions [24] establish that, in Brazil, all data processed and collected exclusively belong to the person described by the data, that is, data which can somehow indicate the individual. Data processing means any production or reception procedure, whether or not they are stored or transmitted, including processing, classification, evaluation or modification techniques. According to [23], data collection by private companies can only occur with prior consent, and can be revoked at any time. The owner must always have access to the data collected and the treatments imposed on them, as well as the purpose of the data processing. All modification and treatment should be cataloged and stored. Currently, there is no characterization of how long the data can be under custody of those who operate them.

In August 2018, Brazil approved its first general data protection law (Law 13,709/2018) [4] after many discussions about privacy, instigated by daily reports of crimes and personal setbacks. Several research institutions were already investigating and offering recommendations regarding this domain [7, 20, 22, 28]. With the enactment of the law, new proposals and provisions on the subject have emerged.

Although there are laws that deal with public and private data regulations peripherally, the consolidation of digital privacy and paralegal discussions led to the formalized Law 13.709/18 [4]. This law brought legal certainty and complements to loopholes that tolerated malicious definitions in public and private systems, which will now be subject to a warning, with deadlines for regularization, and with a fine imposed on those who fail to comply that comprises up to 2% of the company's revenue and limited to fifty million reais, in addition to daily penalty fines. The rigidity of sanctions must be applied according to the gravity of the infraction, considering the advantage sought by the offender, their economic condition, recidivism, degree of damage, participation in the act and their ability to intervene in detriments. The judicial authority is responsible for assessing the actual damages and disputes. A digital data recovery action, for example, can be accepted as an infraction by the network that does not deliver organized information, which can even amount to compensation for relatives of deceased persons who prove their ownership.

From the legal standpoint, death is proved by the certificate extracted from public files (Law of Public Records, 6,015/1973, articles 77 to 88 and CC, article 9, I.). However, for Diniz [10], "extinction is not complete with death; the desire of the deceased survives with their will. Respect is owed to the corpse. Certain rights have effects after death, such as the moral right of the author, the right to image and honor. Military and civil servants can be promoted post mortem."

In this perspective, further investigations into the fate of postmortem digital assets are necessary, and an initial route to such discussion is the analysis of the terms of use and privacy policies of these applications.

2.2 Terms of Use and Privacy Policies

The term of use is the central document of the legal regiment of a social network. It deals with the description of what is the product or service of that site or application, showing how the user's relationship will be online. Its internal rules are defined by providers who stipulate the rights and duties of the user and what is allowed in their environment, such as forbidding the sharing of inappropriate content or copying owned content.

For Barbosa [2], the terms of use are "a series of conditions that define the rules of use and operation of the computer program, which the user must abide by in order to be granted access to the virtual environment." In the view of Yamaguchi, Souza and Pereira Junior [42], the "term of use describes what the application is like, besides informing the 'internal rules' that must be following during its operation."

The terms of use employed by modern social networks discontinue the old habit of drafting long documents filled with complex terms. The texts seek a simplistic tendency; suggesting rules in simple and spontaneous forms, which in principle fulfills the requisites to avoid vices of consent, protecting users from misinterpretations. However, they are tolerant of appropriate or malicious executions when the discussions come from unusual topics such as the death of a user. The thesis is put forward that the fickle yearnings of the common people as to death itself or of a loved one are not understood by the general rules. Several complaints and disputes [14] of these documents are worked out to the operators and the common justice, in the case of Facebook as we will see later, various problems according to the restrictions that an account without a previously registered legacy contact may suffer.

In turn, the privacy policy is the document that must inform the user which data will be requested, how the system will make use of them and the reason for collecting them, determining the purpose of the application in collecting such data, as well as the length of time for which this data will be stored. It should be noted that intimacy is a subjective right protected by law, described in more than one legal edict. In Brasil [4] is explicit in Article 17 of Chapter 3, the security to the holder of their personal data and fundamental rights. For Yamauchi, Souza and Pereira Junior [41], the "privacy policy informs the user of privacy issues related to their data, for example, information regarding the collection and processing of data and the location of servers."

Assets with a declared value are called digital assets [8], which can be something that has been acquired in some business or produced by the user, which belongs to an individual company or person, or to a couple, which must be shared in case of separation or divorce, or even an object of legacy in case of death according to order of civil succession. A 2012 draft bill [5] called for the amendment of the Brazilian Civil Code [6] and determined that all digital data must be included in divorce and inheritance inventories in accordance to Article 1,788. Digital files saved in a deceased person's phone can only be accessed if previously allowed by the person when alive, according to Law n. 9,296 of 1996, known as the "telephone call interception bill". In the absence of this permission, the heirs are granted a court authorization if the situation is justified.

Understanding how the terms of use and privacy policies of social networks address the possibility of user death is a pressing matter [48]. For that reason, an analysis of documents regarding the terms of seven social networks was conducted and is described in the following section.

3   Methodological Decisions

The source of this analysis includes the terms of use and privacy policies of seven social networks selected for this study. These networks were selected according to the usage information and statistics [26], as follows:

1. Facebook – currently the largest social network in the world;
2. Pinterest – a large image sharing network;
3. Instagram – this social network has more than 300 million active users and is very effective for advertising;
4. Foursquare – network in which the user shares their location with friends and is rewarded for visiting different places. Its game version, Swarm offers users challenges and rewards during the use of the platform, which keeps users constantly immersed.

5. LinkedIn – it is also marked as the main social network in the corporate world due to the dissemination of professional experience and job offers;
6. WhatsApp – daily accessed by one third of the Brazilian population;
7. YouTube – the second largest social network accessed in the country.

The metrics used to analyzed differences for each document that safeguards usage and storage of network data were defined in a meeting of members of the research project "DAVI – Dados além da vida" (Data Beyond Life) [44], in the Laboratory of Interactive Virtual Environments of the Computer Science Institute of the Federal University of Mato Grosso, held in May 2017. The members were all users of social networks and were familiar with death-related issues. They addressed the possibilities that could integrate this study, proposing social networks and voting corresponding to a characteristic approach to privacy studies. The digital legacy experts of this group, based on current suggestions found in literature [20, 22, 24, 27], defined that the terms of use and the privacy policies of each system were analyzed on the following topics:

1. Whether there is a transfer of digital assets;
2. Whether there is a record of heirs/inheritance;
3. Whether digital assets/goods are addressed;
4. Whether it is possible to inactivate an account;
5. Whether user privacy is addressed in case of death.

By examining each section of the documents, the authors indicated the perspective addressed for each topic, noting the possibility of transferring data and digital properties to someone after death and, if it is possible, how the user would select people to receive them and how they would be delivered. Furthermore, the authors sought to know if, for cases with services that have a declared financial value, the purchased service or product could be passed on.

When there is a possibility that the user wishes to be forgotten, it was investigated how the network is able to delete the account and the digital traces that may remain after the user's death. When found, information on the assignments of the heirs and the form of death detection were reported.

Based on these criteria, the authors performed an analysis of the legal documents of the social networks selected for this work. Such analysis and results are presented in the following sections.

4 Analysis Through Social Networks

This section presents the analysis of social networks and referenced documents available online, such as terms of use and privacy policies. Some information was complementarily obtained from the Help function in the applications. It should be noted that some of these applications fall into different types of software; however, in this research they are addressed as social networks. It is important to highlight that the data herein presented were collected in 2017. In 2019, this data were updated, in case there were changes.

4.1 Facebook

Facebook allows the user to add, change or remove the legacy contact in a very simple way. With only four steps, it is possible to configure the heir contact by accessing the account settings, entering the name of the heir and sending the invitation. Facebook also remembers the user's privacy settings from time to time through notifications and prompts the user to set up an heir. If the account is transformed into a memorial [46], this heir will be the person who will take care of the account. Their responsibilities can be seen in Fig. 1.

A legacy contact is someone you choose to look after your account if it's memorialized...... br
Once your account is memorialized, your legacy contact will have the option to do things like:

- Write a pinned post for your profile (example: to share a final message on your behalf or provide information about a memorial service).

- View posts, even if you had set your privacy to **Only Me**.

- Decide who can see and who can post tributes, if the memorialized account has an area for tributes.

- Delete tribute posts.

- Change who can see posts that you're tagged in.

- Remove tags of you that someone else has posted.

- Respond to new friend requests (example: old friends or family members who weren't yet on Facebook).

- Update your profile picture and cover photo.

- If you had turned on timeline review, your legacy contact will be able to turn off the requirement to review posts and tags before they appear in the tributes section.

- Request the removal of your account.

You also have the option to allow your legacy contact to download a copy of what you've shared on Facebook, and we may add additional capabilities for legacy contacts in the future.

Fig. 1. Responsibilities of the legacy contact [11]

There are four restrictions for the legacy contact, as depicted in Fig. 2.

Your legacy contact can't:

• Log into your account.

• Read your messages.

• Remove any of your friends or make new friend requests.

Fig. 2. Restrictions of the legacy contact [11].

Currently, Facebook makes it clear, in its term of use, that if death of the user is detected, the account is transformed into a memorial [12, 46]. Moreover, another user can inform of someone's death by filling a form available in https://www.facebook.com/help/contact/651319028315841, which is then analyzed by the team responsible for verifying the authenticity of the request.

After the account is transformed into a memorial page, some elements are changed in the user profile, the expression "In memory" is added next to the person's name, [12] and that profile no longer appears in public spaces, such as *people you may know, birthday reminders* or *notifications*. Depending on the privacy settings of the deceased user, friends can post memories on their timeline [11], just as everything that was shared by the user in life remains visible to the audience configured in the post.

After becoming a memorial account, nobody can enter the account, even if they type in the account login and password. In case the deceased user has not set up a legacy contact, the account remains unchanged, just the way the user left it, and if this

Fig. 3. Example of the profile layout transformed into a memorial

account is the sole administrator of a page, all the page content will be deleted from Facebook. Figure 3 shows an example of a memorial type of profile.

The image of a memorial depicted in the layout above refers to the messages of nostalgia and homages, which seem to be examples of behavior by the Brazilian community, where people like to visit environments, speak with friends in common, see photos and even talk to the deceased individual, all for the sake of reminiscing with a loved one.

Facebook allows user desire regarding account functioning after the user's death, as in the recommendations of [20, 22]. However, the user must notify their wishes to the social network while still alive, otherwise, by default, the account will be transformed into a memorial without a legacy contact to manage it. A family member may contact and request the removal or request to manage the memorial. To specify the desire to delete the account after death, it is necessary to access the privacy settings and establish one's will, as shown in Fig. 4.

Fig. 4. Steps for deleting an account [10]

If friends and family members wish to claim ownership of the memorial or request deletion of the account, they can do so by filling out and sending the form available at https://www.facebook.com/help/contact/228813257197480. The process for deleting an account can only be performed by a direct family member or will executor. After starting the process with the submission of the form, Facebook requires verification to confirm the authenticity of the request.

An interesting artifice is that, even if an account is deleted, its data will remain unreachable by any user, but will still be under social network ownership for ninety days, and if family members choose to request information from a deleted account or memorial, they can do so it, through requests in justice and, later, to the organization (https://www.facebook.com/help/123355624495297?helpref=popular_topics). Figure 5 shows the form for requesting the contents of a deceased person's account.

It is worth noting that, in Brazil, there is still no consolidated jurisprudence or court decision about the topic of the digital legacy in social network in the Supreme Court of Justice, at least until now.

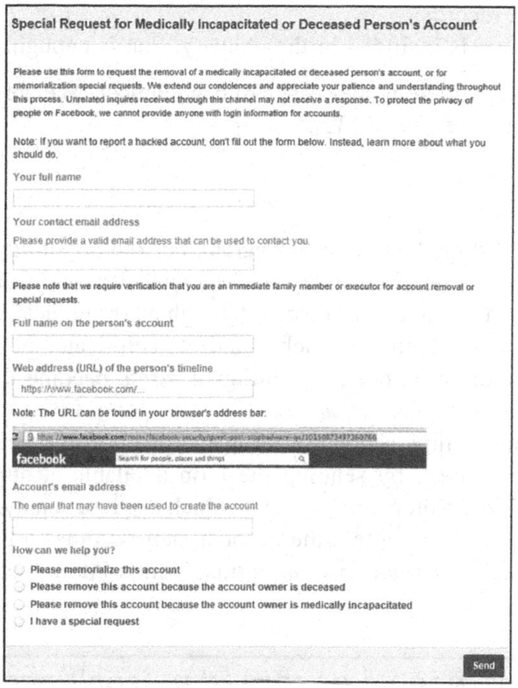

Special Request for Medically Incapacitated or Deceased Person's Account

Please use this form to request the removal of a medically incapacitated or deceased person's account, or for memorialization special requests. We extend our condolences and appreciate your patience and understanding throughout this process. Unrelated inquires received through this channel may not receive a response. To protect the privacy of people on Facebook, we cannot provide anyone with login information for accounts.

Note: If you want to report a hacked account, don't fill out the form below. Instead, learn more about what you should do.

Your full name

Your contact email address
Please provide a valid email address that can be used to contact you.

Please note that we require verification that you are an immediate family member or executor for account removal or special requests.

Full name on the person's account

Web address (URL) of the person's timeline
https://www.facebook.com/...

Note: The URL can be found in your browser's address bar:

facebook   Search for people, places and things

Account's email address
The email that may have been used to create the account

How can we help you?
○ Please memorialize this account
○ Please remove this account because the account owner is deceased
○ Please remove this account because the account owner is medically incapacitated
○ I have a special request

Send

Fig. 5. Requesting content from a deceased person's account

4.2 Pinterest

Pinterest is an image sharing social network generally formed by images available online. Users can share images, repost those of other users and include them in private collections or boards, and comment and perform other actions available in the website.

This network does not allow users to register an heir. Nor is it possible to transform the account into a memorial; therefore, it is impossible to transmit digital assets [31]. In this case, digital assets generated or obtained by the user through the network are deleted, which includes privacy after death, thus assuring the right to be forgotten [25], if this is their concern.

However, if the user wishes to leave a legacy and be digitally remembered, the account owner is barred if another user informs about the user's death via email to care@pinterest.com. In this case, it is necessary to yield to the conditions requested by the system, such as informing the applicant's identification, providing their full name and the deceased user's full name and email with the link of their account, as well as proof of death, which can be a death certificate, obituary or news article. Still, the applicant needs to prove their relationship with the person by providing the following documents [32]:

– Birth or marriage certificate;
– Public mention of the relationship;
– Genealogy;

- Family/household records;
- If the person's name is included in the obituary, that is enough.

In the privacy policy, there is a message of condolence: "We are very sorry to hear about the loss of your loved one" [32].

4.3 Instagram

There is no transfer of digital assets in Instagram, nor the possibility of registering an heir; that is, the data belong exclusively to the social network. However, if a direct relative so wishes, the account can be deleted through a [16] request. In order to do this, it is necessary to present a document such as a death certificate, the deceased person's birth certificate or proof of authority. The digital assets become the property of the system the moment a user dies.

The option of transforming accounts into memorials is also practiced. For this, it is necessary to make a request, by sending the form available at http://help.instagram.com/264154560391256?helpref=faq_content, which will be analyzed by a support team [15]. If the request is accepted, the account then becomes a memorial. Figure 6 illustrates what happens when an account is transformed into a memorial.

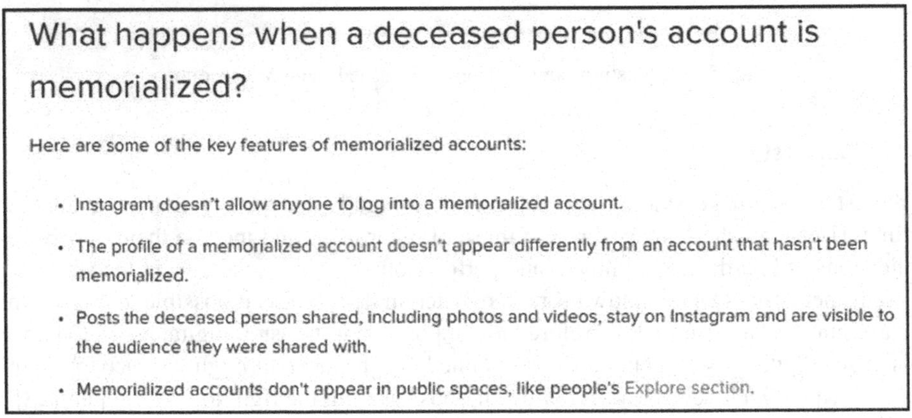

What happens when a deceased person's account is memorialized?

Here are some of the key features of memorialized accounts:

- Instagram doesn't allow anyone to log into a memorialized account.
- The profile of a memorialized account doesn't appear differently from an account that hasn't been memorialized.
- Posts the deceased person shared, including photos and videos, stay on Instagram and are visible to the audience they were shared with.
- Memorialized accounts don't appear in public spaces, like people's Explore section.

Fig. 6. Main features of the memorialized account [15]

In the Help screen, the system shows that "If you find that a post or comment on a memorial profile violates the Community Guidelines or the Terms of Use, you can file a complaint form located next to the post or comment" [15].

Unlike the concept of other memorials, Instagram does not allow homages or interactions with a memorialized account. A converted account will remain unchanged throughout the residual existence of the social network, with privacy settings preserved.

4.4   Foursquare

For this application, the data sent by users is of paramount importance. The system is based on a collaborative concept in which users visit websites or establish a region and issue their opinions and information about them so that other users can follow such recommendations. Therefore, the data sent by the users are essential for the operation of the network. This is the primary prerogative of its privacy policy, and it is made clear that whatever is produced by the user is fully owned by the application [13]. Thus, Foursquare does not have a transfer of digital goods and, as a consequence, there is also no possibility of registering an heir.

However, in the event of a user's death, their account can be deactivated if a family member so requests. In order for this to occur, it is necessary to send an e-mail to <privacy@foursquare.com> with a death certificate and the official documents of the petitioner [13]. If the request is considered authentic, it will then follow that all Foursquare services will be deactivated for such account, leaving it to be located by other users. Additionally, the opinions expressed by the user about places visited by him are also removed. This also affects Swarm, an application connected to this social network by which, in a way, the check-in and user evaluations generate scores that encourages competition among users. Awards and achievements acquired by the user in Swarm are then excluded when death is notified.

4.5   LinkedIn

Without hesitation, the application that is most eager to announce its data asset policy is LinkedIn, which specifies that the owner of the information is the user [19]. It offers a variety of data processing solutions for individuals and companies accessing the application and addresses digital data using two different approaches: one for the benefit of family members and the other for legal purposes, unlike other systems that are reluctant to deliver personal data in judicial proceedings. For LinkedIn, in judicial court hearing, the user will only be notified of the proceedings and will have his or her data promptly delivered to the requesting authority [19]. Moreover, if any person is under risk of serious physical injury or death, and this can be avoided by providing information contained in the network, any person can request an "emergency data request", and is subjected to legal punishment if there is found to be no imminent risk. This social network does not have a record of legacy contacts, only the possibility of requesting the termination of the account, which will remain for thirty days available through the data acquisition method mentioned above. Personal data will only be delivered to government entities and their direct members. There is a form for such a request, available at http://www.linkedin.com/help/linkedin/answer/56372.

Since there is no registration of heirs, this is the only means to transfer data from an inactive account, and privacy is infringed until messages exchanged with other users can be delivered by LinkedIn if the latter understands the request as valid [19].

Friends, family members and colleagues can ask the account to be deleted in case of death, by accessing <https://www.linkedin.com/help/linkedin/ask/ts-rdmlp> and making the request with the obituary or link of a relevant news article. If the allegation is considered true, the account will be deleted, regardless if the user wished their data to persist [22]. There is no memorialized account in LinkedIn.

4.6   WhatsApp

WhatsApp is a multiplatform instant messaging and voice calling application for smartphones. It functions as a social network for it allows the creation of groups. However, it does not store user data. Sent messages are saved in the server, waiting to be downloaded, and are deleted when the 30-day limit has been exceeded [40]. Also, there is no legacy contact registration or transfer of digital assets. On the other hand, privacy after death is protected, for no one can get through the platform to obtain personal data. The account can only be deleted at the user's request while alive. There are no digital memorials, as it does not seem to make sense in this type of social network.

However, after the death of a user, the account remains in existence and functioning, photos and status are kept, and the account can receive messages, serving as a space where family and friends continue to send news and tell stories to the account of the deceased, even though they can never receive an answer. The only way to retrieve the digital data from an account is through the devices from which it was accessed. If there is access to the device, there may be a violation of the privacy of user data because the system works without a login.

4.7   YouTube

YouTube is a video sharing platform, and, like other Google services, it has assistance from Google Inactive Accounts [17], a service dedicated to setting up the digital legacy.

According to terms of use of this application [43], the account owner may decide to have a legacy contact in life to administer it after their death.

Relatives may also request access to the channel of a deceased entity, either to delete or manage it, or just to request data from the platform [17]. Thus, there is the possibility of transferring digital legacies, treating the digital assets according to the user's volition [9], or deactivating the account, if it is their will. The privacy of an account will be kept according to the settings and the legacy contact can change it (Fig. 7).

Many YouTube channels are driven by groups of people, but all have essentially one administrator and, in case of death, it will be up to those interested in the channel management to adapt to its end or request to terminate the account, deleting all content produced and interactions with other users. They can also request access to channel funds if the channel is monetized, and are allowed to be paid the advertising revenue captured with the videos produced before the owner's death.

Submit a request regarding a deceased user's account

People expect Google to keep their information safe, even in the event of their death.

Make plans for your account
Inactive Account Manager is the best way for you to let us know who should have access to your information, and whether you want your account to be deleted. Set up Inactive Account Manager ⧉ for your account.

Make a request for a deceased person's account
We recognize that many people pass away without leaving clear instructions about how to manage their online accounts. We can work with immediate family members and representatives to close the account of a deceased person where appropriate. In certain circumstances we may provide content from a deceased user's account. In all of these cases, our primary responsibility is to keep people's information secure, safe, and private. We cannot provide passwords or other login details. Any decision to satisfy a request about a deceased user will be made only after a careful review.

What would you like to do?

○ Close the account of a deceased user

○ Submit a request for funds from a deceased user's account

○ Obtain data from a deceased user's account

Fig. 7. Request form for a deceased user account [49]

5   Final Considerations

This research aimed to obtain a deeper understanding of how some of the main social networks address death of a user. For this reason, the analysis of the documents governing such social networks in Brazil was carried out, investigating the theme and the limitations found based on pre-established criteria.

In this analysis, the authors noted that only YouTube and Facebook have available options for the transfer of digital assets to third parties. This need has already been discussed in studies by Maciel [22], Prates et al. [34], Meireles and Batalha [27] and de Toledo et al. [46]; particularly the need to respect the user's wish to pass on their data after death. The possibility of registering heirs to receive such inheritances is directly linked to the previously discussed issue. In the case of YouTube, this is done through Google Inactive Accounts.

Some social networks analyzed in this paper address particular issues regarding digital assets or goods in different ways, treating them autonomously in its privacy policies. The agencies responsible for addressing matters regarding privacy policies are laws from the state of California (USA), where all social networks established their forums. This presents a challenge for implementing terms of use and privacy policies that may not match the local laws, as is the case in Brazil [4, 6].

The authors noticed that some strategies employed by Facebook, a social network that is very popular worldwide, can dictate many behaviors adopted by other social networks. According to de Toledo [46], "although this social network models death issues and anticipated volition of the user, the currently existing solution does not fully meet the requirements suggested by the Social Web". This is the case of the transformation of accounts into memorialized profiles, keeping the user's digital assets, which is also possible in Instagram. However, each This solution implies a commitment to the immortalization of network users. On the other hand, protecting the image and the honor of the deceased should be guaranteed, since they remain perennially remembered through memories, as immortal assets that extend far beyond life.

Table 1 shows a general view of the criteria adopted for analyzing the selected social networks. These data are subject to constant updating in the social networks.

Table 1. Comparative analysis of the criteria adopted for analyzing social networks

Criteria	Facebook	Pinterest	Instagram	Fourquare	LinkedIn	WhatsApp	YouTube
Whether there is a transfer of digital assets	x						x
Whether there is a record of heirs/inheritance	x						x
Whether digital assets/goods are addressed	x		x		x		x
Whether it is possible to inactivate an account	x	x	x	x	x		x
Whether user privacy is addressed in case of death	x	x	x	x	x		x

It is interesting to note that users do not always know who owns their data in virtual environments. Yamauchi et al. [41] applied a survey in Brazil to 171 users and, when asked about how they felt regarding the ownership of their data, 84% of users stated that the data belonged to them; 8% believed the data belonged to the companies that owned the data; 4% believed the data was public; and 4%, others. On the other hand, when asked users if they usually read the content about digital legacy in terms of use and privacy policies of digital systems, 52% claimed never to read it; 44% sometimes read it; and 4% read the terms of use and privacy policies. In general, the ownership of digital assets is specified in these documents.

According to Schaub [36], privacy policies attribute different roles to different stakeholders. While users wish to gain control and transparency over sharing and data collection practices, service providers are concerned about showing conformity with data protection regulations and limiting their responsibility. This way, there is mutual effort for both stakeholders to understand these legal documents.

It was noticed that, despite the weaknesses of a few social networks regarding the criteria analyzed, they show some degree of concern with user privacy and allow user data to be deleted after notification of death, with a few specificities, of course. The exception is WhatsApp, since it does not store user data and does not address digital legacy of deceased users.

Brazilian legislation has been mirrored in international models of data protection; however, it has still not drafted a law addressing the transfer of digital assets or formalized the topic into an existing law. All court cases concerning the subject are based in interpretations and executed according to the details that direct the circumstances that will define the progress of the process, with gratifications and constraints to the parties. The subject requires further investigation, since it covers a modern and contemporary topic and, as a precept of the rapid evolution and constant modification of computer science, it is hoped that, driven by discussions proposed in the academic environment and initiated by congress approvals, we will soon have rich artifacts to remedy the complexity of the relationship between digital life and death.

Recent enforcement provisions such as the Internet Civil Registry [3] and the General Data Protection Act [4] do not contain provisions for dealing with digital legacy issues [35]. It should be noted that the current proposals in draft laws currently underway in Brazil suggest that decision-making power regarding the fate of digital inheritance should be assigned to the heirs of the deceased. Although one of them mentioned the immediate deletion of content from Internet application providers after proof of death, such prerogative is attributed to the family of the deceased [35]. For Matta [14], the country requires legislation that regulates the types of goods. In his opinion, regarding privacy legacy, we must not ignore the third party who participated, albeit passively, so as not to transgress a fundamental right. The author reinforces that such an initiative has already begun to be considered in the existence of digital memorials, but the specificities of this transfer should be addressed. Tartuce [38] argues that it is necessary to differentiate the content that involves intimacy and privacy of the person from those who do not so as to perhaps create a possible way of assigning the digital inheritance to the legitimate heirs, whenever possible. For the author, digital data concerning the privacy and intimacy of the person, which seems to be the rule, should disappear with it. In other words, for him, digital inheritance must expire with the person.

Amid the many reflections generated by this research, there is a need to reflect upon death in the digital context with a legal basis. This leads to discussion not only in terms of corporate responsibility for such digital assets, but also for users to perceive the implications of their network data after their demise. For this, taboos must be overcome. For Silva [37], "we cannot ignore the fact that a society in which death no longer makes sense is also a society, as Weber would say, that has lost its meaning."

With these preliminary results, the research study progresses to a new stage, in which it is possible to compare terms of use and privacy policies with current Brazilian legislation [20, 21], noting how the normative process works with terms and contracts signed between providers of digital services/social networks and users while analyzing conflict resolution models in the treatment of the digital legacy in online applications. In addition to this study from the legal standpoint, it is also important to develop research from the technological point of view, since one field supports the other. When considering that each user presents specific needs, the use of usability and/or accessibility techniques help the user to understand the interfaces. However, according to Acquisti [1], they do not ensure correct decision making, and other obstacles may remain to hinder the assertive decision regarding the data privacy and security. In this sense, new paradigms must be investigated and put to the test. Some techniques and paradigms that may be explored include: nudges Thaler [39], Acquisti [1], affordances

Kaptelinin [17], volitional aspects for the user Maciel [22], interaction anticipation Prates et al. [34], and privacy for design Langheinrich [18].

Furthermore, indications of future research include the confrontation of this research with others carried out in the area, if they exist, and a research with users on the subject. In the end, it is about empowering the user to know and think about their digital legacy, as well as help them make informed and assertive decisions regarding the protection of their information by interacting with digital systems naturally and without barriers.

References

1. Acquisti, A., et al.: Nudges for privacy and security: understanding and assisting users' choices online (2016)
2. Barbosa, M.: A Importância do Direito à Privacidade Digital, Redes Sociais e Extensão Universitária, v. 24. Fragmentos de Cultura, Goiânia (2014)
3. Brasil: Law n° 12,965, "Brazilian Civil Rights Framework for the Internet" (2014). http://www.planalto.gov.br/CCIVIL_03/_Ato20112014/2014/Lei/L12965.htm
4. Brasil: Law n° 13,709 "General Law of Personal Data Protection" (2018). http://www.planalto.gov.br/ccivil_03/_ato2015-2018/2018/lei/L13709.htm
5. Brasil: Chamber of Deputies. Bill n° 4,099 (2012). http://www.camara.gov.br/proposicoesWeb/fichadetramitacao?idProposicao=548678. Accessed 12 Nov 2017
6. Brasil: Civil Code, Law n° 10,406. http://www.planalto.gov.br/ccivil_03/leis/2002/l10406.htm
7. Brubaker, J.R., Dombrowski, L.S., Gilbert, A.M., Kusumakaulika, N., Hayes, G.R.: Stewarding a legacy: responsibilities and relationships in the management of post-mortem data. In: Proceedings of the SIGCHI Conference on Human Factors in Computing Systems, Toronto, pp. 4157–4166. ACM (2014)
8. De Oliveira, J., Amaral, L., Reis, L.P., Faria, B.M.: A study on the need of digital heritage management platforms. In 2016 11th Iberian Conference on Information Systems and Technologies (CISTI), Las Palmas, pp. 1–6. IEEE (2016)
9. Digital in: Digital in 2017: Global Overview - We Are Social (2017). https://wearesocial.com/special-reports/digital-in-2017-global-overview. Accessed 14 Mar 2019
10. Diniz, M.: Curso de direito civil brasileiro. Teoria geral do direito civil, 20nd edn. Saraiva, São Paulo (2003)
11. Facebook: Central de Privacidade segurança. Disponível em. https://www.facebook.com/help/1568013990080948. Accessed 24 Sept 2017
12. Facebook: O que acontecerá com a minha conta se eu falecer? https://www.facebook.com/help/103897939701143. Accessed 01 Aug 2017
13. Foursquare Labs, Inc. Política de Privacidade. https://pt.foursquare.com/legal/privacy. Accessed 24 Sept 2017
14. Matta, L.: Herança digital: uma breve analise de bens digitais, sucessão e direito da personalidade. Jus.com.br. https://jus.com.br/artigos/70063/heranca-digital-uma-breve-analise-debens-digitais-sucessao-e-direito-da-personalidade. Accessed 01 Nov 2018
15. Instagran: O que acontece quando a conta de uma pessoa falecida é transformada em memorial? https://help.instagram.com/231764660354188?helpref=faq_content. Accessed 28 Mar 2019
16. Instagran: Solicitação de remoção de pessoa falecida no Instagram. https://help.instagram.com/contact/1474899482730688?helpref=faq_content. Accessed 28 Mar 2019

17. Kaptelinin, V.: Affordances and Design. The Interaction Design Foundation, Irvine (2014)
18. Langheinrich, M.: Privacy by design — principles of privacy-aware ubiquitous systems. In: Abowd, G.D., Brumitt, B., Shafer, S. (eds.) UbiComp 2001. LNCS, vol. 2201, pp. 273–291. Springer, Heidelberg (2001). https://doi.org/10.1007/3-540-45427-6_23
19. LinkedIn: Política de Privacidade. https://www.linkedin.com/legal/privacy-policy?_l=pt_BR. Accessed 24 Sept 2017
20. Maciel, C., Lopes, A., Carvalho Pereira, V., Leitão, C., Boscarioli, C.: Recommendations for the design of digital memorials in social web. In: Meiselwitz, G. (ed.) HCII 2019. LNCS, vol. 11578, pp. 64–79. Springer, Cham (2019). https://doi.org/10.1007/978-3-030-21902-4_6
21. Luger, E., Moran, S., Rodden, T.: Consent for all: revealing the hidden complexity of terms and conditions. In: Proceedings of the SIGCHI Conference on Human Factors in Computing Systems, Paris, pp. 2687–2696. ACM (2013)
22. Maciel, C.: Issues of the social web interaction project faced with afterlife digital legacy. In: Proceedings of the 10th Brazilian Symposium on Human Factors in Computing Systems and the 5th Latin American Conference on Human-Computer Interaction, Porto de Galinhas, pp. 3–12. Brazilian Computer Society (2011)
23. Maciel, C., Pereira, V.C.: Technological and human challenges to addressing death in information systems. In: I GranDSI-BR – Grand Research Challenges in Information Systems in Brazil – 2016–2026, Porto Alegre, pp. 161–174. Brazilian Computer Society (SBC) (2017)
24. Maciel, C., Pereira, V.C.: Digital Legacy and Interaction: Post-Mortem Issues. Springer, Cham (2013). https://doi.org/10.1007/978-3-319-01631-3
25. Maciel, C., Pereira, V.C., Sztern, M.: Internet users' legal and technical perspectives on digital legacy management for post-mortem interaction. In: Yamamoto, S. (ed.) HIMI 2015. LNCS, vol. 9172, pp. 627–639. Springer, Cham (2015). https://doi.org/10.1007/978-3-319-20612-7_59
26. Marketer Chart: Social Network Users in Latin America, by Country, 2015–2020. http://www.emarketer.com/Chart/Social-NetworkUsers-Latin-America-byCountry-2015-2020/199801. Accessed 24 Sept 2017
27. Meireles, S.M., Batalha, S.W.D.S.: Bens digitais legados e a computação em nuvem: uma proposta de características desejáveis para a modelagem de softwares que tratem o legado digital. Universidade de Brasília, Brasília (2016)
28. Nalini, J.R.: Pronto para partir: reflexões jurídico-filosóficas sobre a morte. Editora revista dos tribunais, São Paulo (2014)
29. Öhman, C., Floridi, L.: The political economy of death in the age of information: a critical approach to the digital afterlife industry. Mind. Mach. 27(4), 639–662 (2017). https://doi.org/10.1007/s11023-017-9445-2
30. Ascensão, J.O.: A terminalidade da vida. In: Tepedino, G., Fachin, L.E. (coord.) O direito e o tempo: embates jurídicos e utopias contemporâneas: estudos em homenagem ao professor Ricardo Pereira Lira, p. 156. Renovar, Rio de Janeiro (2008)
31. Pinterest Política de Privacidade. https://policy.pinterest.com/ptbr/privacy-policy. Accessed 24 Sept 2017
32. Pinterest Reativar ou desativar uma conta. https://help.pinterest.com/pt-br/article/deactivate-or-close-your-account. Accessed 24 Sept 2017
33. Prates, R.O., Rosson, M.B., de Souza, C.S.: Making decisions about digital legacy with Google's inactive account manager. In: Abascal, J., Barbosa, S., Fetter, M., Gross, T., Palanque, P., Winckler, M. (eds.) INTERACT 2015. LNCS, vol. 9296, pp. 201–209. Springer, Cham (2015). https://doi.org/10.1007/978-3-319-22701-6_14

34. Prates, R.O., Rosson, M.B., de Souza, C.S.: Interaction anticipation: communicating impacts of groupware configuration settings to users. In: Díaz, P., Pipek, V., Ardito, C., Jensen, C., Aedo, I., Boden, A. (eds.) IS-EUD 2015. LNCS, vol. 9083, pp. 192–197. Springer, Cham (2015). https://doi.org/10.1007/978-3-319-18425-8_15

35. Leal L Proteção post mortem dos dados pessoais? JOTA Info. www.jota.info/opiniao-e-analise/artigos/protecao-post-mortem-dos-dadospessoais-12012019. Accessed 12 Jan 2019

36. Schaub, F., Breaux, T.D., Sadeh, N.: Crowdsourcing privacy policy analysis: potential, challenges and best practices. it - Inf. Technol. 58(5), 229–236 (2016)

37. Silva, J.A.F.: Tratado de direito funerário. Método editora, São Paulo (2000)

38. Tartuce, F.: Herança digital e sucessão legítima - primeiras reflexões - Família e Sucessões. https://www.migalhas.com.br/FamiliaeSucessoes/104,MI288109,41046Heranca+digital+e+sucessao+legitima+primeiras+reflexoes. Accessed 26 Sept 2018

39. Thaler, R.H., Sunstein, C.R.: Nudge: Improving Decisions About Health, Wealth, and Happiness. Penguin, New Haven (2009)

40. WhatsApp: Informação legal do WhatsApp. https://www.whatsapp.com/legal/?l=pt_br. Accessed 24 Sept 2017

41. Yamauchi, E.A., Maciel, C., Pereira, V.C.: An analysis of users' preferences on pre-management of digital legacy. In: Proceedings of the 17th Brazilian Symposium on Human Factors in Computing Systems, p. 45. ACM (2018)

42. Yamauchi, E.A., Souza, P.C., Silva Junior, D.P.: Prominent issues for privacy establishment in privacy policies of mobile apps. In: Proceedings of the 15th Brazilian Symposium on Human Factors in Computing Systems, article no. 26. ACM (2016)

43. YouTube: Central de política e segurança. https://www.youtube.com/yt/policyandsafety/pt-BR/. Accessed 24 Sept 2017

44. DAVI: Data Beyond Life (Dados além da Vida). http://lavi.ic.ufmt.br/davi/en/

45. Brubaker, J.R., Hayes, G.R., Mazmanian, M.: Orienting to networked grief: situated perspectives of communal mourning on Facebook. In: Proceedings of the ACM on Human-Computer Interaction, vol. 3, no. CSCW, article no. 27 (2019)

46. de Toledo, T.J., Maciel, C., Muriana, L.M., de Souza, P.C., Pereira, V.C.: Identity and volition in Facebook digital memorials and the challenges of anticipating interaction. In: Proceedings of the 18th Brazilian Symposium on Human Factors in Computing Systems, p. 31. ACM (2019)

47. Gach, K.Z.: A case for reimagining the UX of post-mortem account deletion on social media. In: Proceedings of the CSCW 2019. ACM (2019)

48. Viana, G.T., Maciel, C., Arruda, N., de Souza, P.: Análise dos Termos de Uso e Políticas de Privacidade de Redes Sociais quanto ao Tratamento da Morte de Usuários. In: Anais do VIII Workshop sobre Aspectos da Interação Humano-Computador para a Web Social, pp. 82–93. SBC (2017)

49. https://support.google.com/accounts/troubleshooter/6357590

An Analysis of UX Based on Users' Emotional Intention and Values, Both Expressed Through Twitter Posts

Elizabeth S. Furtado[1(⊠)], Marilia S. Mendes[2], Denilson C. Oliveira[1], and Lanna Lima[1]

[1] Graduate Program in Applied Informatics, University of Fortaleza, Fortaleza, CE, Brazil
`elizabethsfur@gmail.com, denilsoncursinol@gmail.com,`
`lannalima.br@gmail.com`
[2] Universidade Federal do Ceará (UFC), Russas, CE, Brazil
`marilia.mendes@ufc.br`

Abstract. Texts written by users are often used in investigations of their experiences using a system. When users write about texts based on their own decisions, the texts are a rich context for User eXperience (UX) evaluation of such systems due to the users' spontaneity. Usually, UX goals are evaluated in users' texts, including their perception about the usability of the system. An UX analysis from the perspective of the user's emotional intent and the expression of their personal or social values in the posts has not yet been performed. In this chapter, we analyzed the UX reported on users' Twitter posts relating to these two perspectives. We identified significant correlations calculated from posts that express a particular level of emotional intention of the user and a certain social or personal value. All levels of emotion had a significant relationship with at least 2 of the 12 values analyzed. Results showed that these relationships from texts written by users are useful to analyze the UX of the posts.

Keywords: Human Computer Interaction (HCI) · User experience · Social systems · Emotional analysis · Values

1 Introduction

Hassenzhal [17] describes user experience as a consequence of a user's internal state (expectations, motivation, mood, etc.), the characteristics of the designed system (e.g. complexity, purpose, usability, etc.) and the context within which the interaction occurs. Several studies bring light to the differences between UX and usability, placing usability as more task-oriented paradigm and UX as more hedonic and emotional paradigm. According to Roto *et al.* [41], emotion affects UX more than usability. Among the definitions for emotion Desmet [8] reports that: emotions are human feelings that arise from encounters with products, having beneficial or detrimental consequences for the individual's concerns, her/his main objectives, motives, well-being or other sensitivities. It is essential to collect the user's emotion at the moment of her/his interaction to understand and analyze the experience [5]. In such a study, the

R. P. d. Santos et al. (Eds.): WAIHCWS 2017/2018, CCIS 1081, pp. 79–98, 2020.
https://doi.org/10.1007/978-3-030-46130-0_5

authors uses sensors to measure physiological variables of users, and consequently to assess their emotion [5]. UX assessment methods also follow a similar approach by working with nonverbal measurements (such as assessment by facial expressions) [7].

The focus of this chapter is on the use of verbal measurements, being those in which the user explicitly writes words to verbalize what s/he is feeling. Some works propose to analyze user texts about the description of a product or system in order to study the user's experience with it [16, 35, 48], such as its facets (satisfaction, memorability, learnability, efficiency, effectiveness, comfort, support, pleasure, etc.) [18, 27].

However, in spite of presenting good results, the collection of the texts was performed by sending a request to the users through questionnaires or with reports of experiences in which users are asked to describe their perceptions or feelings about using the system. Even if the user posts spontaneously, describing what is happening or has happened while using the Social System (SS), an analysis of system problems alone does not address the entire user experience. Some works go beyond system analysis. The authors [27] observed that users, when writing spontaneous PRUs (Postings Related to Use) in the SS in interaction, had different objectives and expressed their feelings about the system or about some system errors. These postings revealed that the user's intention of emotion relates to three levels of Norman design [30]: visceral, behavioral and reflective (see the theoretical foundation section of this chapter). The emotional evaluation in PRUs, referred to as intention-based assessment, was concerned with identifying which posts were visceral, behavioral or reflective. User's intention is related to reporting an error, giving an opinion/suggestion or simply showing her/his dissatisfaction [26]. The following problem was raised [58]: the SS does not recommend the determination of a user profile, but a miscellany of users that aim to interact for various purposes, producing information (user posts) useful to gauge system measurements. The authors of [31] investigated the presence of SS values. The concept of value is something that a person, or group of people, considers important in life [14]. The authors focused on analyzing values in the context of SS and presented a classification of personal and social values. Personal values are autonomy trust, informed consent, emotion and affection, identity, presence, privacy, reciprocity, reputation and visibility, and social values are norms, collaboration, sharing, conversation, groups, object, relationship and ownership. The authors of [31] and [32] observed the importance of these levels for UX facets analysis with a SS (e.g., SS appearance, usability, availability, etc.).

Despite many efforts, up to the conclusion of this research, no work has enabled UX professionals to identify UX features with a SS from the integrated assessment of the user's emotional intent and expression of user values in PRUs. The challenge of conducting a UX assessment from these perspectives raises one question to be investigated: what is the relationship between the users' intention to report their use in the system and their expressed values in PRUs during an interaction? This work aims at presenting an investigation to answer this question from the analysis of user posts extracted from the Twitter SS.

Some of the results found were: (1) 48% of the postings were detailing problems about the use; (2) in the analysis by values, the main result revealed a greater amount of expression of the personal value of Emotion followed by Trust, Autonomy, and Knowledge. The highest expression of the social value was Property followed by

Conversation; and (3) in the statistical analysis, we found the correlation between posts expressing a certain value with one of three levels of intention of the user. The significant correlations identified by level were the following:

- A positive correlation between posts expressing the values of Emotion or Trust with the visceral intention of the user; and a significant correlation demonstrating that posts that express the visceral emotional intention of the user do not express either the Autonomy nor Informed Consent nor Knowledge value;
- A positive correlation between posts expressing the values of Property or Autonomy or Informed Consent or Privacy with the user behavioral intention; and a significant correlation showing that posts that express a behavioral emotional intention of the user do not express the Emotion value; and
- A negative correlation between posts expressing the values of Trust and Property with the level of reflective intention of the user.

The main contribution of this chapter is the presentation of how it is possible to characterize the UX with a SS. The approach starts from the analysis of the correlation between the intention of the user and the expressed values in texts written by users and finishes with the analysis of the implication of the results for UX facet evaluation.

The next section presents the theoretical basis, with concepts of UX evaluation and human values. Then we describe the related work. Subsequently, the research is carried out, and finally the results, discussion and conclusion are presented.

2   Theoretical Foundation

The authors of this chapter have been working on the extraction of public posts from a SS which are related to that particular system usage and are called PRUs. An example is: "*I can't share a tweet*". A non-PRU is any post that does not refer to the use of the system, such as: "*Let's go to the movies, @user, you and me?*".

This section presents concepts examined in UX studies in SS in the following three subsections: UX evaluation and the Norman emotional model; Classification of PRUs by users' intention; and Human values expressed in PRUs.

2.1   UX Evaluation and the Norman Emotional Model

The evaluation of the UX comprises of the emotions expressed by users before, during and after their interaction with a system [21]. Emotions are an important factor in life and play an essential role in understanding users' behavior in their interaction with the computer [2]. Voeffray [4] claims that there are variety of emotions, such as anger, contempt, enthusiasm, envy, fear, frustration, disappointment, shame, disgust, happiness, hatred, hope, jealousy, joy, love, pride, surprise and sadness. Ekman [11], on the other hand, limits the amount of emotions to six basic emotions: happiness, sadness, surprise, fear, disgust and anger, whereas others are combinations of these.

Norman and his colleagues [30, 34], in their studies on emotion, characterized the affective behavior of humans at three levels of brain structure: the visceral level, automatic or preprogrammed, making quick judgments, such as what is good or bad, safe or dangerous; the behavioral level, which refers to the brain processes that control most of our actions and; the reflective level, which refers to the interpretation, understanding, reasoning and the contemplative part of the brain [34].

Norman [30] associated these three levels of human processing with aspects of design: The visceral design, which refers to appearances and to the first impact caused by a product; the behavioral design, which refers to use of the product, with many measurements related to its usability and characteristics related to user's activities being considered here; and the reflective design, which considers the rationalization of a product, the affective memory and the meanings attributed to the product.

2.2   Classification of PRUs by User Intention

As described in the introduction, we adopt the classification of PRUs by user's intention [26, 27] to represent the perspective of Norman's emotional analysis in PRUs. In [27], two factors motivated the authors to analyze the PRUs, which are: (i) when users express their feelings about the system, they do not always specify the system error. The post can be an outburst, an impulsive posting, with the main purpose of representing what the user felt at that moment; and (ii) the more the user expresses a feeling in a post, the less s/he shows interest in finding a solution; comparatively, and vice-versa. In [26], a classification of PRUs was made into the categories: visceral, behavioral and reflective. The definitions that emerged from the PRU were as follows:

Visceral PRU has greater intensity of user's feelings, usually to criticize or praise the system. It is mainly related to attraction and first impressions. It does not contain details of use or system features. These are two examples: "My twitter doesn't work, what the <bad language>", "Is Twitter full of bugs today, or am I going crazy?";

Behavioral PRU has lower intensity of user's feelings and is also characterized by objective sentences, which contain details of use, actions performed, functionalities, etc. Two examples are the following: "Twitter, what's your problem!!! Why don't you let me use the question mark!!!!"; and "it's a very cool thing being able to press enter on Twitter" and;

Reflective PRU is characterized by being subjective, presenting affection or a situation of reflection on the system. Three examples are given: "Do you know what I miss on Twitter? An easy way to find the first Tweets of each account."; "Suggestion for Twitter: provide an edit button. So we will not have to erase everything because we missed something." and; "I think I love Twitter more than Facebook, there I don't express myself soooo much".

2.3   Human Values Expressed in PRUs

According to [13], since Plato, value-oriented discourse has varied, its many definitions being used to emphasize good, the end, entitlement, obligation, virtue, moral judgment, aesthetic judgment, beauty, truth and validity. In regard to the area of Human-computer interaction (HCI), the authors [36] propose 10 personal values (e.g., autonomy, trust, informed consent, emotion, identity, presence, privacy, reciprocity, reputation, and visibility) and 8 social values expressed from the interaction among two or more individuals (e.g., Norms/Rules/Policies; collaboration; sharing; conversation; group; object; relationship; and property). Authors broadened this conceptualization by including 4 personal values [31]: social responsibility; knowledge; religiosity; and prestige. Schwartz [45] describes personal values as desirable inter-situational goals that vary in importance and serve as guiding principles in a person's life. In [22], Johnston argues that social values must emerge from two areas of practice: the first concerns social values arising from the domain of professional individuals; and, secondly, the focus is on "significant places." The authors categorize these places into: public and private places; meeting points; and places of entertainment.

We made a comprehensive review collecting definitions for each mentioned value. The amount of definitions of a value depended on their applications and subjectivity. Some values may have different classifications in articles. For example, Trust is considered to be a facet of UX in [27] and a construct of UX in [21]. We consider the definition of the value that is associated with the user's perception of the system in use and not to a system's characteristic (such as the system's Trustability [42]). Table 1 presents the definition only for the 8 personal values and 4 social values used in this chapter. This definition also includes our own definition that was used in the classification of Twitter posts, as well as an example and some relevant references. The classification process will be described in the fourth section.

Table 1. Concepts and examples of personal and social values.

Personal values	Concepts and examples
Autonomy	The etymological origin of the word comes from the Greek term "autos nomos" which implies: self-determination, own rules [6]. It concerns the user's ability to use the SS in a way that is assumed to be a normal interaction to achieve her/his goals. e.g., "I updated my twitter again"; we still consider this value in sentences that praise the possibility or the lack of it, and to use the SS in different platforms
Trust	Feeling from someone who trusts, who believes in the sincerity of something or someone [20]. When there is trust, we will have posts in which the users praise some function or even the whole SS. When there is lack of confidence, it will be expressed when the user realizes that a particular function did not behave the way the user expected, e.g. This Twitter thing shows dislike for the tweets where I gave like, please stop
Informed consent	This value had its importance emphasized initially by [12, 43] with the construction of ethical principles and may designate a state of mind of acquiescence [47]. When there is a lack of permission by the user for the SS to do something with some user's information, or there is also this value when the user states that s/he did not give consent, did not ask, did not request, e.g., What an <bad language> this is about Twitter wanting to publish my icon
Emotion/Affection	It is a state of physiological arousal and of cognition appropriate to this state [40]. In order to categorize the presence of this value in the posts the following criteria were utilized: texts in uppercase; adjectives that express emotion like joking, perfect, etc.; curse words like shit, fuck, etc.; expressive verbs of emotion like give up, complain, drop, cry, help, love, hate, detest, worship, etc.; emoticons like:); interjections (in Portuguese) like "oh", "vixe", "aaaa", "rss", "kkkk", "hahaha' … and nouns that express emotion like God, Lord, love. e.g., {User} #{user} I'm getting angry with this Twitter because it never works when I want it to

(*continued*)

Table 1. (*continued*)

Personal values	Concepts and examples
Identity	Circumstance of an individual being in which s/he claims to be or that which another presumes that person to be. Set of elements that, together, create the individuality and personality of an individual [20]. For [1], in a more philosophical discussion, identity is linked to a person at a time and with certain particular mental properties. While for [19], identity is the concept of the person of who they are, what kind of person they are and how they relate to others, e.g., I want to change my profile photo and twitter cover, but I can never do it
Privacy	According to [44], it concerns the ability to control the access that others have to ourselves, e.g., What's up with Twitter notifying someone else's tweet; we can also add that it concerns the intimacy of a person or a group of people
Reciprocity	[40] states that the essence of reciprocity is the obligation to give, receive and reciprocate. In posts, this value will be present when individuals have a feeling of gratitude or willingness to reward something done, suggested or made available by another individual, e.g., Get to know the new features that will make Twitter safer. Just click and go to our blog post: {URL}
Knowledge	[3] says it is a science, a system of cognitive appropriation of the real and regulated transformation of that real, from the definition that the theory of science makes of its object. The post will express this value if, in its content, we have the search for knowledge: whether with a question or the indication of a response to a previously asked question E.g., some guys hacked my twitter by sending msg to everyone following everyone, these guys are messing around, what do I do?
Social values	Concepts and examples
Norms/Rules/Policies (NRP)	Provides the principle of trust and is necessary to build reliable mechanisms of interaction between people and resources under the rule of NRP value [10]. A post expresses this value when relating some limitation imposed by the SS and is commented on by the user, in a positive or negative way, about some rule, norm or policy, e.g., only thing missing from Twitter, I want to increase the size of posts
Sharing	To be part of something with someone [20]. In posts, it is expressed if there is a {URL}, e.g., want to learn how to change your profile, go here {URL}
Conversation	Possibility of two persons, or a group of individuals, to establish direct communication [20]. It must provide words that explicitly direct the post to a person or a group, for instance a person's name, a group of people, my friends, etc.; e.g., {USER}, does your Twitter work? Here it is very bad
Property	[47] defines ownership as a system of rules governing access to and control of scarce material resources. The expression of this value in a post is referred to when it indicates that there is an intention or even action on something of its possession or even on a SS function that can only be performed by this user or others; e.g., My Twitter keeps stopping

3   Related Work

In this section, we identified articles that made the evaluation of intention in posts of the users, then look at the articles describing and/or treating a certain value regarding a SS.

Being a recent approach, few articles have evaluated the UX in SS by intention from posts of the users. In [26] and [27], this form of evaluation was applied in two systems: Facebook and Twitter. The analysis illustrated characteristics of the intentions of the users of each system when mentioning their use, for example: users show some emotion in regard to the system use and explain the problem, the error, the reason for satisfaction or dissatisfaction, or even to express the need to find a solution. In [27], the intention in posts of the users in an e-learning system with social characteristics (communities, discussion forums, chats, etc.) was compared with social networks. 650 PRUs were selected and classified as visceral, behavioral and reflective. The results showed that in the evaluated system (academic system), users were more interested in reporting system errors, giving details of system usage and presenting fewer emotions than in social networks.

Then we found studies related to values and categorized the selected articles according to their different purposes of use of values in relation to a SS. They were:

- To evaluate the quality of UX with SS. The paper [36] identified the relation existing between values and the following requirements of a SS: accessibility, adaptability, appearance, awareness, availability, scalability, portability and safety. The authors [14, 15, 17, 23, 24] reported the importance of human values in a UX assessment when the SS is in use, but values can also be used for the development of the SS [32]. Herein, works can also be found that study the users' opinions to evaluate UX [8, 9, 18, 25, 49] by making an emotional analysis;
- To evaluate the usability of the SS only [1]. Dealing with the value of knowledge. It creates a learning SS, and evaluates its efficiency to provide an exchange of knowledge between students and teachers;
- To analyze the cultural dimensions of the SS [37]. Data collected in textual evaluations may reveal the context of the user who wrote the text [25], the characteristics of the reported experience (such as the activity in which the user was involved, and the features of the application that affect it) [8], the themes portrayed in the text [9] and the UX goals implied in a good or bad experience [35]. Such data are important in a context-based assessment to know the added value of the system for the user [32], her/his perception of privacy, amongst others;
- To analyze the relationships among values. For instance; if we consider the values of visibility and knowledge, [50] presented statistical results to verify the following hypothesis: in a group of knowledge exchange, those who make available a certain piece of knowledge and are close (geographically) to those who need this knowledge, will have more visibility when compared to those who make it available but are further away;
- To improve the SS (e.g. provide greater security, improve knowledge sharing [46], encourage the value of reciprocity [24], etc.). The author of [14] presented design suggestions when evaluating SS from the point of view of human values; and
- To design the SS. [22] proposed a model of design patterns to integrate information about social values.

None of the studies about the users' opinions evaluated UX for both human values and the users' intention of emotion when describing their use of the system in posts.

In our case, evaluation of intention characterizes the intentions of users when mentioning their use in the system. Values assessment can be used to characterize the users' texts regarding their principles and attitudes that lead their experiences in the SS studied, or even better, to characterize the way users interact and relate in an SS.

4   Conduction of Research

This subsection presents the conduction of the research, detailing the extraction and classification processes of the posts, then the analysis of classified PRUs.

4.1   Extraction and Classification Processes

The extraction of the posts from Twitter was carried out with the support of a tool called UUX-Posts [26]. This tool applies certain patterns to collect posts that refer to user's opinion about the system under analysis or about her/his experience using it. 3,880 Twitter posts were collected, these being 367 PRUs and 3513 Non-PRUs [31]. Then, for this chapter, the collected posts went through a process of manual classification, performed in the following order:

I. Analysis of PRUs in order to confirm if a particular post represented the user's perception about the system during its use or about her/his experience using it;

II. Classification of PRUs by user's intention into one of the levels: visceral, behavioral or reflective;

III. Classification of PRUs into personal values. In this type of classification, a post can have more than one personal value. Another important fact is that the rating for a value can have a positive or negative expression of this value, for example, positive trust value: "that's why I'm a twitter fan it never fails ... rather than Facebook and Instagram which continually fail!!" and negative trust value (mistrust): "Frozen Twitter here ..."; and

IV. Classification of PRUs into social values. In this type of classification, a post can also have more than one social value.

The steps took place from April 1st to October 16th, 2018. The classification was performed by three HCI researchers (aged between 32–54). These three evaluators were part of a research project and evaluated postings in other circumstances [31, 32]. Two evaluators only consulted the third one in case of doubts. Specifically, because there were a large number of classification categories, 12 values in total, in the last two classification steps, we included two additional groups of classifiers, each group composed of three participants, and one responsible for conducting the work. The participants, graduate students (aged between 20–25), had previous training and used the definitions from Table 1. For each evaluated item (a certain value) in a post, the participant should assign one of the following answers: Yes (if the post presented the value) or; No (if the post did not present the value). The responsible participant used the Airtable software to plan the tasks and shared excel files with the participants. A strategy was adopted of assigning a code for each post, as well as for each evaluator, in order to facilitate the management of the collaborative work. The use of the codes enabled the generation of dynamic tables, showing when there were inconsistencies in assignments from responses given by participants.

The groups checked their results between themselves. Then the responsible participant reported the group results to the researchers. Each inconsistency in the classification was discussed with the group, according to the value definition.

4.2 Analysis of Classified PRUs

After the first step, some posts that were not PRUs were detected and discarded, resulting in 349 PRUs. The analyses of classified posts during the execution of the three other steps are organized herein into two items: (1) Analysis of the UX by the intention of the users; and (2) Analysis of UX by human and social values.

4.2.1 Analysis of UX by the Intention of the Users

As a result of the 349 posts analyzed, the type of posts with the highest proportion was behavioral (48%, n = 168 PRUs), followed by visceral (33%, n = 114 PRUs) and reflective (19%, n = 67 PRUs). Some examples of postings for each processing level are shown in Table 2.

Table 2. Examples of representation of the analyzed posts

Type of posting	Representation of the analyzed posts
Visceral	(P1) "Twitter more garbage with every passing day" (P2) "Twitter has more bugs than netflix" (P3) "I don't know what to do with Twitter here, I've uninstalled it, turned off my cellphone and nothing. HELP."
Behavioral	(P4) "why are the numbers in my twitter in bold?? I don't understand" (P5) "{User} twitter boring as <expletive> can't duplicate letter !!!" (P6) "are the twitter medias loading for you?"
Reflective	(P7) "I love Twitter because I can participate in polls that I have no idea what they are for but it's worth giving your opinion" (P8) "I use twitter more to follow news (as a kind of newspaper) than anything!" (P9) "Just having the option to save video for Twitter would be perfect" (P10) "I love Twitter because for me it's a mix of tumbler images and poetic or nasty phrases with random scenes + wtv I wanna say"

In regard to Visceral postings P1–P3 in Table 2. We found the following types of posts: complaints, compliments, comparisons and questions. No suggestion fits at this level. Users complain, give praise or make comparisons in the system demonstrating emotion, but usually without specifying what the error and/or problem is, why the system does not work or what the cause of user dissatisfaction is. Throughout the postings, users did not express any need to find a solution or for an explanation.

For examples of behavioral postings, see P4–P6 (Table 2). Again, no posting regarding suggestions were classified at this level. However, in posting P5, the user shows some emotion in regard to the system use and explaining the problem, the error, the reason for dissatisfaction, or even to express the need to find a solution.

As examples of reflective postings, we have postings P7–P10. At such a level, we found the following types of postings: comparison (P10), compliments (P7, P9, P10) and suggestion (P9). This suggestion is based on the reflection of the system use. In posting P8, the user reports the reason s/he uses Twitter and in posting P7, the user reflects on the motivation to use Twitter as a kind of added value.

4.2.2 Analysis of UX by Human and Social Values

The analysis of posts classified by the values is described as follows.

572 personal values expressed in 349 PRUs analyzed, being 183 personal values at the visceral level, 288 at behavioral level, and 101 at the reflective level. Figure 1 shows the number of 572 personal values. It is important to emphasize that the personal value of Emotion—the main subject of this research—is the most expressed value in the posts (n = 225, 39%). The second most expressed personal value was Trust (n = 161, 28%), followed by Autonomy (n = 84, 15%), then Knowledge (n = 78, 14%), Informed Consent (n = 12, 2%), Reciprocity, Privacy and Identity (n = 12, 1%, 1% and 0%, respectively).

We realize that there is a relationship between the two personal values (Trust and Emotion and affection) most expressed in posts. For instance, in postings P1–P3 (Table 2), when users complain that the system does not work as expected, they usually demonstrate lack of Trust and Emotion. Another analysis that can be made from Fig. 1 concerns the posts when the user explains the problem and her/his reason for dissatisfaction, where s/he can express Knowledge in a request posting (such as P4 and P6 - Table 2). It is common in these types of posts that express Knowledge (according to the definition of this value in Table 1), that there is the identification of the social values of Conversation, Sharing and the personal value of Reciprocity. For example: {User} I started using Twitter because you always speak well of it. I have a lot of questions to ask you #petitcomite. The analysis of this relationship among the values was statistically proven, as shown in the next section. Finally, value analysis can demonstrate how users' opinions about their experiences affect other SS users.

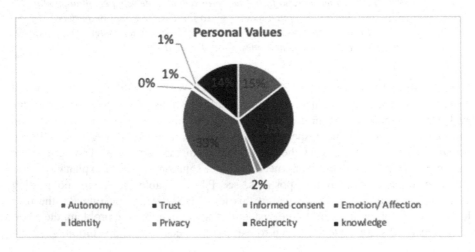

Fig. 1. Personal values found in posts.

Regarding the social values, 377 values were identified, expressed in 349 PRUs analyzed, being 102 of the visceral type, 218 of the behavioral type, and 57 of the reflective type. The social value of Property was the most expressed value in the posts (n = 246, 65%). This value is found in the posts: P3, P4, P5, P7, P8 and P10 (Table 2). We notice in several posts that express the value of Property, that they also express the values Autonomy, Informed Consent and Trust. For example, {User} this twitter problem of getting duplicate photos is a bunch of crap. Here, the twitter user is lacking confidence in the SS because their photos (Property) are being duplicated without their consent. The second most expressed social value was Conversation (n = 90, 24%), followed by NRP (n = 28, 7%), then Sharing (n = 13, 4%).

5 Results

5.1 Relationship Between Classifications of Intention of the User and of Human Values

Considering that the research question is to determine the users' intention and what the types of values expressed by them are related to, the starting point was to analyze the relationships between the PRU classifications of user's intention and of values. We counted how many PRUs are in each combination of values and types of user's intention. In general, certain human values are more expressed in the intention of users to report their use in SS than others. For instance, the personal value of Informed Consent was expressed in 12 behavioral posts and none in visceral or reflective posts. These 12 posts expressing this value represent only 4.2% of the amount of expression of personal values (n = 288) in behavioral posts. However, for these 12 posts exclusively classified at the behavioral level, we may say 100% of Informed Consent value represents such a level.

The analysis of the amount of expression of a certain value by level leads us to the most significant relationships between the perspectives studied. In particular, Fig. 2

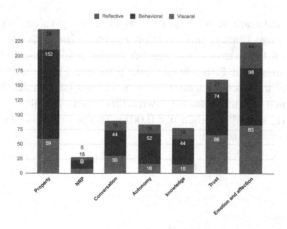

Fig. 2. The user's intention by Value

depicts the expression of a certain numerical value that occurs in visceral, behavioral and reflective levels. In the case of Emotion and affection, this is expressed in all the levels with (n = 83), (n = 98), and (n = 44). Regarding the social value of Property, we have an expression (69.7%) of social values (n = 218) at the behavioral level, when compared to visceral (57.8%) with an expression of social values (n = 102) at this level and reflective (61.4%) with an expression of social values (n = 57) at this level. The greater expression of the Property value in behavioral is also followed by the other values, such as Emotion and affection, Trust, Autonomy, Conversation, knowledge and NRP.

The complexity of the analysis can increase with the inclusion of so many variables from each perspective. So, in the following paragraphs, we will present the statistical analysis, which can help evaluators to identify which of these most expressed relationships are significant for Twitter UX analysis.

We calculated the correlation analysis with the phi coefficient according to the explanation given as follows. The process of assigning values to the posts generated a database of binary observations, for example, when we ask the question: does post A present the Knowledge value? To enable parametric analysis, the numerical value 1 was assigned when the answer was Yes (Y) and 0 when the answer was No (N). A correlation between binary variables is called phi and is represented by the Greek symbol. To illustrate the correlation calculation, we will use the example of calculating the correlation between the values Knowledge and Conversation.

In this example:

YY, where 40 posts that presented Conversation also presented Knowledge,

YN, where 38 posts presented Conversation and did not present Knowledge,

NY, where 50 posts did not present Conversation and presented Knowledge and,

NN, where 221 posts were neither Conversation nor Knowledge.

We then apply the following formula for the correlation between binary variables:

$$\varphi = \frac{ad - bc}{\sqrt{(a+b)(c+d)(a+c)(b+d)}}$$

The statistical software R was used to calculate the p-value. We used the rcorr function of the Hmisc library, this function returns a list with the elements r, the correlation matrix, n the matrix of the number of observations used in the analysis of each pair of variables, and P, the asymptotic p-values. The significant relationships between values and the user's intention were as follows (see Tables 3, 4, and 5). The value for significance of correlation is shown with certain symbols ('*' when $p < 0.05$, '**' when $p < 0.01$, and '***' when $p < 0.001$). The positive correlations are in bold and the negative ones are in italic.

Table 3. Expression of significant personal and social values in visceral posts

User's intention	Correlation with	phi coefficient	Significance	
Visceral	Autonomy	−0,163	2,19E−03	**
	Trust	**0,164**	2,07E−03	**
	Informed consent	−0,131	1,40E−02	*
	Emotion	**0,121**	2,34E−02	*
	Knowledge	−0,154	4,01E−03	**
	Behavioral	−0,671	0,00E+00	***
	Reflexiva	−0,339	7,32E−11	***

Table 4. Expression of significant personal and social values in behavioral posts

User's intention	Correlation with	phi coefficient	Significance	
Behavioral	Property	**0,422**	0,00E+00	***
	Visceral	−0,671	0,00E+00	***
	Reflexiva	−0,470	0,00E+00	***
	Informed consent	**0,196**	2,32E−04	***
	Autonomy	**0,155**	3,67E−03	**
	Emotion	−0,124	2,10E−02	*
	Privacy	**0,108**	4,46E−02	*

Table 5. Expression of significant personal and social values in reflective posts

User's intention	Correlation with	phi coefficient	Significance	
Reflective	Trust	−0,145	6,81E−03	**
	Property	−0,195	2,47E−04	***
	Visceral	−0,339	7,32E−11	***
	Behavioral	−0,470	0,00E+00	***

Considering that the closer to 0 the correlation is, the weaker it becomes, it is possible to highlight a few correlations in each of these tables, specifically those under 0.250. In Table 3, the two strongest correlations can be interpreted as follows: a post that expresses a user's emotional intention of the visceral type is inversely proportional to the behavioral intention and the reflective intention. That is, the more visceral a post is, the less behavioral and reflective it will be. In fact, a post can only be classified into a single type of user's emotional intent.

Analyzing the correlation between Emotion (subject of this chapter) and visceral intention (see Table 3), we see that the correlation is weak (phi = 0.121, $p < 0.05$), because there is a very similar distribution of posts in the four combinations discussed above. For example, for the combination Y (exists) and N (does not exist) representing the presence of this value and that intention, we have: 83 posts are YY, 94 are NN, 142 are YN and 30 are NY. The correlation is positive because the sum of YY and NN is greater than the other two combinations.

We found significant correlation between Trust value and visceral intention, but it was also weak (0.164, $p < 0.01$). At the visceral level, people are very sensitive to their feelings, and the product's appearance [30]. We notice people do not tolerate the lack of confidence by expressing their indignation. The correlation between Knowledge value and visceral intention is also weak (phi = 0.154, $p < 0.01$). It is negative because there are more posts where there is value and there is no intention and vice versa. A similar justification may be given for the correlations between Autonomy value and visceral intention and between Informed Consent value and visceral intention.

In Table 4, we found significant correlation between Property value and behavioral intention (phi = 0.422, $p < 0.001$). This may be attributable to the fact the behavioral level is the part that contains the brain processes that control everyday behavior [35], being activity-oriented. The expression of Property value in a post refers to when it indicates that there is pretension or even action on something or even on a SS function that can only be performed by this user. The other three values (such as Autonomy, Privacy and Informed Consent) also had a weak correlation, with the behavioral emotional intention of the users. Posts classified as such values tended to express a user's feeling of control (or lack of) in the SS. The correlation between Emotion value and behavioral intention is also weak (phi = -0.124, $p < 0.05$) and negative, because there are more posts where there is value and there is no intention and vice versa.

In Table 5, we again see an inverse correlation between reflective and behavioral. The correlation between Emotion value and reflective intention is very weak, so it has been hidden from Table 5. The inverse correlations between Trust value and reflective intention (phi = 0.145, $p < 0.01$) and between Property value and reflective intention (phi = 0.195, $p < 0.05$) may be attributable to the fact people do not try to explain the phenomena when expressing these values.

5.2   Relationship Between Personal and Social Values

In this subsection, we apply the same procedure to identify the significant relationships between personal and social values. All the correlations were below 0.250, except for these relationships with the Knowledge value. In the case of the correlation between Knowledge and Conversation, the analysis was performed by considering the following combinations: 40 posts are YY, 221 are NN, 38 are YN and 50 are NY, being positive because the sum of YY and NN is bigger than the other two combinations. There is a correlation between Emotion and Knowledge, and we could infer that posts that express a visceral emotional intention do not express the Knowledge value. In this study, no statistical evidence was found to confirm that posts that express Knowledge value also express a reflective emotional intention; see the discussion section.

In the next section, we will describe the implications of this result for the UX evaluation considering only the 12 significant correlations found in the Tables 3, 4 and 5, between a certain value and a certain user intention.

6   Implication of Results to Evaluate UX

According to [26], to find problems and analyze solutions in a textual evaluation, the posts should be classified according to their functionality and quality of use criteria (the facets of UX). The classification by functionality aims to identify the functionality or cause that motivated the user to publish their post. For example, the following posting: "It's really annoying that Twitter is duplicating the photos in the gallery", the functionality identified is: "duplicate photos in the gallery". This type of classification makes it possible to identify problems, but the type of problem is identified by the facets of UX, including the usability facets present in each post [26].

Thus, the 349 posts were classified by the authors of this chapter, into the following facets of UX: Efficacy, Efficiency, Security, Utility, Memorability, Satisfaction and Learning in [38], Aesthetics [4] and Frustration [4]. A post can identify more than one type of problem (facet). The post "How annoying! Why are the twitter letters so small! I can't see as well as the old update" was classified as frustration, utility (lack of) and aesthetics.

After the classification of the facets, first, we made the UX analysis with the intentions. The results were: the highest percentage of such problems found (N = 168, 62%) was in the behavioral intention, followed by reflective (N = 114, 23%) and visceral (N = 67, 15%).

Then we made the UX analysis for each of the 12 significant relationships between a certain value and a certain user intention. The relationships were: (i) between the values of Autonomy or Informed Consent or Knowledge, Trust or Emotion with level of visceral intention of the user; (ii) between the value of Property or Autonomy or Informed Consent or Privacy or Emotion with level of user behavioral intention, and; (iii) between the value of Trust or Property with level of reflective intention of the user. The calculation was as follows: For each PRU, where there was the presence of a certain value and a certain user intention, we checked the associated facet(s). From the 12 relations considered, the relation of Informed Consent value and the visceral intention was excluded, because there was no associated facet.

In regard to the results of the remaining 11 relationships, it is important to emphasize that for all relationships, except for relationships of values with reflective intent, the greatest number of types of problems encountered were in the Frustration and Utility facets, sometimes followed by the facets of Efficiency and Effectiveness. As most of the problems are in the Behavioral type posts (this was also observed in [26]), here, we emphasize the importance in considering the values of Property, Autonomy, Informed Consent, and Privacy for identifying the quality of the problems in use, specifically relating to the usability of the system under analysis.

In the case of the relationship of values with visceral intention, the second most identified facet was Satisfaction, except for the relationship of the Knowledge Value with visceral intent. In reflective posts, users tend to express less of their feelings about problems encountered while using an SS, to the point of examining, for example, whether the error is actually in the SS [26]. However, the result here was different. In the relationship of Trust and Property values with reflective intent, the most identified problems imply Satisfaction, Frustration and Aesthetics.

7 Discussion

In this section, the research carried out in regard to the following items is discussed:

Users' Feelings and Their Intention When Posting a Message. In [56], the authors started a discussion about the verbal description of a feeling and defined feeling as one of the components of emotion, not representing the emotional state of an individual, but rather a verbal attribution that a person makes about an emotional episode. According to the authors, the feeling is the conscious interpretation where the individual realizes what s/he feels at the moment, and this can be transmitted in a verbal way, for example, when a person says that s/he feels "happy" to have been able to make a purchase on the Internet [39]. In this work, the user's feelings expressed in the postings were not evaluated, be they happy or frustrated, but her/his intention when posting that message e.g., if s/he wanted to express her/his feelings about the system or report a problem or functionality in the system. In addition, the emotion's dimension (such as arousal) can be positive or negative. For instance, arousal measures the level of calm/excitement, and ranges from very calm to neutral to highly aroused emotions. We did not treat this aspect here;

Classification of Posts in Human Values. Considering the formal representation of each concept [32], it is possible to determine patterns that can be used to classify posts (e.g., check for a link, "http", to classify in the social value of sharing). On the other hand, the characteristics of the values may present challenges. In the case of the Emotion personal value, the value may be implicit (e.g., "Twitter faster than my tortoise") or explicit (e.g., "I love using Twitter"). The existence of emotion and/or affection is subjective (e.g., "I want to change my profile photo and twitter cover, but I never can!"), so we specified some definition rules in Table 1 and worked with explicit emotion. However, it is important to have an expert evaluator when there is a difference of interpretations by the previous evaluators. We also encourage practitioners to use the triangulation of results to obtain different perspectives and confirm the findings, allowing for more rigorous results;

Beyond the Analysis of Users' Emotional Intention and Values. Comparing this work with related work that analyzed UX from the emotional and/or values perspective, we emphasize that the facets of UX identified in the postings were not classified by the joint analysis of the perspectives. In [26, 27, 31] and [32], facets were related only to emotional levels and not to values as well, as presented in Sect. 6. In this chapter, we improve the conceptual description of each value, initially described in [31] and [32]. Checking and comparing classified Twitter posts with the description of each value allowed us to better define each value resulting in Table 1. We now have a much more reliable database, available for public access; and

Correlation Between Knowledge Value and Reflective Intention. Here, the classifier considers that there is a reflective intention of the user in a text, when the post expresses the user's personal opinion or even suggestion for the system, such as: "I guess", "I think", "I would like to have ..." As in the following example: "I think the only thing that is missing from Twitter for it to be perfect is the tweet edit option".

The reader might suppose that if this kind of reflection exists, then the value of knowledge should also be expressed in the post. However, in this chapter, we did not find significant correlation between Knowledge value and reflective intention. We attributed this to the definition of this value (see Table 1), where a post expresses knowledge if an answer or question is written in such a post. Extending this value's concept may change this result.

8 Conclusion

We proposed to answer the question related to the challenge of analyzing the quality in use of a SS following the vision of the Norman-oriented intention of use, adapted for postings, and the expression of human values. The question was: what is the relation between the users' intention of use with a SS and the expressed human values?

It was verified that all PRUs express values and the intention of the users with the Twitter SS correlating them. The highest expression of the personal value was Emotion followed by Trust, Autonomy, and Knowledge. The highest expression of the social value was Property followed by Conversation. In the statistical analysis of the correlations, we found the following evidences: (i) The highest expression of the value of Property is in behavioral posts; (ii) We found significant correlations, which were weak, between the other 6 values studied (these being Autonomy, Trust, Informed consent, Emotion, Knowledge and Privacy) and the levels of visceral, behavioral and reflective intention of the user; and (iii) The personal value of Knowledge has a correlation with the Conversation social value.

The main contributions of this work are:

- Known correlations between posts expressing the users' emotional intention and their values and the identified UX facets. Results can guide evaluators to identify which relationships are relevant for analyzes of one or more facets (see Sect. 6), so the evaluator can conduct future qualitative studies with users. For example, a test scenario for the user to try using a SS could be: you share "your" profile (property) and find that there is a photo in it that you do not trust. Show me how you would solve this? Here, the property value of the task that the user has to perform would allow the evaluator to analyze the facets of user satisfaction and frustration;
- Known correlations between the perspectives studied here that can be useful in the elaboration of other collection instruments such as questionnaires, observations, etc.;
- Known correlations between values. These findings can be used to minimize the effort of analysis, for instance, if the relation between two values is significant, the UX can be characterized by an analysis of the relationship between these values;
- Known correlations between posts expressing Emotion value and the intention levels. There is evidence that there is a positive correlation between posts expressing Emotion value and visceral intention, and a negative correlation between posts expressing Emotion value and behavioral intention. It can be useful to evaluators to elaborate test scenarios that invoke such behaviors from users;

- An approach that supports UX researchers to understand why some human values are more expressed than others. For instance, the personal value of Emotion is less likely to be found in reflective intention as posts that express a visceral emotional intent do not express knowledge value; and
- The teaching of HCI evaluation methods, considering the categories of textual classification described in this text.

This study considers the classification by user's intention and human values, so another question can be raised for future works: will a given human value always be more expressed in visceral, behavioral and reflective postings compared to other SSs? The answer will depend on further analysis, with other postings and other SSs. For example, we note that the SS can influence the relationship between values. In the case of the user autonomy value, it can be more expressed or not according to the NRP value of a certain SS, which specifies what the user can and can not do in the system itself. Another example refers to the actions that the user can take within the SS (such as follow, unfollow, change profile), which serve to characterize certain values (her/his identity, trust, etc.). Thus, the application of this approach in another SS may require an adaptation, detailing the definition of values, described in Table 1.

This challenge for the generalization of these results will guide the next steps of this research. In addition, the relationships with Emotion and Knowledge personal values need to be reviewed in new assessments to gauge certainty for HCI professionals.

References

1. Baker, L.R.: Persons and Bodies: A Constitution View. Cambridge University Press, Cambridge (2000)
2. Baranauskas, C., Souza, C., Pereira, R.: GranDIHC-BR, pp. 27–30 (2012)
3. Baremblitt, G.F.: Progressos e retrocessos em psiquiatria e psicanálise. Global, Rio de Janeiro (1978)
4. Bargas-Avila, J., Hornbæk, K.: Old wine in new bottles or novel challenges: a critical analysis of empirical studies of user experience. In: CHI 2011, pp. 2689–2698. The ACM Press (2011)
5. Maia, C.L.B., Furtado, E.S.: An approach to analyze user's emotion in HCI experiments using psychophysiological measures. IEEE Access **7**, 36471–36480 (2019)
6. Cardoso, C.: A cidade-estado antiga. Ática, São Paulo (1987)
7. Cristescu, I.: Emotions in human-computer interaction: the role of non-verbal behavior in interactive systems. Revista Informatica Economica **2**, 110–116 (2008)
8. Desmet, O.: Measuring emotion: development and application of an instrument to measure emotional responses to products. In: Blythe, M.A., Overbeeke, K., Monk, A.F., Wright, P.C. (eds.) Funology: From Usability to Enjoyment. Human-Computer Interaction Series, vol. 3, pp. 111–123. Springer, Dordrecht (2003). https://doi.org/10.1007/1-4020-2967-5_12
9. Donath, J.: Identity and deception in the virtual community. In: Kollock, P., Smith, M. (eds.) Communities in Cyberspace. Routledge, New York (1999)
10. Dron, J.: Designing the undesignable: social software and control. Educ. Technol. Soc. **10**(3), 60–71 (2007)
11. Ekman, P.: An argument for basic emotions. Cogn. Emot. **6**, 169–200 (1992)

12. Faden, R., Beauchamp, T.: A History and Theory of Informed Consent. Oxford University Press, New York (1986)
13. Frankena, W.: Value and valuation. In: Edwards, P. (ed.) The Encyclopedia of Philosophy, vol. 7–8, pp. 409–410. Macmillan, New York (1972)
14. Friedman B., Peter, H., Kahn J., Boring, A.: Value sensitive design and information systems. In: Human-Computer Interaction in Management Information Systems: Foundations, pp. 348–372 (2006)
15. Friedman, B.: Value-sensitive design. Interactions **3**, 16–23 (1996)
16. Hassenzahl, M., Diefenbach, S., Görtz, A.: Needs, affect, and interactive products. J. Interact. Comput. **22**(5), 353–362 (2010)
17. Hassenzahl, M., Tractinsky, N.: User experience -a research agenda. Behav. Inf. Technol. **25** (2), 91–97 (2006)
18. Hedegaard, S., Simonsen, J.: Extracting usability and user experience information from online user reviews. In: Conference on Human Factors in Computing Systems (CHI 2013), pp. 2089–2098 (2013)
19. Hogg, M., Abrams, D.: Social Identification: A Social Psychology of Intergroup Relations and Group Processes. Routledge, London (1988)
20. Holanda, A.B.: Dicionário Aurélio da Língua Portuguesa, 5° edição (2010)
21. Hornbæk, K., Hertzum, M.: Technology acceptance and user experience: a review of the experiential component in HCI. ACM Trans. Comput.-Hum. Interact. **24**(5) (2017). Article no. 33
22. Johnston, C.: What is Social Value? A Discussion Paper. Australian Government Publishing Service, Canberra (1992)
23. Ketola, P., Roto, V.: Exploring user experience measurement needs. In: 5th COST294-MAUSE Open Workshop on Valid Useful User Experience Measurement (2008)
24. Kleinberg J.: Challenges in mining social network data: processes, privacy and paradoxes. In: Em KDD/USA, pp. 4–5 (2007)
25. Korhgen, H., Arrasvuori, J., Väänänen, V.: Let users tell the story. In Proceedings of AMC CHI 2010 Extended Abstracts, Atlanta, pp. 4051–4056. The ACM Press (2010)
26. Mendes, M.S., Furtado, E., Furtado, V., de Castro, M.F.: How do users express their emotions regarding the social system in use? A classification of their postings by using the emotional analysis of norman. In: Meiselwitz, G. (ed.) SCSM 2014. LNCS, vol. 8531, pp. 229–241. Springer, Cham (2014). https://doi.org/10.1007/978-3-319-07632-4_22
27. Mendes, M.: MALTU - Um modelo para avaliação da interação em sistemas sociais a partir da linguagem textual do usuário. Tese (doutorado). Universidade Federal do Ceará, Programa de Pós-Graduação em Ciência da Computação, Fortaleza (2015)
28. Mendes, M., Furtado, E.S.: UUX-Posts: a tool for extracting and classifying postings related to the use of a system. In: Proceedings of the 8th Latin American Conference on HCI (2017)
29. Moser, C., Fuchsberger, V., Tscheligi, M.: A value-based UX evaluation. In: CHI 2012, pp. 5–10 (2012)
30. Norman, D.: Emotional Design: Why We Love (or Hate) Everyday Things. Basic Books, New York (2004)
31. Oliveira, D.C., Furtado, E.S., Mendes, M.S.: Uma Investigação da Relação entre Valores Humanos e a Intenção Emocional do Usuário em suas postagens no Twitter. In: WAIHCWS, 8 2017, 1. Anais do VIII Workshop sobre Aspectos da Interação Humano-Computador para a Web Social, Porto Alegre, pp. 58–69, December 2017. ISSN 2596-0296
32. Oliveira, D.C.: MASSVA: Modelo de Avaliação de Sistemas Sociais sob a ótica dos Valores humanos a partir das postagens dos usuários. Tese doutorado. Unifor (2018)

33. Olsson, T., Salo, M.: Narratives of satisfying and unsatisfying experiences of current mobile augmented reality applications. In: Proceedings of AMC CHI 2012 Extended Abstracts, pp. 2779–2788 (2012)
34. Ortony, A., Norman, D., Revelle, W.: Affect and proto-affect in effective functioning. In: Fellous, J.M., Arbib, M.A. (eds.) Who Needs Emotions? The Brain Meets the Robot, pp. 173–202. Oxford University Press, Oxford (2005)
35. Partala, T., Kallinen, A.: Understanding the most satisfying and unsatisfying user experiences: emotions, psychological needs, and context. Interact. Comput. **24**, 25–34 (2012)
36. Pereira, R., Baranauskas, C.: Softwares sociais: uma visão orientada a valores. In: IHC, pp. 149–158 (2010)
37. Pereira, R., de Miranda, L.C., Baranauskas, C., Piccolo, L.S.G., Almeida, L.D.A., Dos Reis, J.C.: Interaction design of social software: clarifying requirements through a culturally aware artifact. In: Information Society (i-Society), pp. 293–298 (2011)
38. Preece, J., Rogers, Y.: Design de interação: além da interação homem-computador. Bookman (2013)
39. Riediger, M.: Experience Sampling. RatSWD Working Paper, no. 62. http://library. mpibberlin.mpg.de/ft/mr/MR_Experience_2009.pdf
40. Rokeach, M.: The Nature of Human Values. Free Press, New York (1973)
41. Roto, V., Rantavuo, H., Vaananen-Vainio-Mattila, K.: Evaluating user experience of early product concepts. In: International Conference on Designing Pleasurable Products and Interfaces, pp. 199–208 (2009)
42. Santos, R.M., de Oliveira, K.M., Andrade, R.M.C., Santos, I.S., Lima, E.R.: A quality model for human-computer interaction evaluation in ubiquitous systems. In: Collazos, C., Liborio, A., Rusu, C. (eds.) CLIHC 2013. LNCS, vol. 8278, pp. 63–70. Springer, Cham (2013). https://doi.org/10.1007/978-3-319-03068-5_13
43. Schachter, S., Singer, J.E.: Cognitive, social, and physiological determinants of emotional state. Psychol. Rev. **69**, 379–399 (1962)
44. Schoeman, F.: Privacy and Social Freedom. Cambridge University Press, Cambridge (1992)
45. Schwartz, S.H.: Are there universal aspects in the structure and contents of human values? J. Soc. Issues **50**(4), 19–45 (1994)
46. Sorenson, O., Rivkin, J., Lee, F.: Complexity, networks and knowledge flow. Res. Policy **35**, 994–1017 (2006)
47. The Belmont Report: Ethical Principles and Guidelines for the Protection of Human Subjects of Research 1978. The National Commission for the Protection of Human Subjects of Biomedical and Behavioral Research
48. Tuch, A., Trusell, R., Hornbæk, K.: Analyzing users' narratives to understand experience with interactive products. In: Proceedings of AMC CHI 2013 Extended Abstracts, pp. 2079–2088. The ACM Press (2013)
49. Xavier, R.: Uma abordagem híbrida para a avaliação da experiência emocional de usuários. 161 f. Dissertação (Mestrado em Ciência da Computação), São Carlos-SP, Brasil (2013)
50. Ying, Y., Ziran Z.: Contemporary social design principles in HCI design. In: Control, Automation and Systems Engineering (CASE), pp. 1–4 (2011)

What to See in a Scientific Event? A Social Recommendation Model of Technical Sessions

Aline Tramontin[1(✉)], Roberto Pereira[2(✉)], and Isabela Gasparini[1(✉)]

[1] Graduate Program in Applied Computing (PPGCA), Department of Computer Science, Santa Catarina State University (UDESC), Joinville, SC, Brazil
aline.tramontin@gmail.com, isabela.gasparini@udesc.br
[2] Department of Computer Science, Federal University of Paraná (UFPR), Curitiba, PR, Brazil
rpereira@inf.ufpr.br

Abstract. Scientific/Academic events promote the meeting of researchers for the dissemination of their work to a scientific community. These events are dynamic, where several sessions can happen simultaneously and participants may have difficulty choosing which sessions to attend. Recommender Systems can support participants in this choice by offering recommendations based on information from sessions, participants' profile and social relationships. This paper presents a Social Recommendation Model of Technical Sessions for Scientific Events. The model was partially implemented and was applied on the IHC 2017 and IHC 2018 events, considering co-authoring relationships. The application of the model was evaluated via a questionnaire and triangulated through captured usage data, where users provided their perceptions about the utility of coauthoring network to recommend sessions. Results suggest the model is promising and capable of supporting the implementation of relevant social recommendation mechanisms.

Keywords: Recommender model · Social recommendation · Academic events · Scientific events

1 Introduction

Scientific events bring together researchers, students and other stakeholders, and are composed of different types of sessions. Several topics are addressed, sometimes as subsets of large areas of study, and each session may contain presentations related to themes in these large areas. One of the goals for someone to participate in scientific events is to increase one's network of academic collaboration.

In the social perspective, attending events helps people to make new connections, favouring social capital (i.e. investment in relation to the expected returns [1]). Participation in scientific events also contributes to social relationships, as they connect researchers and promote potential collaborations, increasing their network of academic collaboration [2]. Generally, in academic events there are sessions occurring simultaneously, which makes it difficult to choose which one to participate.

R. P. d. Santos et al. (Eds.): WAIHCWS 2017/2018, CCIS 1081, pp. 99–119, 2020.
https://doi.org/10.1007/978-3-030-46130-0_6

Recommender Systems (RS) are increasingly present in the daily life of users connected to the world wide web. The increasing possibilities of access to information via different types of devices (smartphone, smart TV, tablet, desktop, laptop) allows users to be protagonists, creating their own digital content in social media sites, as well as other types of systems that produce data that need to be analyzed and processed, thus generating an information overload. This overload makes it difficult to choose and access information deemed relevant by the user. At that time, RS have a key role: to help the user to find items relevant to him/her quickly.

A RS is designed to help the users to find items relevant to their interests. Usually, the system focuses on a specific type of item and, therefore, the design, graphical user interface and recommendation technique used to generate the recommendations are all customized to provide useful and effective suggestions for this type of item [3].

There are problems independent of the domain in the RS context: the scarcity of evaluations and the cold start. The scarcity of evaluations occurs when the number of items evaluated is much smaller than that of items available in the system, making it difficult to identify the similarities between people. The cold start problem occurs when a new user or item is entered into the system and there are no evaluations of the item or no items evaluated by the user, so it is not possible to recommend items or find similar users. In the case of RS for scientific events, the problems above due to the short period of time an event exists, a lack of participation history and assessments, and the lack of navigation or interaction data to create/update the user profile.

Social networks allow the user to interact and share information, providing data that can be used by RS, as well as similarity among friends, frequency of interactions, participation in events, among other contextual data that contribute to the improvement of the recommendation. Therefore, social networks become a rich source of information for RS to identify users' profile e offer them relevant information.

This paper presents the Social Recommendation Model of Technical Sessions for Scientific Events, in Portuguese *Modelo de Recomendação Social de Sessões para Eventos Científicos* (MRSSEC). Usage scenarios have been defined that help to illustrate and explain how the model can be applied to different situations of participation in scientific events, the model was applied in a real setting to show the model feasibility.

The analyzes evaluate the user's perception regarding the relevance of the session recommendation generated through the application of MRSSEC in a small scientific event. No comparisons were made with other models or approaches, and the focus of the analyzes was to evaluate the application of the model in a specific context.

This paper is organized in the following way: in Sect. 2 we present the Related Works, in Sect. 3 we present the methodology, in Sect. 4 we present our Social Recommendation Model, in Sect. 5 we present the Usage Scenarios, in Sect. 6 we describe the model application, in Sect. 7 we present the Discussion and, in Sect. 8 we present the considerations about the research.

2 Related Works

In this section we present researches that use the social context in the process of recommending sessions in scientific events.

Farzan and Brusilovsky [4] present a paper that explores social navigation and social search technology in the context of conference attendance planning. A community-based system called "Conference Navigator" was developed for the E-Learning conference series organized by the Association for the Advancement of Computing in Education. The system helps conference participants to schedule appropriate sessions, reducing chances of neglecting articles that are important for the user. The system is built as an intermediary service between the user and the AACE conference planning system, which enables conference participants to navigate the entire program and plan their own programming.

When using the system, users must first choose a community or create one. The system provides two access modes: Schedule Browser and Personal Schedule Planner. In both modes, users can search for interesting documents and sessions as well as navigate through the conference schedule. Farzan and Brusilovsky's [4] research has shown that social navigation can help researchers attending a conference to find relevant documents to read and presentation. However, they do not use social data or location data in the recommendation process.

Pham et al. [2] present a modified version of the Collaborative Filtering algorithm, called Context-Aware Mobile Recommender Services (CAMRS), that combines the social context extracted from social networks within the space of conference participants and delivery recommendation services on mobile devices. The approach considers the mobility and sensitivity to location, time, user and social context. The social context is inferred and refers to the community of on-site researchers, co-authorship in publications, citation networks, research projects and links of mutual collaboration.

The research activities of target user are used for neighborhood (community) formation. Researchers who have similar interests or who are working on similar topics are identified through the co-authoring network and citation network. Two types of links can be selected as members of the target user's community: direct pairs and indirect pairs. Direct pairs are authors with whom the target user has collaborated or referenced directly, being measured by the existence or nonexistence. Indirect pairs are authors that are distant in the network but are similar to the target user. Link prediction methods were used to predict collaboration (direct and indirect pairs) and *Jaccard* coefficient to measure similarity between indirect co-authors in citations and co-authoring. However, they do not use social data from friendship social network.

Asabere et al. [5] present a solution called Social Aware Recommendation of Venues and Environments (SARVE) to improve intelligent attendance at conferences through recommendations on mobile devices. SARVE recommends sites and presentation session environments to participants using community detection techniques. Conference attendees specify their search interests via their mobile devices by entering keywords (tags). SARVE uses four types of context: location, time, user, and social relationships. The location context involves the detection of the exact location of the presentation session. Asabere et al. [5] use the user-based Collaborative Filtering algorithm and Pearson's correlation to identify similarity between two users (closest neighbors) involving a presenting user and a participating user. After more similar users were found through the item and user array, user-based Collaborative Filtering techniques generate a top-N recommendation list for the participating user. However, they do not use social data from the friendship social network, only the community of researchers at the event venue.

In the presented papers, it is observed that the recommendation of presentation sessions that incorporate the social context is a subject under study and with the possibility of exploration. Besides community data it is possible to use social data of the target user from different sources, friendship social networks, citation networks, co-authoring networks, as well as contextual data such as location and time.

Regarding the context, compared to MRSSEC, the presented papers that consider Context Information to improve the recommendation based on the user's situation are: Pham et al. [2] and Asabere et al. [5]. These consider the Local Context, Temporal and Social context. In MRSSEC the Local context is explored, because in large events contextual location information can provide recommendations that help the target user to find relevant sessions near him/her and Social Context, because social contextual information makes it possible to know the target user better from his/her relationships. Farzan and Brusilovsky [4] do not present the use of information based on the user's situation.

Following, we present a social recommendation model that takes into account explicit and implicit relationships. The model deals with the case where the user is not a member of a social network, implicitly connecting the user with the other participants of the event and comparing the similarity of topics of interest between these partici-pants and the target user. However, the main difference of the proposed model in relation to the related works is its design for flexibility and applicability to any type of scientific event.

3   Methodology

This work is classified as exploratory research and has applied nature, being charac-terized as an experimental development work, as it seeks to generate knowledge through the development and experimentation of MRSSEC in a real situation. The approach to the problem of this work is qualitative, the data was collected through questionnaires (Appendix) with open and closed questions and triangulated through automatically captured usage data. The objectives of this research are explanatory, aiming to understand the phenomena explored from the perspective of the participants, identifying the perception of users about the relevance of recommendations. Thus, the question that guides this research is: Can the use of social elements in the session recommendation process generate relevant recommendations for the participants of a scientific event?

4 Social Recommendation Model

In this section, we introduce the MRSSEC, a social recommendation model that considers different types of relationships: (i) implicit, from social networks/database; (ii) explicitly, provided by the user and (iii) implicit, connecting users participating in the event to an implicit social network.

MRSSEC is composed of three essential components: (1) User, (2) Session and (3) Social Network. The User component is the target user of RS and is responsible for providing the necessary data to find and know the user, which are: Name, Surname, Institution, Topics of Interest and Location. The Session component has the attributes of the sessions so that sessions can be identified and recommended for the target user. The essential attributes of a session are: Session Title, Time, Place, Chair, Topics of Interest, Presentations (Authors, Title, Keywords, Institutions). The Social Network component is responsible for providing data about the social relationships of the User component, making it possible to know their relationships and to provide social recommendations.

Social networks or databases can be academic/scientific, friendship or professional. Academic/scientific networks can be: co-authoring, citation, projects, academic orientation or social networks of scientific research. The Social Networking component can also be derived from the event's attendance and presentation history.

MRSSEC is a flexible model and can be fully or partially implemented. In MRSSEC there are two ways to analyze the relationship: implicitly and explicitly. The Implicit Relationship is measured according to the characteristics of the network, for example, in a social network that allows direct interactions between users, data of duration or frequency of contact between the users can be extracted and the Tie Strength (strength of the relationship) can be calculated. The MRSSEC is shown in Fig. 1.

In Fig. 1, the input data is the User data and Technical Sessions data, then data are processed based on the Relationship and Similarity of topics of interest. The algorithm can receive explicit data provided by the user and/or implicit data analyzed in the Social Networking component. The user can explicitly indicate which authors want to "Follow", thus defining Influence by Authority (a kind of influence based on trust, respect and knowledge).

Implicitly, through the input data, the user is located in the Social Network component and the Tie Strength calculation is performed. This calculation can be obtained in two ways, through (i) Frequency of Interactions and/or through (ii) Neighborhood Overlap, the Social Network (or social database) is a mandatory component for the use of the model. In this way, the verification of the existence of implicit relationships is also mandatory.

The Similar User Favorites component is obtained by comparing the topics of interest of the target user with the topics of interest of other users of the event, implicitly connected in the application of the model. Subsequently, data are combined prioritizing the social inputs and then the recommendation can be presented.

MRSSEC can be implemented partially, but due to the essential social component, it is indispensable the implementation of Implicit Relationship.

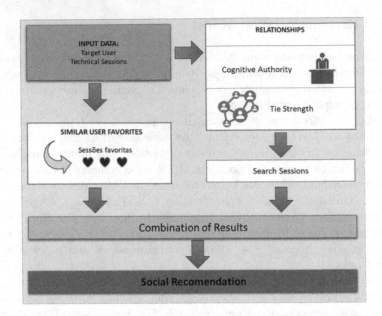

Fig. 1. The social recommendation model of technical sessions for scientific events

4.1 Relationships

Social relations between individuals may be called social ties. Social ties can be implicit, identified through social interactions in a network, or explicitly indicated by the user.

In MRSSEC the explicit relationship represents a cognitive authority relationship recognized from one individual to another, i.e. users indicate who they want to "Follow" according to their personal experiences, trust, reputation, popularity, among other aspects that individuals deem pertinent to consider and that are beyond external questioning. Each person determines his/her own authorities: no one can determine who is an authority for another person other than itself [6].

Through the implicit relationship the Tie Strength between the target user and the other members of the network can be calculated analyzing only the direct pairs. The Tie Strength can be calculated by the frequency of interactions between the members of a network or by overlapping the neighborhood, depending on how the members of the network are connected, if by means of collaborations, having one or more links in common, or through a friendship or professional link [5, 7]. Thus, the top-N relationships are considered Strong Ties in the Social Network (in this step we exclude the authors already selected explicitly by the user). After users' relationships are identified, the sessions in which these relationships are present are retrieved.

4.2 Similar User Favorites

Users present in a same event are implicitly connected by sharing common interests, making it possible to identify a local implicit social network [8]. This network allows to analyze the similarity of the topics of interest of the target user and the topics of interest of other users present in the event, generating a similarity matrix based on content.

For producing more precise results, the similarity between the target user and other users is calculated by means of the cosine similarity [9]. In this technique, the content is represented by a vector of terms $d_j = (w_{1,j}, w_{2,j}, \ldots, w_{t,j})$ arranged in a vector space of k dimensions, where k is the number of terms, the near items are considered similar. Equation 1 for the calculation of the similarity of the Cosine is defined as [10]:

$$sim(d_c, d_s) = \frac{\sum_{i=1}^{k} w_{i,c} w_{i,s}}{\sqrt{\sum_{i=1}^{k} w_{i,c}^2} \sqrt{\sum_{i=1}^{k} w_{i,s}^2}} \tag{1}$$

Where: $sim(d_c, d_s)$ is the result of the distance of the vectors, ranging from [0, 1]; $w_{i,c}$ is the present term in position i of item c; $w_{i,s}$ is the present term in position i of item s. The most similar top-N users and their favorite sessions will be selected.

4.3 Location

MRSSEC considers the location of the User component and the Location of the Session component. This feature allows the mobile user at large events to receive session recommendations taking into account the physical proximity of the user. The location can be implicit or explicit. Implicit when the location is captured by sensors (Wi-Fi, GPS, Bluetooth) and explicit when users manually informs their location (QR Code, Menu Option, Check-in). This feature can be configured according to the size and purpose of the event.

4.4 Combination of Results

After selecting sessions based on relationships (Strong Ties and Influence by Authority) and the favorite sessions of the most similar users, results are combined and filtered to be recommended to the target user. According Fig. 2, in the recommendation process social criteria are prioritized: the Authority Influence (1) is the most relevant criteria as it is an explicit action where the user indicate the authors he or her wants to follow. The Tie Strength (2), obtained implicitly from Social Network calculation, is applied in the sequence and, finally, the Similarity of Topics of Interest (3) is applied, where sessions are recommended based on the most similar users identified according to the topics of interest from local social network.

If Location feature (4) is enabled in the application, it can be used as another criterium for recommending sessions, however, the priority of social criteria must be respected. Lastly, a Top-N list of sessions will be generated and the presentation of the recommendation should take into account the priority of social criteria in all model applications.

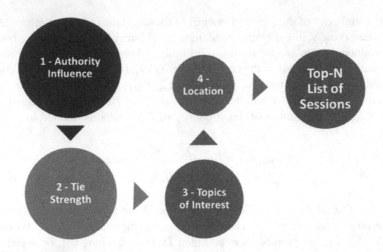

Fig. 2. Combination of results to generate the Top-N list recommendation

5 Usage Scenarios

Scenarios were created to demonstrate the use of MRSSEC. According to Rosson and Carrol (2002, apud Barbosa and Silva 2010) [11], "a scenario is a narrative, textual or pictorial, concrete, rich in contextual details, a situation of use of the application, involving users, processes and actual or potential data." In this section, scenarios where MRSSEC can be applied will be presented. Table 1 presents 8 possible scenarios of use.

The other possibilities of Usage Scenarios (5, 6, 7 and 8), according to Table 1, resemble the four scenarios already presented, differing only by the non-use (by the user) or non-implementation (by the system developer) of the MRSSEC Location feature. The first scenario illustrated in Table 1 were selected.

Table 1. Possible combinations of usage scenarios.

	Relationship			
Scenario	Explicit	Implicit	Topics Interest	Location
1	X	X	X	X
2	–	X	X	X
3	X	X	–	X
4	–	X	–	X
5	X	X	X	–
6	–	X	X	–
7	X	X	–	–
8	–	X	–	–

5.1   Usage Scenario 1

Usage Scenario 1 demonstrates the full application of MRSSEC according to Fig. 3. Rose is a graduate student at a public university and has submitted her first research paper to an academic event in co-authoring with her professors, Mary and John. With the acceptance of her paper, Rose went to the event to present her paper and to attend to the others presentations.

Upon arriving, Rose was informed about a mobile application to help participants find presentation sessions and other activities. She registered in the application by informing some personal data (name, surname and e-mail) and her institution.

Rose allowed the system to locate her in a social network of friendships. In the system, she selected some topics of interest and the author she wishes to follow at the event, Odete, one of the pioneers in research publications related to Rose's interests.

The system located Rose's coauthors, Mary and John, in the event-authoring database and presentation sessions in which they have works to present, recommending sessions based on frequency of interactions obtained from co-authoring relationship. From Rose's social network of friends, the system found more common relationships among the friends considered as strong ties: Ellen has a work to be presented in the current event. The system recommended Ellen's work for Rose, indicating it as a social recommendation.

The system also presented recommendations based on the similarity of topics of interest. For this, the system found users who selected topics of interest similar to those selected by Rose and recommended to Rose the sessions these users liked. The system also presented to Rose the sessions in which the author Odete is present.

The event takes place in a large pavilion, with an auditorium, several venues, and other places with presentations and exhibitions of works. Rose has the system on her mobile device and checked in by a QR-Code when entering Venue Z to watch a

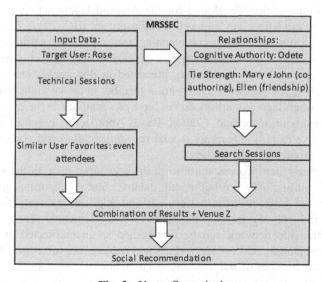

Fig. 3. Usage Scenario 1

presentation. Rose's location was identified by the system and Rose receives a presentation session recommendation that will occur in the same venue after the current session. Usage Scenario 1 is exemplified in Fig. 3.

6   Model Application

MRSSEC seeks to be a flexible model for social recommendations in the context of scientific or academic events, and validation and adaptation to other contexts are not explored within the scope of this research.

MRSSEC was applied at the XVI Brazilian Symposium on Human Factors in Computer Systems (IHC), in 2017. To provide social relationships, the database of IHC full papers publications in Brazil was used.

The analyzes presented are intended to evaluate the user's perception regarding the relevance of the session recommendation generated through the application of MRSSEC in a small scientific event.

This section presents the model application in a real event to evaluate the proposed model.

6.1   IHC 2017

The model was partially instantiated (as on scenario 8, see Table 1) for the event IHC 2017, that took place between October 23 and 27 in Joinville, Santa Catarina, Brazil. The application was carried out with the objective of obtaining the perception of target users in relation to the social recommendation.

In order to apply the model, it is necessary to define the Social Network component. For this instantiation we used the IHC co-authoring network.

For this application, the model was instantiated in a mobile app, AppIHC, which is an open source application developed for the Android Operating System, using the Material Design guidelines, to support participants in IHC 2017, offering general information about the event and recommending sessions for the participants to attend [12], the first version of the application was developed only in Portuguese.

The social approach by co-authoring presented in this application has two main disadvantages: 1. when the target user is not a member in the co-authoring network of the event, or 2. when their co-authors do not have presentations in the event. In order to compensate for this disadvantage, Content-Based Approach is executed in parallel as proposed by Oliveira [13]. Therefore, social recommendation and content-based recommendation complement each other.

The recommendation process starts from the user input data. In the sequence, the target user is identified in the co-authorship database and the algorithm to identify the High Frequency of Interactions is performed. This application exemplifies the Usage Scenario 8, where only the Implicit Relationship is implemented (Table 1).

The co-authorship network can be represented as an undirected graph with the following representation: authors are vertices and publications are edges. The objective is to quantify the number of publications in co-authorship (interactions), that is, how many edges each pair of the network has. Thus, according to Fig. 4, the co-authorship relationship between two authors, vertices *u2* and *u3*, is represented by a prominent link as they have more than one paper together.

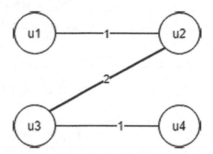

Fig. 4. Tie strength representation in co-authorship network

For the application, the greater the number of publications in co-authorship the stronger the relationship between the authors. The recommendation to the target user is generated based on the publications of his/her co-authors (except the ones she or he is an author as well). Pairs are selected and the tiebreaker is held by the most recent co-authorship.

The Tie Strength calculation is a measure that identifies the co-author who has the highest quantity of papers authored with the target user u. Let be $C(u)$ the set of co-authors of u and $V_{u,k}$ the quantity of publications u has with a user $k \in C(u)$, the Strong Co-author Relationship is defined by Eq. 2:

$$SRCoauthoring(u) = \{k : u \in C(u), \max(V_{u,k})\} \qquad (2)$$

The IHC 2017 had 250 participants, and 108 participants used the application. The algorithm identified 35 participants, previously enrolled in the event, who are co-authors in the IHC database, but only 14 users installed the application and received a co-authoring recommendation. This reduced number of users is partially due to operating systems restrictions, as the AppIHC was developed for Android only. After the event, a questionnaire was sent to the 14 co-authors who used the application, and 8 users answered the questions presented in Table 2. The analysis of the questionnaire is qualitative, seeking to analyze the user's perception of the recommendations received, and AppIHC usage data are analyzed to help understand the user's perception of the social recommendation.

The social recommendation by co-authoring was added implicitly in the application. When using AppIHC, the user received recommendations through text and icon in the event schedule, presented per day according to Fig. 5 (in Portuguese).

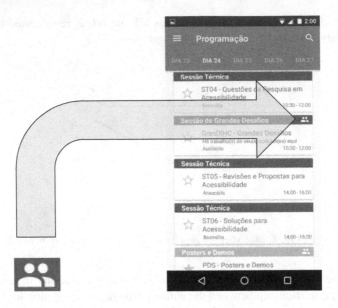

Fig. 5. Social icon and social recommendation

Table 2. Closed questions.

Question	Yes	Did not say	No
Q1- Did you notice the indication that in a given session there was your co-author (s)?	5	2	1
Q2- Did this information influence your decision-making process to which sessions to watch?	1	2	5
Q3- Do you find it useful to co-authoring to recommend sessions?	5	2	1

Data was combined with the recording of activities in the application and the responses of the questionnaire, showing that although some users considered they were not influenced to attend a presentation session because of coauthoring information, they liked the recommended session favorited it, indicating that it was relevant for them and they want to easily locate their coauthors.

MRSSEC uses social data to improve recommendations. These data can be derived from social relations, social interactions, participation in events, among other data that contribute to the improvement of the recommendation process. The model proposed in this paper also uses social data provided explicitly by the user and analyzes the similarity between the participants of the event through the topics of interest.

The application of MRSSEC in the event IHC 2017, although partial, provided capturing usage data and through a questionnaire it was possible to verify that social data can generate useful recommendations for the target user.

6.2 IHC 2018

AppIHC was also used in IHC 2018. In the version of AppIHC 2018 were added features related to this research, for example, the user can select, in addition to topics of interest, favorite sessions and favorite authors. Therefore, it was possible to obtain a database with topics of interest, favorite authors and favorite sessions of each user.

The event took place in Belém, Pará, Brazil, from October 22 to 26, 2018. During the event, usage data were collected from 98 users, and through the AppIHC 2018. Users answered questions related to the recommender system: I consider important the social-based recommendation functionality in an event application. Twenty-six users answered this question, of which 18 users said yes, they consider important, 5 were neutral and 2 users did not consider important. A user submitted the questionnaire without answering this question.

In order to simulate the recommendations by co-authoring, the same database of the previous event (IHC 2017) was used, and co-authoring data of the complete papers presented in IHC 2017 were also used. The Tie Strength calculation were accomplished according Eq. 2, presented in Sect. 6.1. The model was implemented according to scenario 5 (see Table 1, Sect. 5), therefore, only the location was not implemented.

IHC 2018 had 294 registered users, 98 users installed the app, 2 registered users did not participate in the event and 1 application user was not registered in the event. During the event, 4 users received recommendations. However, due to the communication problem with AppIHC 2018 the recommendations were not presented during the event. Thus, after the event, recommendations were generated for registered users who used the application, 77 users received recommendations, and 18 users did not receive any type of recommendation. The recommendations that were generated for the 77 users were sent by email, attached with the schedule and a link to answer a questionnaire.

The questionnaire questions were divided into 3 sections according to the type of recommendation: (i) Tie Strength, (ii) Cognitive Authority, and (iii) Similar User Favorites. Each participant was instructed to answer only the sections that represent the type of recommendation received, as many participants received more than one type of recommendation. Therefore, the number of answers is greater than the number of respondents.

Of the 77 users (population) who received recommendations, 46 (sample) answered the survey, representing 60% of the population. However, two participants did not answer the questions according to the recommendation received, thus the number of participants with valid answers was 44, representing 58% of the population.

In order to obtain user perception, they were asked to answer the question "Are the recommendations relevant?". Responses were presented in Likert scale: 1-Fully Irrelevant, 2-Irrelevant, 3-Indifferent, 4-Relevant and 5-Fully Relevant. Thus, Fig. 6 presents the answers by type of recommendation was generated. Figure 6 shows that

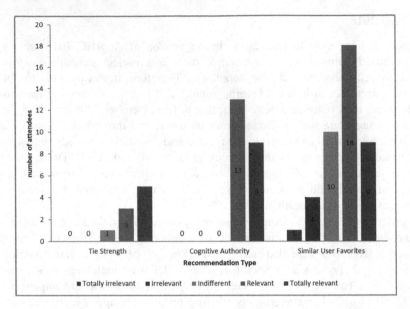

Fig. 6. Relevance of recommendations by type of recommendation

only in the recommendation by Similar User Favorites there is indication of Totally Irrelevant and Irrelevant, for recommendation by Tie Strength and Cognitive Authority there were no indications of irrelevance.

In AppIHC 2018 were verified the number of sessions favored by the research participants. Therefore, an analysis was performed to identify the recommended sessions after the event that were favored by the participant during the event. Of the 46 participants who received recommendations after the event, 24 participants favored at least one session during the event. Of these 24, 17 participants received the recommendation of at least one session that had been favored.

Figure 7 shows the list of 17 users who received recommendations from favorite sessions, the number of favorite sessions in blue and the number of favorite sessions that were recommended in red. For user number 17, for example, 15 sessions from 18 sessions he favored during the event were recommended to her/him after the event. Favourite sessions indicated by the participant during the event represent an explicit evidence of relevance for the recommendations offered by the MRSSEC.

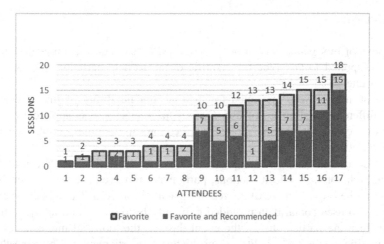

Fig. 7. Favorite x favorite and recommended number of sessions (Color figure online)

7 Discussion

Through the analysis of each type of recommendation it was possible to verify that most participants considered the Recommendations relevant.

Of the 44 participants, 39 received at least one recommendation considered Relevant or Fully Relevant. An explicit evidence of relevance was indicated by participants who favored sessions during the event; 17 participants received the recommendation of at least one session that had been favored. For each type of recommendation generated, most participants stated that they had attended between 30% and 50% of the sessions, being considered a positive percentage range for the application of the experiment.

The results demonstrate the importance of prioritizing social criteria, reinforcing the belief that cognitive authorities tend to offer items of greater interest to the granting authority user and that existing social ties contribute to generate relevant recommendations.

However, there are limitations and threats to the validity of the experiment. One threat to the validity of the experiment is that the model was partially implemented in the first experiment. Regarding the second experiment only user's location was not implemented. Both experiments were applied to the same small event. Therefore, further experiments are necessary to verify the adherence of the complete model and in all scenarios presented and with different audiences.

A limitation of the experiment is the size of the sample. In both the first and second experiments few participants answered to the survey, which could have more conclusive results if more participants had participated.

Another limitation is that the recommendations were not generated in real time in the second experiment because more usage data could have been collected in addition to the feedback that could have been collected during the event.

8 Conclusion

The purpose of this paper was to present MRSSEC, a social recommendation model that can be applied to any type of scientific event, to help participants choose which sessions to attend.

Usage scenarios were presented to illustrate the flexibility of the model, which allows 8 different possibilities of use. One of the scenarios was applied for the IHC 2017, implemented for use in AppIHC application, and another simulated with real data of IHC 2018.

MRSSEC uses social data to improve recommendations. These data can be derived from social relations, social interactions, participation in events, among other data that contribute to the improvement of the recommendation process. The model proposed in this paper also uses social data provided explicitly by the user and analyzes the similarity between the participants of the event through the topics of interest.

In scientific events there is little or no history of participation. Choosing the most relevant sessions can be a difficult task, especially at large events or when sessions occur simultaneously. The academic conferences are dynamic, the participants are moving, participating in different presentations in different environments and schedules. RS can assist in choosing which sessions to watch, as they use data about the participant, about sessions and social data. The model presented in this paper can inform designers of recommending systems to design their systems taking into account social elements relevant for the users.

Regarding the guiding question, "Can the use of social elements in the session recommendation process generate relevant recommendations for the participants of a scientific event?", based on the applied experiments, it is possible to say that the social elements used in MRSSEC contribute positively to the session recommendation process by providing relevant recommendations to the participants of scientific events.

Thus, the main contributions of this paper include the definition of a flexible Social Recommendation Model of Technical Sessions for Scientific Events, applicable to any scientific event. The model has important differentials, such as the Cognitive Authority, which is the explicit indication of a relationship of trust, admiration, among other user reasons for authors; Similar User Favorites, which broadens the diversity of the recommendation and increases the chances of finding serendipities relevant to the user's interests. The use of different sources of social data, such as social networks or databases in which relationships can be extracted, and the similarity of topics of interest between users implicitly connected to a local social network are also different from existing work, seeking assist participants in these events to easily find relevant sessions.

As future works we seek to extend the model. First by recommending sessions to authors from the same university. Recommend the most discussed topics, which can be verified through the user's interaction with the system, recommend sessions of authors referenced in the target user's article. Another suggestion of improvement for the model is in the case of parallel sessions, to present to the target user an option where he/she can indicate which session is more relevant, so MRSSEC can build a profile for the target user.

Acknowledgment. We thank the financial support of FAPESC, public call public FAPESC/CNPQ No. 06/2016 support the infrastructure of CTI for young researchers, project T.O. No: 2017TR1755 - Intelligent Educational Environments with Integration of Learning Analytics and Gamification Techniques. The present work was carried out with the support of the Coordination of Improvement of Higher Education Personnel - Brazil (CAPES) - Financing Code 001.

Appendix - Recommendation Evaluation Questionnaire

Avaliação da Recomendação Social de Sessões do IHC 2018

Prezado(a) participante,

Este questionário faz parte de uma dissertação de mestrado que criou um Modelo para Recomendação de Sessões Técnicas de Eventos Científicos com base em Elementos Sociais. Como uma experimentação do modelo, capturamos os dados do aplicativo do evento, AppIHC2018. Como você participou do IHC e usou o AppIHC, verificamos que o sistema de recomendação poderia sugerir sessões à você. Deste modo, encaminhamos a você um email com um arquivo .pdf contendo as recomendações geradas.

Este questionário tem como objetivo avaliar a recomendação social que lhe foi enviada por e-mail, e não o uso do aplicativo durante o IHC 2018 (Belém, Pará).

O formulário é composto por 3 seções relacionadas as recomendações. Por gentileza, responda a seção de questões de acordo com as recomendações que você recebeu.
  1 - Sessões em que há coautores seus;
  2 - Sessões em que há trabalhos de autores que você segue;
  3 - Sessões que outros pesquisadores favoritaram (baseado em seus tópicos de interesse).

Muito obrigado por sua participação!

Aline de Paula Araújo Tramontin (mestranda, PPGCA - UDESC)
Isabela Gasparini (orientadora, PPGCA - UDESC)
Roberto Pereira (coorientador, Depto. Informática - UFPR)
Contato: aline.tramontin@gmail.com

*Obrigatório

Termo de Consentimento *

Aceito participar da pesquisa e entendo que todos meus dados individuais serão sigilosos. Apenas os pesquisadores deste projeto terão acesso aos dados brutos. Solicitamos a sua autorização para o uso de seus dados para a produção de textos técnicos e científicos. A sua privacidade será mantida.

☐ Aceito participar desta pesquisa

1 - Sessões em que há coautores seus:

Se você não recebeu recomendações baseadas em 'Coautores', siga para as próximas seções do formulário!

1.1 - As recomendações são relevantes:
(1) Totalmente irrelevante (2) Irrelevante (3) Indiferente (4) Relevante (5) Totalmente relevante

           1   2   3   4   5

Totalmente Irrelevante ◯ ◯ ◯ ◯ ◯ Totalmente Relevante

1.2 - Se você achou as recomendações relevantes, mesmo que parcialmente, aponte-nos o(s) motivo(s):

☐ Tenho interesse na linha de pesquisa em que meus coautores trabalham atualmente

☐ Gosto de prestigiar as apresentações de meus coautores

☐ Acho interessante saber que meus coautores estão presentes no evento

☐ Outro: _____

1.3 - Se você não achou as recomendações relevantes, diga-nos o(s) motivo(s):

Sua resposta

1.4 Você assistiu a alguma das sessões recomendadas?

◯ Nenhuma sessão recomendada

◯ Menos de 30% das sessões recomendas

◯ Entre 30% até 50% das sessões recomendadas

◯ Mais de 50% das sessões recomendadas

◯ Outro: _____

2 - Sessões em que há trabalhos de 'autores que você segue':

Se você não recebeu recomendações por 'Autores que você segue', siga para a próxima seção do formulário!

2.1 - As recomendações são relevantes:
(1) Totalmente irrelevante (2) Irrelevante (3) Indiferente (4) Relevante (5) Totalmente relevante

| 1 | 2 | 3 | 4 | 5 |

Totalmente Irrelevante ○ ○ ○ ○ ○ Totalmente Relevante

2.2 - Se você achou as recomendações relevantes, mesmo que parcialmente, aponte-nos o(s) motivo(s):

☐ Atuo ou tenho interesse em atuar na mesma linha de pesquisa em que os autores que sigo

☐ Tenho interesse na mesma linha de pesquisa em os autores que sigo

☐ São autores renomados e/ou prestigiados pela comunidade do IHC no Brasil

☐ São meus coautores e gostaria de encontrá-los no evento

☐ Outro:

2.3 - Se você não achou as recomendações relevantes, diga-nos o(s) motivo(s):

Sua resposta

2.4 - Você assistiu a alguma das sessões recomendadas?

○ Nenhuma sessão recomendada

○ Menos de 30% das sessões recomendas

○ Entre 30% até 50% das sessões recomendadas

○ Mais de 50% das sessões recomendadas

○ Outro:

3 - Sessões que outros pesquisadores 'favoritaram':

Baseado em seus tópicos de interesse

3.1 - As recomendações são relevantes:
(1) Totalmente irrelevante (2) Irrelevante (3) Indiferente (4) Relevante (5) Totalmente relevante

    1   2   3   4   5

Totalmente Irrelevante   ○ ○ ○ ○ ○   Totalmente Relevante

3.2 - Se você achou as recomendações relevantes, mesmo que parcialmente, aponte-nos o(s) motivo(s):

☐ As sessões recomendadas possuem trabalhos relacionados aos meus tópicos de interesse

☐ As sessões recomendadas possuem trabalhos de autores do meu interesse

☐ Outro:

3.3 - Se você não achou as recomendações relevantes, diga-nos o(s) motivo(s):

Sua resposta

3.4 - Você assistiu a alguma das sessões recomendadas?

○ Nenhuma sessão recomendada

○ Menos de 30% das sessões recomendas

○ Entre 30% até 50% das sessões recomendadas

○ Mais de 50% das sessões recomendadas

References

1. Lin, N., Cook, K.S., Burt, R.S.: Social Capital: Theory and Research. Routledge, Abingdon (2001)
2. Pham, M.C., Kovachev, D., Cao, Y., Mbogos, G.M., Klamma, R.: Enhancing academic event participation with context-aware and social recommendations. In: International Conference on Advances in Social Networks Analysis and Mining (ASONAM 2012), pp. 464–471. IEEE Computer Society (2012)
3. Ricci, F., Rokach, L., Shapira, B.: Introduction to recommender systems handbook. In: Ricci, F., Rokach, L., Shapira, B., Kantor, Paul B. (eds.) Recommender Systems Handbook, pp. 1–35. Springer, Boston, MA (2011). https://doi.org/10.1007/978-0-387-85820-3_1

4. Farzan, R., Brusilovsky, P.: Where did the researchers go? Supporting social navigation at a large academic conference. In: Proceedings of the nineteenth ACM conference on Hypertext and Hypermedia (HT 2008), pp. 203–212. ACM, New York, NY, USA (2008)

5. Asabere, N.Y., Xia, F., Wang, W., Rodrigues, J.J., Basso, F., Ma, J.: Improving smart conference participation through socially aware recommendation. IEEE Trans. Hum. Mach. Syst. **44**(5), 689–700 (2014)

6. Toledo, D.F., Pereira, R., Oliveira, J.R.E.: Identifying cognitive authority in social networks: a conceptual framework. In: Proceedings of the 14th Brazilian Symposium on Human Factors in Computing Systems, p. 42. ACM (2015)

7. Granovetter, M.: The strength of weak ties. Am. J. Sociol. **78**(6), 1360–1380 (1973)

8. Bernardes, D., Diaby, M., Fournier, R., FogelmanSoulié, F., Viennet, E.: A social formalism and survey for recommender systems. ACM SIGKDD Explor. Newsl. **16**(2), 20–37 (2015)

9. Jannach, D., Zanker, M., Felfernig, A., Friedrich, G.: Recommender Systems: An Introduction. Cambridge University Press, Cambridge (2010)

10. Adomavicius, G., Tuzhilin, A.: Toward the next generation of recommender systems: a survey of the state-of-the-art and possible extensions. IEEE Trans. Knowl. Data Eng. **17**(6), 734–749 (2005)

11. Barbosa, S.D.J., da Silva, B.S.: Interação humano-computador, p. 384. Elsevier, Rio de Janeiro (2010)

12. Sohn, R.: Aplicação Móvel para Apoiar Participantes de Eventos Científicos. Universidade do Estado de Santa Catarina, Joinville (2017)

13. Oliveira, B.: Sistema de Recomendação Baseado em Conteúdo: Recomendando Sessões em Eventos Científicos. Universidade do Estado de Santa Catarina, Joinville (2017)

MobiBus: A Mobile Application to Keep Track of Buses in Small Cities

Artur Kronbauer[1,2](✉), Jorge Campos[1,2], Gleison da Silva[1], Raimundo Lima[1], and Isaac Moreira[1]

[1] Bahia State University, Rodovia BR-110, KM 03, Alagoinhas, Bahia, Brazil
arturhk@gmail.com, jorgapcampos@gmail.com, gleison.fernandesb@gmail.com,
rvini.andrade@gmail.com, isaacdouglas@gmail.com
[2] Salvador University, R. Dr. José Peroba, 251, Salvador, Bahia, Brazil

Abstract. Major cities have been investing in vast financial resources to improve their information systems regarding public transport, especially regarding bus schedules and time of arrival. Medium-sized cities, however, do not have the financial resources to buy or develop applications that can provide accurate information to the users of the public transportation system. In this sense, this article presents a proposal based on the concepts of crowdsourcing, mobile computing, and social networks, to offer a viable solution to the problem, both technically and economically speaking. The developed application allows people to exchange information about the public transportation service, obtain the location of the bus and the estimated time of arrival of a bus at a certain location. As a contribution, it is expected to occur democratization of information about the public transport system, even in cities with little financial resources to invest in this area. An experiment with real users of the Alagoinhas public transport system suggests that the MobiBus App can alleviate the inconveniences caused by a long waiting time at the bus stops, making users feel more secure.

Keywords: Intelligent Transportation Systems · Advanced Systems of Public Transport · Crowdsourcing · Collaborative systems · Social networks

1 Introduction

Mobility, in an urban context, is concerned with meeting the need of people's movement, the democratization of access to public transportation, respect to the environment, and improvement of the quality of life of their citizens [2]. Therefore, urban mobility has become one of the recurrent themes in discussions concerning city development models.

Aiming at ensuring the mobility of goods and people, major cities have developed a complex and multimodal transportation system. In this system, it is used in a coordinated way various transportation modes (e.g., public, private, mass or

© Springer Nature Switzerland AG 2020
R. P. d. Santos et al. (Eds.): WAIHCWS 2017/2018, CCIS 1081, pp. 120–137, 2020.
https://doi.org/10.1007/978-3-030-46130-0_7

individual). The economic growth experienced by emerging markets over the last decade, however, encouraged the migration of rural population to urban areas. This phenomenon generates a huge demand for public transportation and the acquisition of vehicles at a rate much higher than the capacity of cities to adapt its road infrastructure. Unfortunately, private cars have become the solution for common citizens to escape from an increasingly chaotic and inefficient public transportation system. The strategy used by most countries to overcome this situation and to improve urban mobility has been increasing the use of modern information and communication technologies in the public transportation system [17].

Major cities have been incorporating the technology of Intelligent Transportation Systems (ITS) to monitor, manage, and analyze the transportation network. ITS can be defined as the collection of advanced applications in which information and communication technologies are applied in the field of road transportation networks, including infrastructure, vehicles, and users. ITS encompass many specialized subsystems [1], the most known being Advanced Traffic Management Systems (ATMS), Advanced Traveler Information Systems (ATIS), Commercial Vehicle Operation (CVO), Advanced Vehicle Control Systems (AVCS), Electronic Toll Collection (ETC), and Advanced Systems of Public Transport (ASPT). ASPT is closely related to the realm of this work. ASPT incorporate major advances in geographic and intelligent transportation systems, mobile and ubiquitous computing, and communication technologies to provide solutions that encourage the use and allow the analysis and management of the public system. The main goals of ASPT are safety, efficiency, and effectiveness. Concerning the bus system, ASPT aims to minimize waiting time, increase security, and enhance information about itineraries and schedules.

ASPT address three major segments of the bus transportation system: the user segment, the segment of bus companies, which operate the system, and the segment of regulatory agencies, which supervise the quality and efficiency of the system. Each segment has different needs and expectations. Passengers, for instance, are interested in knowing the best itinerary or combination of itinerary to go from one place to another, a precise estimated time of arrival of the next bus, the duration of the intended trip under actual traffic conditions, and the situation of the coming bus (e.g., it is full or dirty, it has accessibility equipment). Moreover, passengers are anxious to be heard about their complaints and willing to voluntarily collaborate with the system improvements. On the other side, bus companies and regulatory agencies are interested in analyzing the efficiency and quality of the system, bus schedules compliance, the behavior of each driver, the frequency and duration of buses' trip, and in be aware of passengers' suggestions and complaints.

Despite the size and complexity of the public transport system, the problems experienced by users of these systems are similar. Alagoinhas, for instance, a city located in northeastern Brazil, has a population of something around 150 thousand inhabitants. The users of the collective transportation system in Alagoinhas have the same complaints about the service as their fellows of big metropoles around the world, that is, the excessive waiting time for the vehicles and the inaccuracy of their schedules. Also, bus stops at Alagoinhas do not have any source of information about bus timetables, forcing people to spend a long time waiting for the bus, which at certain times and places can be quite dangerous for the user. The use of information and communication technologies in the context of ASPT could help to minimize many of these problems. The technology used by big metropoles, however, requires a huge amount of investment, an investment that most small and medium cities cannot afford.

In order to overcome some of the problems faced by small and medium cities, this paper presents a crowdsourcing-based solution that uses the voluntary contribution of the users of the public transportation system to generate information about bus schedules and delays. The proposed solution is strong based on existing mobile devices and in the public participation [5], thus it does not require investments in infrastructure and can be easily implemented by any city. To evaluate the potential of the proposed solution, an experiment was carried out with the participation of users of the public transportation system of the city of Alagoinhas. The results of the experiment are promising and the expectation is that the system can be adopted in cities of any size.

The remainder of this article is structured as follows: Sect. 2 deals with related work; Sect. 3 presents the proposed application; Sect. 4 describes the steps used to develop a case study to validate the application presents and discusses the results of the case study; and Sect. 5 presents conclusions and discusses future work.

2   Related Work

Crowdsourcing is a type of online participatory activity in which an individual or a company proposes to a group of individuals to accomplish a task voluntarily [5]. The crowd participates with its work, time, knowledge or experience. Engaging in the task always brings mutual benefits. On one hand, participants receive a recompense, which can be personal satisfaction, pecuniary rewards, social recognition, self-esteem, or the development of individual competencies. Initiators of the crowdsourcing process, on the other hand, obtain the benefit of using data and information brought by the participants, which depend on the type of activity performed.

Crowdsensing is the capability of ordinary citizens to use sensors to capture and communicate information about themselves, the environment, or the infrastructure. Crowdsensing is crowdsourcing of sensor data from mobile devices. Devices equipped with various sensors have become ubiquitous. An emerging category of personal and connected devices, such as smartphones and embedded vehicles devices, are incorporating a myriad of sensors which allow the measurement of all sort of things (e.g., a user heart frequency and the number of steps during a walking, a vehicle gas consumption, traffic flow status, and road conditions such as potholes and bumps [7].

The combination of information coming from humans and data gathered by sensors have a distinct nature. Contributions from humans are always participatory, that is, a person must devote some time to accomplish a task. Data from sensors are opportunistic, that is, sensors work in the background, while mobile devices usually collect and process the data and send them to a Web service somewhere in the Cloud. In the context of applications for Advanced Systems of Public Transport, both pieces of information are relevant. There are a countless number of Web and mobile applications that use participatory and opportunistic information coming from the crowd of users and their sensors. We will discuss here some applications strong related to our work, although some of them are based on information about the transportation network, bus schedules and itineraries that, in most cities, are not yet widely available or in the worst-case scenario, does not even exist.

CittaMobi [10] is a mobile crowdsensing application used to precisely forecast the arrival of buses at each bus stop. The time of arrival of each bus is computed based on the current position of the bus and the traffic condition of the road network. These pieces of information are continuously updated, which gives a good estimate of the time of arrival. In addition, the user can count on information regarding events along the road network; can search for buses passing through a given bus stop, can check if the coming bus is adapted to wheelchair users; visualizes all nearby buses with estimated time of arrival; and records favorite bus stops and itineraries to make searching easier. CittaMobi is available in only 26 major Brazilian cities.

O Moovit is a mobile crowdsensing and crowdsourcing application that aims to improve urban mobility and facilitate the use of the public transportation system. Moovit is a very popular transportation application, being present in 58 countries and 700 cities, and with more than 10 million Brazilian users [3]. Moovit allows users to plan their travels mixing different types of transportation modes. Using its crowdsensing capability, Moovit gives users reports about the current condition of the road network, precise information about the trip and how long it will take to the user's destination. Moreover, users can share your route and view other users of the app and even talk to them. Moovit also has an app for carpool sharing, letting users find other users who will take a similar route to share the cost of the trip.

Another popular application widely used to obtain traffic information is Waze. Waze is a crowdsensing and crowdsourcing application that aims to improve urban mobility by giving precise information about traffic conditions along with the road network. When users travel running the Waze application, their location and speed are sent to Waze to estimate the average speed of the via. Its feature is captured opportunistically, that is, there is no need for the user to intervene manually. Besides, users can actively collaborate doing insertions and manual edits of some kinds of information available in the application, such as relating a car accident, maintenance services on the road, or the price of the fuel at a certain gas station [4].

All initiatives presented so far are commercial solutions backed by the infrastructure of big companies. Thus, some functionalities and services provided by these solutions are not yet available and cannot be implemented in small cities, especially in cities from developing countries. An inspiring initiative is the application OneBusAway [6]. OneBusAway provides real-time information about buses from the Seattle region of the United States. This application aims to have a precise forecast for bus schedules. The position of each bus is obtained by an embedded GPS device and sent regularly to a central server. The server considers bus locations and traffic conditions of the road network and broadcast to all users the estimated time of arrival of each bus. The flow of information, in this case, is the outdated Internet model to exchange information known as top-down, that is, the information is produced by the owner of the process and made available to the community to consume it. In this model, there is no way for the user to contribute to the process. Internet 2.0 inverts the flows of information and creates the user-generated content (UGC), which becomes the base of the crowdsourcing technology.

An alternative to the use of position devices in each bus is the work of [15]. In this work is presented the use of DSRC (Dedicated Short-Range Communication) as a mechanism to provide vehicle location. DSRC is a kind of short-range communication system used specifically in the field of transportation. The idea is to have a DSCR device at each bus station. This device can gather all kinds of information about the vehicle. In this work, however, the information is used only to capture the position of the bus as it passes by the bus station and estimates the time of arrival at the next bus station along the itinerary. This kind of solution works only in cities that have already a DSCR network.

Sandheep et al. [13] presented a crowdsourcing and crowdsensing application to estimate the time of arrival of buses. The system uses the device's embedded accelerometer to detect every bus stop. Whenever the device detected a vehicle stop, the GPS sensor is activated and the coordinates of the stop are sent to the server. The server runs a scheduling algorithm and updates the timetable. Every time the user of the application enters a source and a destination, the corresponding bus schedule is displayed. There are some drawbacks to this approach. Since the position of each bus station is already known, it is cheaper to keep the GPS activated than to continually run an algorithm to detect stops. Moreover, the algorithm that detects a bus stop based on accelerometer data can produce many false positives, that is, a stop caused by a traffic jam has the same acceleration pattern of a stop at a bus station.

Crowdmap [14] is another crowdsensing application aiming at the public transportation system. The focus of Crowdmap is to gather data about the travel and road conditions along the bus itinerary. Crowmap automatically senses route signatures and events like speeding, braking, making turns, and speeding up to infer the condition of the pavement and the driving behavior. Although the information gathered could be used to estimate the time of arrival, these pieces of information are mainly used to maintain an inventory of road conditions and users' travel preferences.

Inspired by the features offered by the large proprietary systems and in the potential that crowdsourcing and crowdsensing technologies represent for intelligent transport systems, this work presents MobiBus. MobiBus is designed to address the needs of users of the public transportation systems of small and medium-sized cities. We used as a basis for developing the demands pointed out by research conducted with the users of the system and the idiosyncrasies of the public transport system of the city of Alagoinhas, Bahia - Brazil. We believe, however, that the solution adopted can be used in urban agglomerates with similar characteristics. In the next section, we discuss the design of MobiBus.

3   MobiBus Architecture

One of the major challenges faced by municipalities is to implement mobility actions in which public transport is made available with quality and becomes the preferred means of transportation [11]. The popularization and universalization of public transport (i) allow the free locomotion of people; (ii) facilitate access for people with physical disabilities; (iii) provide transportation for people who are not qualified to drive; (iv) reduce congestion and levels of pollution; (v) promote energy saving; and (vi) reduce the demand for new roads and parking lots.

Although it is possible to observe several investments in the area of public transportation in large urban centers in Brazil, most small and medium-sized Brazilian cities work with very small budgets and present a chaotic reality in this sector. The most recurrent problem in these urban settlements is the insufficiency of itineraries, aging of the fleet, lack of comfort, insecurity, unavailability of information regarding itineraries and inaccuracy of schedules [11]. MobiBus was developed to contribute to public transport services of medium-sized cities. The goal of MobiBus is to be a mobile application that meets the demand for information about schedules, itineraries, and problems without demanding large investments from the public sector.

MobiBus is an application based on the voluntary contribution of users of the public transport system. Before being made available to the general public, however, it is necessary to register base information regarding the infrastructure of the city's public transportation system. The initial charge of MobiBus system consists of registering the location of each bus stop and buses' itineraries. These pieces of information are usually registered by the municipal bodies but can be made by any citizen who has this kind of information and skill. Once all base information is in place, MobiBus is fed by users of the system in a voluntary contribution scheme.

MobiBus users need to log-in and defines the itineraries that they are interested in obtaining information. Once the itineraries have been defined, the user becomes an Observer of the public transport system. A MobiBus Observers receive information about locations and the expected time of arrival of buses in which they have declared the interest. Figure 1 illustrates all steps involved in the process of using the MobiBus application.

When Observers board one of the buses, they must make check-in on the application. The check-in goal is to register the vehicle/itinerary in which the observer has boarded. Upon check-in, the Observer assumes the role of the Collaborator (step 1). Initially, the mobile application sends Collaborator's location to a Web Server (step 2). Collaborator's locations continue to be sent to the server at 10-s intervals, ensuring a continuously update of the position of the bus in which the Collaborator is traveling. The positions of all buses with Collaborators inside are sent to all Observers who have registered interest in these itineraries (step 3).

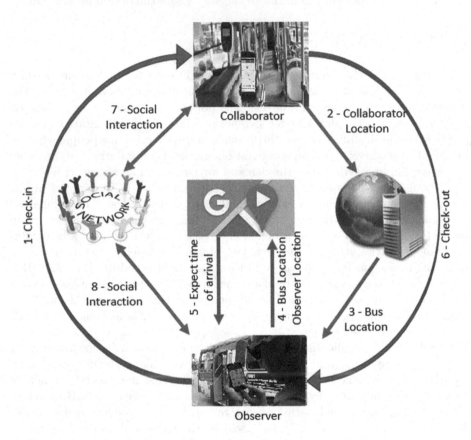

Fig. 1. Overview of MobiBus architecture

The MobiBus application running on Observers' devices receives the position of the buses along the itineraries chosen during the login process. The application running on the Observer's device places a request via Google Maps API requesting the travel time between the bus position and the Observer position (step 4). The Google routing service has been configured to return the route and the estimated time of arrival using the public transport system, which gives a more realistic estimate of the time of arrival. Information returned by the Google routing service is displayed on the map of the Observer device (step 5). Contributors remain in this state as long as they are inside a bus. When Collaborators drop-off from the bus, they need to register this fact by making a check-out. A check-out turns the Collaborator into an Observer of the system (step 6). Both

Collaborators and Observers can participate in the MobiBus social network to communicate problems and socialize their opinions about the public transport system functioning (steps 7 and 8).

Considering the functionalities discussed above, it was decided to split the MobiBus platform into five units, that is, Collaboration, Observation, Persistence, Management, and Social units (Fig. 2). Despite the functional motivation to create independent units, the modularization of the system also allows the replications of this proposal using different technologies. It is because the implementations of any software artifact of one unit do not interfere with the implementations of other units.

The MobiBus platform is based on the Service-Oriented Architecture (SOA) [16]. SOA is an architectural approach that provides interoperable and modular services to enhance maintainability, flexibility, and usability of the code. To standardize the exchange of data between the platform's units it was used JavaScript Object Notation (JSON).

The Collaboration, Observation and Social units (2 are executed on the users' devices and implement most of the functionalities discussed earlier in this paper. For the development of the application a hybrid solution was chosen, that is, part of the application performs natively, and part is multiplatform, allowing the application to run in different mobile platforms using the same source code. This hybrid approach uses HTML5, CSS3, and JavaScript. For the construction of the application, it was chosen Bootstrap, an open-source front-end framework developed by the Twitter team [8]. Bootstrap is compatible with HTML5 and CSS3, enabling the creation of responsive layouts grids. Grids give the possibility to organize the user interface with up to 12 columns and each column can behave differently in different devices' resolutions.

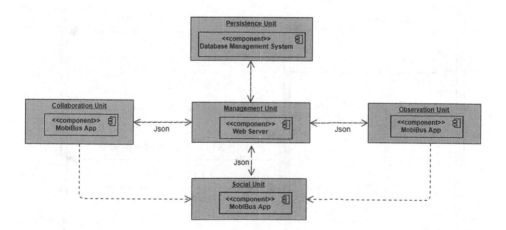

Fig. 2. The MobiBus modularization

The Persistence Unit stores the data related to the users' check-in and check-out, messages exchanged in the social network of the application and locations of the buses with Collaborators inside. It was used MySQL Database Manager in the Persistence Unit. The cloud environment used was Google Compute Engine, which provides high-performance virtual machines in innovative data centers that use Google's infrastructure.

The Management Unit relies on a Web Server for providing the integration and coordination of all units. The Web Service is based on Laravel, a free open-source PHP framework for Web systems development. Laravel uses the Model-View-Controller (MVC) architecture standard. In order to be able to use Laravel together with the Web Service and to guarantee the scalability and availability of the system, we have adopted the Google App Engine. This platform allows the development and execution of applications developed using several programming languages (Java, PHP, Node.js, Python, C#, .NET, Ruby and Go).

The MobiBus application was developed with simplicity and ease of use in mind. Thus, the user interface has only a few commands. Although users of the application can play separate roles in the system, actions associated with each role are simple and run automatically most of the time. In Fig. 3, for example, you can view the sequence diagram of steps performed on the platform by Collaborators. Collaborators check-in and receive the status of the action executed. In the case of successful check-in, the application automatically submits Collaborators' locations every 10 s, creating a systematic cycle until the Collaborators check themselves out.

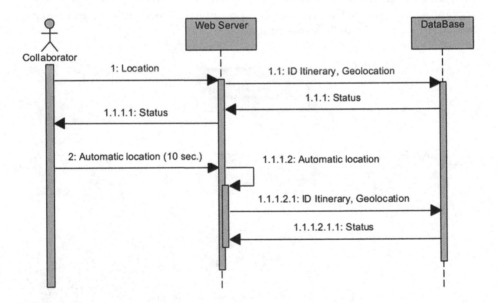

Fig. 3. Collaborator sequence diagram

Figure 4 shows the sequence diagram of the steps performed when an observer receives an update of a coming bus. The Observer initially register in the Web Server the itineraries they are interested in. Every time that there is an update of the location of a bus in one of the registered itineraries, the observer location, and the bus location are sent to a Google Maps server. The Observer receives back the distance and expected time of arrival of the bus.

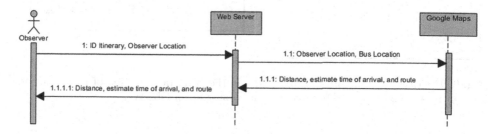

Fig. 4. Observer diagram sequence

The social network of the platform was created so that users (Collaborators and Observers) can post information about the public transportation system of the city. This feature currently supports only text messaging. In Fig. 5 it is possible to contemplate the sequence diagram of the steps performed to post of a message in the social network.

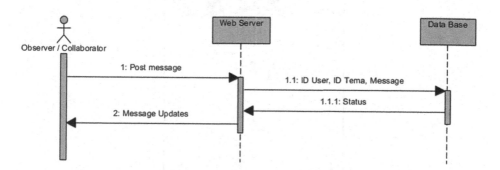

Fig. 5. Social network diagram sequence

The materialization of all functionalities described so far was obtained through simple and succinct screens. Initially, users need to choose which itinerary they are interested in monitoring (Fig. 6a). Once the itinerary has been defined, the user must choose whether to play the role of Contributor or Observer (Fig. 6b).

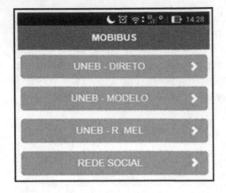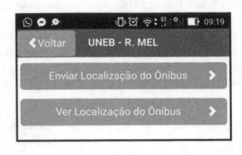

Fig. 6. Interface to configure the role of the in the App: (a) selection of itineraries of interest and (b) selection to become a Collaborator or an Observer

As Observers, users can view on a map their instantaneous location obtained directly from the location sensor of their device. This location is the same geographic coordinate sent to the Web Server at 10-s intervals. As an Observer, users receive the exact location of the bus, how far the bus is from their location and how long it will take to the bus arrives. All these pieces of information are presented on a map (Fig. 7).

Fig. 7. Observer view of the bus position and expected time of arrival

4   MobiBus Evaluation

The evaluation of the MobiBus application was done through an experiment with users of the public transportation system of the city of Alagoinhas, Bahia. The experiment was carried out using questionnaires to identify the user experience (UX) with the public transportation system before and after the use of MobiBus. The experiment reported in this work was divided into six distinct phases, based on the guidelines proposed in the DECIDE framework [12] that guided the steps performed during all phases of the experiment:

- **Determine the goals of the analysis** - The focus of the experiment was to obtain information regarding the efficiency, effectiveness, usability, and experience of MobiBus users.
- **Explore the questions to be answered** - Based on the goals to be achieved, a set of questions was developed that guide the analysis of the data, as well as to prove the potential of the application proposed in this study.
  1. How often do you use public transport?
  2. What is your level of satisfaction with the public transportation system in the city of Alagoinhas?
  3. Has the public transportation system provided in Alagoinhas already brought losses to your daily routine?
  4. Has the MobiBus application helped to diminish any inconvenience caused by the collective transportation system of the city of Alagoinhas?
  5. How satisfied are you with MobiBus?
  6. Did MobiBus help to reduce waiting time at the bus stop?
  7. Did you feel more secure using MobiBus since you have an estimate of time of arrival of the bus?
  8. Do you consider MobiBus useful to the population?
  9. How important is MobiBus to assist the users of the public transportation system in the city of Alagoinhas?
- **Choose the evaluation approach and methods** - The chosen approach to obtain the data was the application of a questionnaire, with the questions proposed in the previous item, using the scale of Likert [9] with 5 points, varying from "Very Satisfied" to "Very unsatisfied".
- **Identify and manage practical issues** - At this stage, a document was specified during the experiment, containing explanatory text about the work proposal, how to download the application and simple instructions for using MobiBus.
- **Decide how to deal with the ethical issues** - At this stage, an Informed Consent Form was prepared so that the volunteers expressed their interest in participating in the experiment and made the data available for futures evaluations. All participants were of legal age and with good physical and mental capacity.
- **Evaluate, analyze, interpret and present the data** - The data collection was made between 02/05/2018 to 05/17/2018, with the participation of 21

users, of whom 10 were female and 11 were male. Regarding schooling, it was observed that 2 participants have a graduate degree, 14 are undergraduate students, 3 have concluded high school and 2 have only elementary education. The sample was formed by students and employees of the State University of Bahia (UNEB) - Campus II - Alagoinhas. The type of sample is non-probabilistic by accessibility since the participants of the experiment coexist with the authors of this article.

The first question refers to the frequency in which participants of the case study use the public transportation system in the city of Alagoinhas. The results indicated that 76.2% of participants use the system frequently and 23.8% use only occasionally.

The results regarding the participants' satisfaction with Alagoinhas's current public transportation system can be seen in the graph of Fig. 8. The numbers are not encouraging at all, since more than half of the interviewees find the public transport system bad or terrible, indicating that the system is not attractive nor appropriate, and probably does not provide quality and updated information to its users.

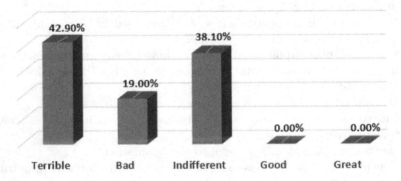

Fig. 8. Level of satisfaction with the current public transportation system of Alagoinhas

The third question asks if the research participants have already suffered some kind of loss with the collective transportation service provided in Alagoinhas. The results indicated that 63.6% were greatly impaired, 27.3% were moderately impaired, 4.5% were slightly impaired and 4.5% did not suffer losses with current collective transportation. The data allow us to confirm the importance of thinking about solutions that aim to improve the users' experience in the use of the public transportation system in Alagoinhas.

The fourth question "Has the MobiBus application helped to diminish any inconvenience caused by the collective transportation system of the city of Alagoinhas?". This question intends to measure the impact of the MobiBus application as a tool that can help to mitigate the problems caused by the service. In this regard, the results show that more than 70% of the users are satisfied or very satisfied with the application (Fig. 9).

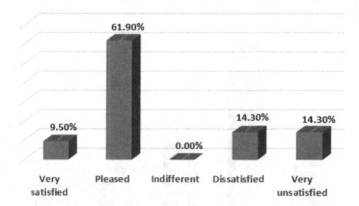

Fig. 9. Percentage of satisfaction with the help of MobiBus to the public transport service

MobiBus was designed to be easy to use and less annoying as possible since the application relies on the voluntary collaboration of the users. Crowdsourcing and collaborative applications have become the way to get information about anything, helping to understand and solve complex problems. People are willing to collaborate but not to be annoyed. In this context, participants were asked if MobiBus is easy to use. The graph of Fig. 10 indicates a high level of satisfaction with the usability of the application.

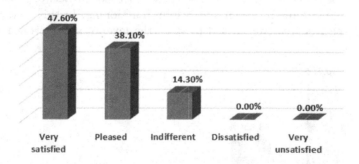

Fig. 10. Percentage of satisfaction with the ease of use of MobiBus

The main goal of MobiBus is to provide real-time information about the location of the buses, distance and expected time of arrival at the user location. This goal is twofold: minimizing the wasting of time and enhancing public safety.

In this regard, question 6 asked if the application helps to reduce waiting time and question 7 asked the user feels more secure since the application gives an estimate of time of arrival of the bus. The data in the graph of Fig. 11 shows that MobiBus is effective in estimating the time of arrival with more than 60% pleased or very satisfied.

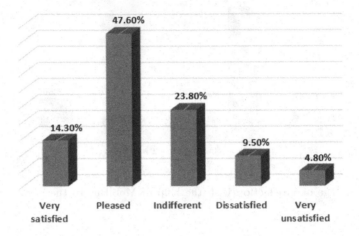

Fig. 11. Percentage of satisfaction with the help of MobiBus in relation to waiting time

Question 7 relates the feeling of security with the knowledge of the time of arrival of the next bus. This question does not use a Likert scale to evaluate this feeling but only two possible answers, that is, yes, I do feel more secure, and No, I do not feel more secure. For this question, 81% said they feel more secure and 19% do not believe that the application helps to enhance public safety.

MobiBus also enables users to make posts in a social network, socializing information and complains about the system functioning. In this way, the participants of the research were asked to state the level of satisfaction regarding

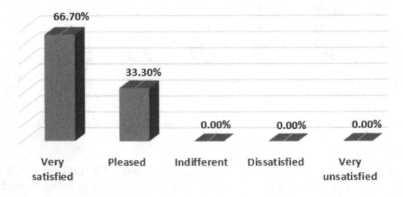

Fig. 12. Level of satisfaction with usability of MobiBus

the public utility of MobiBus. The graph shows that 100% of the participants find the application useful or very useful (Fig. 12). This feedback is important to a crowdsourcing application that rewards its users with the fact that the application produces relevant information to MobiBus community.

The last question is related to the relevance of the application to assist users of the public transportation system. All participants of the experiment believe that the application is either relevant or very relevant to their daily lives as users of the public transportation system (Fig. 13). It is very rewarding to know that the proposed tool is known to be of public utility and has been well received by its users.

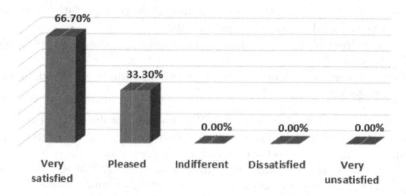

Fig. 13. Degree of MobiBus relevance

5   Conclusions and Future Works

The process of urbanization in Brazil generated pressure for investments in urban mobility far superior to the financial capacity of most small and medium-sized municipalities.

In this scenario, it is important to emphasize the importance of offering quality public transportation services. Good public transportation services are attractive to users, reduce the number of cars on the roads, contribute to the environment, reduce the flow of traffic, and improve the quality of life of citizens.

Major cities have relied on the help of ITS to improve, among other things, the services and management of the public transportation system. Once again, smaller cities do not have the resources to invest in the usual mechanisms and tools provided by ITS and can only rely on innovative solutions that explore the capacity of the users of the system to contribute to its improvement voluntarily.

Taking as an example the public transportation system of the city of Alagoinhas, we have identified many deficiencies and complaints which are common for almost every city of the same size. One of the main shortcomings is the lack of forecast and availability of buses' schedules. Moreover, the inaccuracy of schedules and the long waiting time on bus stops have exposed users to many risks related to their safety.

In this scenario, we have developed and tested MobiBus, a mobile crowdsourcing application to help users of the public transportation system. MobiBus relies on the voluntary contribution of the users of the public transportation system to generate information about the expected time of arrival of buses. Moreover, MobiBus maintains a social network of its users, so they can share comments and complains about the transportation system functioning. To evaluate the potential of the proposed solution, an experiment was carried out with the participation of users of the public transportation system of the city of Alagoinhas. The results of the experiment allow us to conclude that MobiBus meets the expectations of the users in the following aspects:

- MobiBus alleviate some troubles caused by public transportation services.
- Users were satisfied with the use of MobiBus.
- MobiBus helped to reduce waiting time at the bus stop, increasing users' feeling of security.
- The users considered MobiBus useful as a tool to improve the public transportation system.

The segmented architecture of MobiBus and the results of the experiment show a good potential of implementing MobiBus in other similar cities with a great chance of having a good acceptance by their citizens.

As future work, we are planning to improve the user interface, while keeping it simple. The main improvements in the user interface contemplate the incorporation of accessibility functions for the visually impaired and addition of new functionalities such as a warning button for emergencies on the bus. MobiBus works with and free version of the Google API to estimate the time of arrival of the bus. The Google API free version has a limited number of requisitions per month. Aiming at avoiding the use of a paid version of the Google API, we are considering the usage of an open and free routing service such as Open Street Map Routing API (OSRM) to estimate the time of arrival of the bus. We are planning also to implement and evaluate MobiBus in another medium-size city using a larger number of participants. Finally, our research group is developing a mobile application to evaluate the driver's behaviors while driving. The proposed application analyzes the driver's behavior based on five variables (fuel consumption, carbon dioxide emission, speed, longitudinal acceleration, and transverse acceleration). We are planning to adapt this application to evaluate the behavior of the bus driver.

References

1. Aquino, W., de Aquino, N.B., Pereira, W.F.: Considerações sobre o uso de its. Revista dos Transportes Públicos **23**(91), 33–37 (2001)
2. Araújo, M.R.M.D., Oliveira, J.M.D., Jesus, M.S.D., Sá, N.R.D., Santos, P.A.C.D., Lima, T.C.: Transporte público coletivo: discutindo acessibilidade, mobilidade e qualidade de vida. Psicologia Sociedade **23**(2), 574–582 (2011)

3. Campos, A., Soares, E., Martins, G., Yoshida, L., Oliveira, M., Zaina, L.: Avaliação de comunicabilidade, usabilidade e retorno emocional no transporte público: Um estudo do moovit. In: Symposium on Human Factors in Computing Systems, vol. 4, p. 07, October 2016
4. Costa, C.S., de Oliveira Fernandes, V., Junior, M.J.A.: Aplicação de crowdsourcing na gestão e no planejamento de transportes: conceitos, potencialidades e parcerias do waze. Revista Brasileira de Geomática 3(2), 68–80 (2015)
5. Estellés-Arolas, E., González-Ladrón-De-Guevara, F.: Towards an integrated crowdsourcing definition. J. Inf. Sci. 38(2), 189–200 (2012)
6. Ferris, B., Watkins, K., Borning, A.: Onebusaway: results from providing real-time arrival information for public transit. In: Proceedings of the SIGCHI Conference on Human Factors in Computing Systems, pp. 1807–1816. ACM (2010)
7. Ganti, R.K., Ye, F., Lei, H.: Mobile crowdsensing: current state and future challenges. IEEE Commun. Mag. 49(11), 32–39 (2011)
8. Krause, J.: Introduction to Bootstrap. In: Krause, J. (ed.) Introducing Bootstrap 4, pp. 23–32. Springer, Berkeley (2016). https://doi.org/10.1007/978-1-4842-2382-6_2
9. Likert, R.: A technique for the measurement of attitudes. Arch. Psychol. 1(140), 1–55 (1932)
10. Lopes, B.G., De Marchi, P.M.: A tecnologia como meio de inclusão dos deficientes visuais no transporte público. Iniciação-Revista De Iniciação Científica, Tecnológica E Artística Edição Temática Em Tecnologia Aplicada. São Paulo 5(4) (2015)
11. Pires, A., Pelegi, A., Vasconsellos, E., Néspoli, L.: Mobilidade humana para um brasil urbano. Agência Nacional de Transportes Públicos ANTP. Produção editorial e gráfica PW Gráficos e Editores Associados Ltda São Paulo (2016)
12. Preece, J., Rogers, Y., Sharp, H.: Interaction Design: Beyond Human-Computer Interaction. Wiley, Chichester (2015)
13. Sandheep, S., John, H., Harikumar, A., Panicker, J.V.: Bustimer: an android based application for generating bus schedules using crowdsourcing. In: 2017 International Conference on Technological Advancements in Power and Energy (TAP Energy), pp. 1–6. IEEE (2017)
14. Verma, R.: Crowdmap: Crowdsourcing based city traffic map generation. In: 2017 9th International Conference on Communication Systems and Networks COMSNETS, pp. 582–583. IEEE (2017)
15. Wang, L.y., Yao, D.y., Gong, X.b., Zhang, Z.: A research on bus information service system using DSRC. In: Proceedings. The IEEE 5th International Conference on Intelligent Transportation Systems. pp. 365–369. IEEE (2002)
16. Welke, R., Hirschheim, R., Schwarz, A.: Service-oriented architecture maturity. Computer 44(2), 61–67 (2011)
17. White, P.R.: Public Transport: Its Planning, Management and Operation. Taylor & Francis, New York (2016)

Challenges for the Implementation of Accessible Web and Mobile Systems

Bruno Gomes[1], Juliete Rios[2], and Kamila R. H. Rodrigues[1,2(✉)]

[1] Federal University of São Carlos, São Carlos, SP, Brazil
bdesigner_web@hotmail.com, kamila.rios@gmail.com
[2] University of Araraquara, Araraquara, SP, Brazil
juliete.rios@gmail.com

Abstract. This paper discusses the accessibility in the implementation of systems for the web and mobile devices, as well as seeks to understand why, despite the various accessibility tools available in the literature, most systems are still not accessible. The work is inspired by Challenge 2 of the GrandIHC-BR, but also corroborates the sustainability aspects identified in Challenge 1, especially in the social pillar. It is hypothesized that the main reasons for the low accessibility in computational solutions may include the lack of time of the development team, a supposed increase in the project budget, as well as the lack of knowledge and the lack of interest on the part of the developers. A Systematic Mapping and two exploratory surveys were conducted with developers looking for to assess the context and hypotheses. These professionals reported on their experience and how to use accessibility features in their projects. The research pointed out that the lack of accessible systems is caused, mainly, by the low knowledge of the developers on the techniques of accessible programming.

Keywords: Web accessibility · Mobile accessibility · Challenges · Systematic Mapping

1 Introduction

According to the IBGE Demographic Census (conducted in 2010) [11, 12], in Brazil there are approximately 45 million and a half people with at least one type of disability of those that were surveyed (auditory, motor, visual, mental/intellectual), which represents 23.9% of the population [12]. To this number is added to the elderly population, which must also be considered due to the difficulty of adapting to new technologies. There are approximately 7.5 million elderly people who do not have any kind of disability. This number represents 3.9% of the Brazilian population [18].

These data illustrate that thinking about accessible computing solutions has never been so important. Having a page or an application without accessibility means leaving, for example, at least a quarter of the Brazilian population without access to day-to-day facilities.

A survey carried out in 2011 by the Brazilian Internet Governance Committee (CGI.br) shows that of the 6.6 million pages with gov.br domain, only 4.82% have

R. P. d. Santos et al. (Eds.): WAIHCWS 2017/2018, CCIS 1081, pp. 138–158, 2020.
https://doi.org/10.1007/978-3-030-46130-0_8

some kind of compliance with accessibility criteria, that is, 95.18% of government pages were not accessible to the entire population [3].

The use of new technologies and services, however, is increasingly present in people's daily lives. Ordinary activities are carried out through technological devices, and the use of cell phones and computers is increasingly intrinsic. Companies have invested in services that can be accomplished through such devices. Examples of such services include paying bills or making a transfer without having to go to the bank, shop in the comfort of your own home or even chat online with that friend who lives on the other side of town. These are simple and easy tasks for a good part of the population, however, there is a portion of the population that still faces difficulties in using these technologies. Elderlies and people with physical or intellectual limitations, as cited above, have difficulties in using certain websites and mobile applications because they have not been developed in an accessible way, that is, in a way that everyone (or the largest possible audience) can use.

The World Wide Web Consortium (W3C) consortium is working to develop standards for the web in general. The accessibility theme has a special attention of this team, who classified the term accessibility as the possibility and condition of reach, perception and understanding for the use, in equal opportunities, with security and autonomy, of the physical environment, transportation, information and including information and communication systems and technologies, as well as other services and facilities [27, 29].

Accessibility and Digital Inclusion was also one of the five challenges proposed in the GrandIHC-BR (Great Challenges of Research in IHC in Brazil) in 2012 by researchers in this area [10]. In 2017, the same IHC community met again at the IHC'17[1] symposium to assess the impact these challenges had on the academic community and the market after five years of its proposition. The community also discussed what obstacles still need to be addressed.

The first challenge of the GrandIHC-BR, in turn, brings the theme of sustainability. With the title *Future, Smart Cities and Sustainability* [19], this challenge addresses the impacts of computational solutions on the processes and methods used to design, deploy and maintain such solutions. Sustainability is supported by three pillars: economic, environmental and social. The latter deals with issues related to the care and opportunity given to minorities, or to decent working conditions offered by businesses. Research in this area points to the need for studies that show that the exclusion of minorities does not contribute to a more just, egalitarian society that aims to guarantee a better future for all [21]. Such studies can help disseminate aspects such as digital accessibility and/or exclusion of minorities (e.g. women, the disabled and the LGBT public) - in different areas and also in computing - once that they are related to the idea of justice and equality.

Inspired by the fourth challenge of SBC (Brazilian Computation Society) [24], as well as in the first [19] and second challenges of GrandIHC-BR [1, 2], this paper seeks to contribute to the understanding of the barriers that still exist for the implementation of accessibility in digital solutions. In this sense, we investigated the difficulties

---

[1] http://ihc2017.ihcbrasil.com/pt/trilhas/grandes-desafios-em-ihc/.

encountered by developers in providing accessibility features to their systems. Although the industry and literature currently provide a variety of programming languages, frameworks, tools, and techniques that assist the developer during the implementation of his applications, it is still difficult to find systems web and mobile applications that can be used by any user, including people with disabilities and difficulties various [29].

It is important to note that there are accessible solutions, but these solutions are usually developed for people who have specific disabilities, such as hearing/vision loss, and also for people with mobility limitations. These systems facilitate the access of disabled people to the technologies and allow them to be included. However, what is perceived is the predominance of systems that are not accessible to the disabled in general [29].

In the light of the above, this paper analyzed aspects of accessibility on the web and on mobile devices and sought to understand the difficulties encountered in accessible development, since a very small number of Websites and mobile applications follow existing accessibility standards. The authors of this research assumed that the difficulties could be classified as follows: (1) The developer does not know accessibility tools and techniques; (2) The developer does not have time to implement such resources in the project; (3) The budget is insufficient to address accessibility issues; (4) The customer has no interest; (5) The developer has no interest; and/or (6) The developer did not see this content in the undergraduate or technical course [29].

Based on the hypothesis that these are the barriers to the problem addressed, an exploratory research was carried out in the literature through a Systematic Mapping to identify papers with reports in this direction. In a second moment, online questionnaires were made available so that developers could report their main difficulties and thoughts on the subject. The questionnaires aimed to verify the hypothesis pointed out in the abovementioned difficulties. In a third step, a website was developed with the objective of comparing some of the results and discusses obtained through exploratory research with developers. Details of this moment are not described in this paper, but can be read in the work of Gomes et al. [29].

This research is justified by the lack - in the literature - of works and resources to diagnose and foster the practice of developing accessible systems, although there are frameworks, guidelines and methods for this. Understanding why developers still do not implement accessibility in their projects can be a first step in encouraging more citizen-driven practices between these professionals and the companies that develop systems in general.

This paper is divided as follows: The Sect. 2 reports the theoretical references, the Sect. 3 describes accessibility norms and guidelines, the Sect. 4 describes a mapping carried out in the literature, the Sect. 5 describes the exploratory questionnaires conducted, the Sect. 6 brings a discussion on the data and the Sect. 7, finally, presents the final remarks.

2 Theoretical References

Societies in technological development have a dialectical relationship, in which social changes promote advances in technology research, while technology promotes changes in social relations [17]. Changes in legislation and international growth in the conflict for human rights have put the question of the inclusion of mentally and physically handicapped people more and more on the agenda. It is necessary providing conditions for people with disabilities or with reduced mobility, so that everyone can use public and collective spaces. This concern also exists in virtual environment, since accessibility on the web consists of allowing the access and use of virtual environments, products and services to anyone and in different contexts [27].

A more inclusive society has therefore demanded developers who use the accessibility features, making Information and Communication Technologies (ICTs) also inclusive. This behavior, however, requires a commitment of developers and companies to the construction of accessible codes. The reality, however, is that most systems do not have this inclusive feature.

Nielsen [20] mentions that, beyond the issues of citizenship, there is also a commercial reason for the creation of accessible systems. The author mentions that with the increase in life estimates, more people with difficulties and deficiencies become users of systems and, therefore, the number of clients in this area of business is increased. For Nielsen [20], making the web more accessible to users with various limitations boils down to some extent to adapt HTML: to encode meaning rather than appearance. As long as the web page is encoded for meaning/semantic, alternative browsers may present that meaning in ways that are optimized for the capabilities of individual users and thus make it easier to use the web for the disabled [29].

Creating accessibility features increasingly becomes a competitive strategy for companies that wish to retain a greater number of consumers/customers. Dias [9] also mentions that the tools and resources that provide accessibility to the codes increase very little the cost of software production and may even result in profit. Accessibility should be considered a good practice and be part of any project, especially if it is considered that the simple gesture of incorporating special HTML tags into the code would increase the possibility of access to it [29].

Santos and Pequeno [23] discuss the development of accessible tools based on the logic of social inclusion and access to education. The authors argue that, in addition to a commercial issue, accessibility is - above all else - a matter of citizenship. The authors mention DOSVOX[2] as a software for the education of blind people and also point to JAWS[3], a screen reader also for this audience.

Torres et al. [25], in turn, studied accessibility on the web and realized that adaptations are necessary for users with limited mobility, hearing impaired and visually impaired. Each of these user groups has specific needs and different accessibility demands.

---

[2] http://intervox.nce.ufrj.br/dosvox/.
[3] https://www.freedomscientific.com/Products/Blindness/JAWS.

Granollers and Lorés [30] propose of a new point of view to measure the usability of an interactive system. The proposal is specifically based on the process model of Usability Engineering and Accessibility, u+eEPM. The model provides the basis and methodologies that allow to know how a development team should proceed to design usable and accessible interactive systems following the clearly defined UCD (User Centered Design) process. The u+eEPM is organized in a series of phases which are repeatedly carried out. According the authors, prototyping and evaluation being two key phases for usability and accessibility that are applied from the same instant that each new development is started.

Britto and Pizzolato [6] propose an open source website that discloses a set of web accessibility recommendations for people with Autism Spectrum Disorder (ASD). The website is called GAIA and is intended to help web developers design more accessible interfaces for this user profile. The recommendations were elaborated through a review process of papers published between 2005 and 2015 and included international recommendations, commercial or academic software and peer-reviewed papers. The authors identified 107 recommendations that were grouped into 10 categories using the affinity diagram technique. The recommendations were normalized into categories according to similarities and duplicate statements, generating a set of 28 unique recommendations.

Nielsen [20] points out that accessibility guidelines are not always followed and points out that this tends to occur due to lack of time and the need to satisfy other issues of website design. However, similar Dias [9], Nielsen also emphasizes that accessible websites are inexpensive.

It is a consensus among the authors of the literature that implementing resources that make systems, in general, more accessible do not necessarily imply time or effort that impedes the progress of the project. It is also a consensus that the lack of time and of interest of large companies and/or developers to turn their attention to the theme may be among the factors that corroborate that projects do not have accessibility as a requirement. It should be noted here that most of the existing assistive technologies, and that helps the disabled to use web systems, for example, are open source, which could be easily integrated with the projects and not generate an additional cost to them [29].

The following section discusses the main accessibility standards currently available for the web and mobile devices.

3 Accessibility Guidelines

There are standardized standards for creating accessible resources and tools for information systems. One of the regulatory organizations is the aforementioned W3C [27]. According to the booklet produced by that group, it represents an international consortium in which affiliated organizations, together with a full-time staff, as well as the public, work cooperatively to develop standards for the web. W3C has published more than one hundred standards. "All standards developed are free and open, aiming to ensure the evolution of the web and the growth of interoperable interfaces" [27].

At the Brazilian context, the law 13,146/2105 [5], known as the Disabled Persons Statute, deals with accessible formats for digital files. In article 68, paragraph two, accessible formats are those that "can be recognized and accessed by screen reader software or other assistive technologies that may replace them". These formats should allow for reading with synthesized speech, character enlargement, different contrasts and Braille printing [5].

Still in the Brazilian context, the ordinance 3, dated May 7, 2004, regulates the accessibility in websites linked to Public Administration groups, through the Electronic Government Accessibility Model (e-MAG in Portuguese). This model is based on W3C recommendations [27], and suggests, among other items, how the site should be accessed for people with movement control, paralysis or amputation of an elderly member, as well as people with visual impairment, since these people access websites without the use of a mouse, keyboard, audio and even without a monitor. Also with regard to accessibility on the web, the decree 5.296/2004 [4, 5] establishes as mandatory accessibility in the portals and electronic websites of public administration on the Internet. These sites should allow "the use of the visually impaired, guaranteeing them full access to the available information".

In 2008, Web Content Accessibility Guideline (WCAG 2.0) [27] was launched. According to this document, there are four principles for accessibility on the web. Pages should be: perceivable, operable, understandable and robust. These principles are currently part of ISO/IEC 40500: 2012 [13]. Subsection 3.1 describes such principles.

In the context of web development, HTML (HyperText Markup Language) aims to give meaning to information. This language marks the information through tags, however, it is not the function of HTML to format this information. This responsibility is from CSS (Cascading Style Sheets), which brings layout specifications such as fonts, colors, positioning of elements and sizes of images. JavaScript, in turn, is a language that helps user interaction with the web system, and the interaction of buttons, forms, and alert messages to the user [29].

A well-developed website allows the user to find what they are looking for easily and this task should be easy for users with disabilities as well. However, how can you tell the visually impaired user, for example, which is the most important part of the website? Also, do screen readers who assist these public be able to interpret the entire content of the developed website?

In order for these vehicles to be accessible to all, the WAI-ARIA (Accessible Rich Internet Applications Suite) [28] comes up with the role of increasing accessibility in dynamic content, and is used in conjunction with HTML5. WAI-ARIA helps you bookmark the website so that you can find out where elements such as the header, footer, and navigation menu are located. This effort is relevant because it helps to define the importance of each element of the web page. Afterwards, screen readers can inform the visually impaired when reading the website [29].

All web site marking proposed by WAI-ARIA is made up of two components: *Role* - which defines the type of element the user is interacting with, and *State/Properties* - that defines the state of the element. Within these components there is the *collapse* attribute, where you can inform the status of the element (e.g. open or closed). An example of collapse is a menu that has submenus: if collapse is not used, screen readers cannot interpret submenu options. With the use of the collapse the readers begin to interpret the open or closed state and, with this, also read the submenu for the disabled. According to the authors of the WAI-ARIA [28], this feature:

> [...] defines a way to make web content and applications more accessible to people with disabilities. Especially with the help of some technologies like Ajax, HTML, JavaScript among others, it makes content dynamic and with advanced UI controls. Some features that the sites contain are currently not available to some users with disabilities, especially for people who depend on screen readers and people who cannot use the mouse. WAI-ARIA addresses these accessibility challenges, for example, by defining new ways of providing features for assistive technology (WAI-ARIA [28]).

It is observed, therefore, that there are technologies and specialized software for people with different types of disability. Thus, the lack of resources cannot be used as a justification for developers do not implement accessible solutions. What these professionals demand is, in fact, a greater commitment to inclusion and citizenship, as well as specialized knowledge on the subject, and initiatives to present and discuss the theme to their teachers, clients and leaders.

3.1   WCAG 2.0

The WCAG 2.0 Guidelines provide development accessible to all people. Following these standards, it is possible to produce websites more comprehensive. These same guidelines can be used in the development of mobile applications [8, 27].

There are four principles and twelve guidelines that compose the basis of web accessibility and seventeen guidelines for mobile development. The guidelines contain basic goals to be achieved so that the content becomes accessible, and for each guideline there are success criteria that are defined in three levels of conformance: A, AA, and AAA. For a site to be considered accessible it is mandatory to have all level A guidelines. The AA level are guidelines where use is indicated, but not mandatory. Already the level AAA, is also not mandatory, but greatly improve the accessibility of the page. The WCAG principles are described below.

Principle 1: Perceivable. The content of the interface must be presented in a user-understandable way. This principle advocates that everything displayed on the screen needs to be viewed by any user. For example, in web pages images, graphics and audios need a textual description to convey the information. Colors should be used with adequate contrast, spacing, width, alignment, and the font should be well-presented. For mobile applications, content must fit the screen size and allow the user to zoom up to 200% without damaging the content, the contrast between colors should also be considered.

Principle 2: Operable. This principle states that all components must be operable by the user. This means that the person can interact with everything without encountering obstacles. For web pages, all information must be accessible from the keyboard and should also provide ways to help the user navigate. In mobile applications, the distance between components should be adequate to avoid erroneous touch, and actions that require gestures should be as simple as possible so as not to limit the user with motor impairment.

Principle 3: Understandable. This principle points out that texts need to be understandable, the language of the page, as well as unusual words and abbreviations, need to have a correct pronunciation. When typing something wrong the system should correct or suggest a correction to the user. Labels should be used for user input fields, thus avoiding possible errors. In mobile applications, screen orientation should not be fixed in portrait or landscape, all screens should follow the same layout pattern and if there are custom gestures, there should be a tutorial always available for consultation.

Principle 4: Robust. This principle points out that web pages must support the technologies used by the user to access the site. Developers can not implement requirements that hinder the operation of user support technology. In mobile applications, it is recommended that the keyboard change according to the input type of the data so that possible errors are avoided and the formats are correct, it is also appropriate to use check boxes or radio buttons to decrease the user's need to enter [27].

As described in the sections above, there are a number of tools, resources and technologies that help the developer to implement accessible projects. But, even with the various options for applying accessibility in projects, this is not a widely implemented requirement.

Looking for understand this impasse, a Systematic Mapping in the literature was carried out, as well as exploratory survey with professionals of the area to understand what reasons avoid them from implementing accessibility in their web and mobile projects. Section 4 briefly describes the mapping conducted and Sect. 5 provides data and reports of surveys with questionnaires carried out in the context of this work to evaluate the hypotheses identified as obstacles.

4   Systematic Mapping

According to Kitchenham [14], a Systematic Mapping (SM) is a way to identify, evaluate and interpret existing research in the literature. It can be done to summarize existing evidence on a particular subject. It can also identify flaws in the study object and suggest new research, as well as compare if the theoretical evidence is in accordance with the practical evidence. The latter will be the objective of this study. An SM is composed of three phases: planning, conduction and presentation.

The purpose of the systematic mapping carried out in the context of this work was to identify the difficulties that developers and companies encounter in creating accessible websites and mobile applications, as well as to verify the most reported problems and how they were avoided by companies and developers that already follow the existing standards.

The following questions were elaborated to guide the development of this SM:

- Q1 - What are the difficulties faced for developing web pages and mobile applications following accessibility standards?
- Q2 - How have these difficulties been avoided by companies/developers who follow the standards?
- Q3 - What are the motivations for implementing accessibility standards?

In order to cover all possible ways of handling the topic, the following words were selected to create the search string: Web, mobile, accessibility, WCAG and develop * (the * symbol considers all variations of the word). Thus, the following string was formed:

(Web OR mobile) AND accessibility AND WCAG AND develop∗

The following Inclusion (IC) and Exclusion Criteria (EC) were defined and applied in the title, abstract and keywords of each study returned in the search databases. Are they:

- IC1 - Studies should contain the search string in their title, abstract or keywords;
- IC2 - Studies should be available for online reading;
- IC3 - The studies should address the topics web accessibility or mobile accessibility;
- IC4 - Studies should discuss about problems faced to develop in an accessible way;
- IC5 - Studies should discuss about companies that implement accessibility.
- EC1 - Exclude studies with a language other than Portuguese, Spanish and English;
- EC2 - Exclude duplicate studies;
- EC3 - Exclude studies which talk about other types of accessibility.

The search for primary studies was carried out in the CAPES/MEC Portal of Periodicals. The search string elaborated in the planning stage was applied, returning a total of 1.033 studies. We did not define the year of the papers as inclusion criterion. Exclusion criterion EC1 filtered the results and 617 studies were maintained. The search for the studies that answered the research questions defined for this work was started. Thus, the other inclusion and exclusion criteria were applied resulting in 5 selected papers, which are described in Table 1.

Table 1. Selected studies from systematic mapping.

Paper	Title	Authors	Base search	Questions answered
P1	*An approach to the integration of accessibility requirements into a user interface development method*	Raúl Miñón, Lourdes Moreno, Paloma Martínez, Julio Abascal	*Elsevier*	Q1
P2	*Factors explaining adoption and implementation processes for web accessibility standards within eGovernment systems and organizations*	Eric M. Velleman, Inge Nahuis, Thea van der Geest	*Springer*	Q3
P3	*Improving web accessibility: a study of webmaster perceptions*	Jonathan Lazar, Alfreda Dudley-Sponaugle, Kisha-Dawn Greenidge	*Elsevier*	Q1
P4	*Web Accessibility for People With Disabilities An Introduction for Web Developers*	Jeff Carter, Mike Markel	*IEEE*	Q1/Q3
P5	*Web accessibility implementation in private sector organizations: motivations and business impact*	Marie-Luise Leitner, Christine Strauss, Christian Stummer	*Springer*	Q1/Q3

After evaluating the studies, it was sought to answer the questions outlined in the SM.

Q1 - What are the difficulties faced for developing web pages and mobile applications following accessibility standards?

This question was answered by four of the studies. P3 was considered to be of greater relevance within the web. Specifically, for mobile devices, none of the works answered this question.

In study P3, Lazar et al. [15] conducted a survey with webmasters to understand the perception of accessibility in that group. The main difficulties reported were the challenge of balancing accessibility with graphic design, difficulties in convincing clients/management about the importance of accessibility, technical challenges, lack of funding, time, training and adequate tools. The study also reports that some interviewees created their own barrier by considering unnecessary and inadequate accessibility, arguing that they will only use accessibility if forced to do so by their managers.

In study P1, Miñon et al. [18] state that a high level of accessibility is difficult to achieve because of the lack of adequate development methods, as well as creative and training tools. The authors present a model of accessibility requirements and an extension for a tool, with the purpose of assisting in the development and adoption of accessible websites.

In the study P4, Carter and Markel [7] report that companies do not develop accessible websites because they are not interested in this market. These companies believe that there is no advantage in developing for the public with special needs. According to the authors, there is also the belief that accessible sites are "boring" because they point out that it is not possible to use graphic elements. Another reason for not accepting accessibility is to believe that project costs are higher.

In study P5, Leitner et al. [16] show that the failure to implement accessibility is due to the lack of awareness of those responsible, as well as the lack of support from management, misunderstanding that they do not have a profitable audience that will use these resources and interference in the layout.

Based on the questions pointed out by these works as difficulties for the implementation of accessibility, we carried out an online survey to understand these issues in the Brazilian context. Questionnaires for web developers and other for mobile developers were elaborated and made available.

In both questionnaires, the reported situations that most obstruct the use of the guidelines are lack of team knowledge, clients do not request and the belief that more time is needed for development.

Section 5 describes in more detail the elaboration of the questionnaires and the results obtained through them.

Q2 - How have these difficulties been avoided by companies/developers who follow the standards?

In the studies returned there were no answers to this question. However, through the survey conducted by the questionnaires, it was possible to identify that there were no main problems to implement the guidelines between companies and developers that already adopt accessibility. This demonstrates that after acceptance, it is often simple to put accessibility guidelines into practice.

Q3 - What are the motivations for implementing accessibility standards?

Three studies answered this question. P2 [26] and P5 were considered to be of greater relevance, since both addressed the topic web accessibility through interviews. No work was found in this SM dealing with such issue on mobile devices. The authors of the first paper classified the reasons for implementing accessibility standards into five categories:

Adoption factors: Having the resources and tools that collaborate in the implementation of standards is the main reason and that facilitates the acceptance of the adoption of accessibility. Compatibility with existing web services or infrastructure is also a key reason in this category. Another reason is the pressure received for having competitors who implement accessibility;

Factors related to the design process: knowledge about the theme by managers and leaders makes it easier to accept accessibility in projects. The benefits of an accessible website are pointed out, for example: better ranking in search engines, faster website and satisfied people, because they find the information in which they need;

Factors related to the organizational structure: Accessibility standards were requirements in the projects, which led to the implementation. The importance of the accessibility theme has also been demonstrated as a reason for adopting the norms;

External factors: legislation is considered a reason for implementation of accessibility, as well as requirements of users of the websites;

Personal factors: when the project participants have personal motivations to request accessibility.

In the second study, Leitner et al. [16] group the reasons into three categories: economic, social and technical motivation. In the first category, as was presented in the previous study, organizations think about competition. In this case, they differ, since the other company has not yet implemented the standards. There is the fear of building a negative image or giving the impression of an institution that does not care about inclusion. Others consider the website as the gateway, so they need to be accessible to anyone.

Among the social motivations pointed out in the study is consumer awareness, which is being more judicious in purchasing decisions, preferring companies that have a social commitment. Other reasons reported, also in the previous study, are the influence of a key personality and the support of top management. The technical motivation reported was quality, since with the implementation of accessibility, the websites become simpler and, consequently, have more clarity and usability.

In the P4 study, Carter and Markel [7] point out three main reasons that lead to the use of accessibility, the opening of the market to a new public, for ethical reasons (since it is considered the right thing to do) and the guarantee of access to the whole audience, consequently there is increased access to the webpage.

The questionnaires created point out that the main motivations for using web accessibility are when the client requests, for social inclusion and compliance issues. Among mobile application developers, the key scenarios that lead to the use of the guidelines are social inclusion, increased user numbers, and when customers request it. These issues will be detailed in Sect. 5.

5   Exploratory Surveys

Two exploratory surveys with developers were conducted in the context of this work, looking for verify the hypotheses raised here. One survey was conducted in 2017 and the other in 2018. The following subsection describes the results obtained.

5.1   Survey 1

To verify the research hypotheses adopted in this study, an online questionnaire, was elaborated and made available to developers' communities. The questionnaire was available for 30 days between July and August 2017. Developers from specific groups (such as forums and social networks) were invited via a link to access the research [29].

The questionnaire was divided in three parts. In the first part, we wanted to identify the demographic profile of the participant; in the second part, we wanted to have knowledge about their experience in the area of software development and the use of accessibility features. Finally, in the third part, we tried to identify the reason why developers did not implement accessibility in their projects. Each of the difficulties mentioned in the hypotheses was exposed to the participants in order to verify them [29].

In the questionnaire elaborated, the developer was also asked to indicate his/her position on the mentioned difficulties. Considering each of these difficulties, an affirmation about it has been elaborated, for example: "Do you believe there is enough time in the projects to develop using accessibility tools/strategies?" The developers could answer "Yes", "No" or "Not always". Following each statement, they could comment on it and report experiences on the aspect discussed (lack of knowledge, time, cost, lack of customer and developer interest). Developers could also point to difficulties other than those cited in the questionnaire (identified through the study in the literature and from the experience of the authors of this work). Subsequently, the data were tabulated and analyzed [29].

In total, 25 people answered this questionnaire. Among the 25 people, 21 had a degree in Information Technology (IT), 12 of them with postgraduate degrees in the areas of Web Software Development, MBA in IT and Computer Networks Specialization, some already acting as projects. 11 participants pointed out that they work as freelance/autonomous and 17 works in a corporation. Most participants have over 6 years of IT experience (12 out of 25 participants). The technologies and languages which these developers most relate are: HTML, CSS, JavaScript, PHP and Java [29].

When asked about their experience with accessible development and the use of tools/resources to promote such a requirement, 18 of the 25 participants replied that they did not include accessibility strategies and/or did not use tools to support this requirement. The six participants who used some accessibility tool or strategy, cited the use of features such as: contrast control, font size control, WAI-ARIA, shortcut keys, system for reading texts and for text translation in LIBRAS (Signs Brazilian Language) [29].

Among those 6 participants who declared to apply accessibility features, 5 of them focused on the visually impaired or low vision group, while 3 were concerned with developing systems that help the group of individuals with mobility limitations, and only 2 were concerned about the group of the hearing impaired [29].

For those developers who did not use accessibility strategies/tools in their projects, the questionnaire asked what the reasons were. The data collected reveals that there are developers who do not use accessibility features because they do not believe this is the focus of the developing system, or because they do not think it necessary or even because it is not a requirement requested by the client. In addition, they pointed out the commercial reasons, the lack of interest of the managers, but, mainly, the lack of knowledge of him/her or the team in which he/she works on the techniques or tools for such. One developer revealed: "*I have never looked at this need and, as no client of mine has ever questioned or quoted this point, accessibility has never been included in any project I have participated in*" [29].

When asked if they knew about tools for the development of accessible projects, only 3 of the 25 participants answered positively. These participants pointed out that they use the following tools: WebLibras[4], HandTalk[5], ReadSpeaker[6], NVDA[7], Jaws (See footnote 3) and DosVOX (See footnote 2) [29].

It should be emphasized here that HTML itself offers simple accessibility techniques that can be easily incorporated at the time of development. Tags like ALT represent a good example of HTML features for accessibility. The ALT tag is used to describe images and screen readers read this description for the visually impaired user [29].

Another salutary data collected through the questionnaire refers to the time available in the projects to develop using resources and accessibility tools in the code. 14 of the 25 participants pointed out that there is not always time to deal with this requirement, while 5 were categorical in saying that there is no time. One participant reported: *"Implementing accessibility features requires a lot of code details and testing in development and later deployment, and it is not always possible to add that time to the project scope"*. Another participant pointed out: *"Time is always scarce, so if the product is not designed and designed from the start with these characteristics, it is difficult to spare time to implement them afterwards"*. On the contrary, 5 participants stated that there is enough time [29].

It is important to highlight the aspects pointed out above by the participants, that some resources such as the use of the ALT tag already mentioned, as well as several others foreseen in the HTML, do not demand extra time from the developers and nor does it explicitly need to implement such a requirement. The authors of this work believe that the accessibility requirement should always be considered and included and that the use of accessible HTML and WAI-ARIA tags, once learned, are automatically incorporated into the professional's repertoire and are therefore used automatically. In this sense, we advocated about the teaching of these resources in the process of training professionals, since many pointed out the lack of knowledge. In this sense, it is important that undergraduate teachers and technical courses approach, although in a little way, some of the resources that enable the creation of accessible codes [29].

Another difficulty reinforced by the developers in the questionnaire, and which represents a hypothesis of this work, is that the accessibility resources are not used because they were not planned in the general budget of the project. 5 of the 25 participants reported that there is no budget, while 11 participants pointed out that there is not always a budget available in the projects to develop using accessibility tools/strategies. One participant reported: *"In some cases the cost of accessibility makes the project budget unfeasible"*. This argument was also used by other participants and another one revealed: *"The problem is in the scale of the project to cost offset, given the number of customers with the special need"*. 6 participants, however, have stated that

---

[4] http://www.weblibras.com.br.

[5] https://www.handtalk.me.

[6] https://www.readspeaker.com/pt-pt/.

[7] https://www.nvaccess.org.

there is budget to work such requirement and that it should be thought from the beginning of the project [29].

The reports about the lack of budget for the development of accessible projects can point out some lack of interest and knowledge of the developer and his superiors on the theme and the demand behind it. Applying special HTML tags and/or WAI-ARIA features should be a standard development behavior and at no additional cost, as they represent a good programming practice, including regulatory agencies that point to guidelines [29].

Another possible difficulty presented to the participants as being an obstacle to accessible development was the interest of the clients in this aspect. Only 1 of the 25 participants reported that clients are often interested in developing a project that includes accessibility requirements. The other participants pointed out that clients do not have or always have an interest. One participant reported: "*I believe that clients, for the most part, demonstrate an interest in accessibility when it is a basic requirement for customer service, that is, when accessibility is directly linked to the scope of the business*". Other participants revealed that only large companies and the government are looking for such a requirement, but pointed out that demand for this kind of resource has been increasing [29].

A developer and CEO in the web and mobile solutions development branch, when interviewed by the authors of this work, revealed that most of the time accessibility issues are not implemented due to lack of customer interest and demand and also, collection and supervision of competent groups, so there is no interest of developers and even owners of companies to study, implement and sell projects with such a requirement. This professional argued that encouragement was needed and he reported: "*developing software is such an immense and laborious task [...] that we stick to the basics [...]. We may even have the knowledge, but this is not demanded of the client for us, and ends up being a secondary issue, [...]. The problem is not only the knowledge of the developer regarding accessibility mechanisms, but the lack of knowledge of the market in relation to accessibility mechanisms. The market does not demand this [...]. Those who make the decision do not have this kind of knowledge [...] *". The CEO and developer concluded: "*The battle must be fought from the point of view of those who demand service*" [29].

Although the participants affirm that the client has no interest in having their projects accessible (only when this is an explicit requirement), it is important to note that clients do not always know what this requirement represents and what it means to make an accessible project available, even if the initial target audience is not deficient. In addition, customers believe that an accessible project, in fact, can cost you more. Those responsible for selling services in companies should be committed to inform and explain to the customer about this requirement, how much it allows a greater reach of the public and that the use of this should not represent an additional cost to the project. What is perceived, however, goes against this discourse. Developers who answered to the questionnaire stated that once the client has an interest in getting an accessible project, he/she must pay an additional amount for it. We do not share such discourse, since - as described previously - the techniques are simple and do not justify such onus. We believe that the work of conscientization can be based on who produces the technology and not only on whom it acquires the same, so the battle must be on all fronts [29].

Finally, questioned about their interest in developing accessible projects, 13 of the 25 participants answered that they are interested, mainly due to the growing demand: *"I realized that this kind of implementation really is extremely necessary nowadays. The quantity of people falling into this category is much higher than it appears to be"*. Asked what they attributed to the small supply of accessible projects, participants answered in several directions, including: low financial returns, lack of basic training, ideology and ethics of professionals, high cost, still limited social inclusion, small market and even a possible lack of culture of the Brazilians to think about the other [29].

The following subsection describes the same exploratory survey conducted in 2018 and involving web developers and also developers for mobile devices.

5.2   Survey 2

One year after the first exploratory research with developers, two new questionnaires were elaborated with the objective of observing if there was a change of thought and behavior on the part of the developers in the context of Brazil. These questionnaires also sought to understand the accessibility requirement in the context of mobile development. Similar to the questionnaire in Sect. 5.1, the questionnaires contained three parts each. The first one fancied to understand the profile and experience of the developers, the second part questioned the participant's knowledge about accessibility and whether it was used in their projects; the third part fancied to understand which were the difficulties to develop in an accessible way and which situations motivate this development.

The questionnaires were released via e-mail, online development forums, on social media (e.g. Facebook, LinkedIn and WhatsApp) and became available for 21 days. In all, 39 developers answered to the web accessibility questionnaire and 15 developers responded to the accessibility questionnaire for mobile devices. Most of the participants live in the southeast region of Brazil, are male, are in the age group of 18 to 35 years and have a complete higher education.

When questioned about how they work in the job market, most web developers have answered that they have been in private business for less than 4 years, while most mobile developers have been working freelance for less than 2 years. The most widely used technologies among web developers are JavaScript and PHP, while Java is more common among mobile developers.

When asked about the knowledge of the accessibility guidelines, most of the participants know little or do not know. Only a quarter of the participants apply the standards in their projects. Between mobile developers, 60% do not know that it is possible to apply accessibility in mobile applications, as described in Table 2.

Table 2. Knowledge about the Web Content Accessibility Guidelines.

Knowledge level	Web	Mobile
Know and apply in projects	10 (25,6%)	2 (13,3%)
Know, but do not apply to projects	3 (7,7%)	0
Know little	15 (38,5)	9 (60%)
Don't know	11 (28,2%)	4 (26,7%)

Asked about having received any training related to the development of accessibility applications, 60% of the developers said they had never received training. Asked about the problems faced in accepting the guidelines, only 14 participants answered (among web and mobile developers), most of whom said they had no problem or complaint. There were also those who said that they already adopted standards as good development practices.

About the difficulties in developing accessible projects, most say lack of knowledge of the team. Regarding the situations that lead to the actual use of the guidelines, customer solicitation is among the main reasons pointed out by web developers, while mobile developers believe that it is social inclusion.

At the end of the questionnaires, participants were asked to add something about their use and difficulties in developing accessible projects. Here are some of the participants' reports: P1 - *"The biggest problem I have encountered today is the lack of interest from customers, who always want everything in the shortest possible time at the lowest possible price, making it impossible to work with these guidelines"*. P2 - *"The workshops I participated in recently did not focus on accessibility features. That should be a topic present in all of them "*. P3 - *"I often forget that I do not have access difficulties"*. P4 - *"I do not see technical difficulties, but rather common sense and better understanding of business by those who manage the companies"*.

6   Discussion

From the Systematic Mapping and the questionnaires applied, it was possible to notice that few developers know and apply the accessibility guidelines in your projects. This work brings a diagnosis of this scenario since it sought to clarify what reasons this happens and which situations can help increase the number of accessible projects.

One of the main complaints of the developed MS was the lack of knowledge of the team. This information was confirmed in the questionnaires, especially in what was conducted in 2018, in which 60% of the respondents replied that they had never received any training on accessibility. In fact, this is a poorly covered topic in classrooms and technology events, making it harder to reach all accessible pages and applications.

Another reason for the low adhesion of accessibility is the fact that clients or management do not request such a requirement. This fact demonstrates that the issue is not considered important among the stakeholders. To think that there is no target audience is a mistaken thought, because a quarter of the Brazilian population, for example, does not have access to these webpages or applications, meaning a considerable number of possible new clients are being disregarded.

According to Pressman [22], expenditures on a project increase as the requirements errors are propagated, that is, requirements must be carefully surveyed. This also applies to accessibility requirements. When raised still in the requirements phase, there may be no additional costs. If it is a project to include accessibility in any webpage or application already existent, Pressman points out that the cost will be higher. However, these costs are converted into a return on investment as more users will have access to the solution developed. However, it is important to think about accessibility from the start, and once the team is trained, accessibility development will be natural and without main efforts.

It is need to think that including accessibility in projects is not just a matter of acquiring more users or complying with legislation, it is also a question of ethics and empathy, as this is an audience that already faces difficulties in everyday situations, so how much the fewer barriers there are, the more quality of life these people can have. A team that understands the importance of proposing accessibility is critical for a better engagement in this issue and for there to be no assignment of blame between the parties.

7 Final Remarks

In a society that excludes their disabled, the systems developer earns a social role to realize that you can create accessible projects, democratizing thus access to information. Based on this premise, we analyzed the main difficulties encountered by the market and the developers to develop software that can meet the different difficulties and deficiencies that exist for the target audience.

A study in the literature, combined with exploratory survey with developers, allowed a better understanding of the scenario and the main claims of these professionals for the low adherence to the accessibility resources. The results obtained through the online questionnaires pointed out the lack of interest of the clients and of the knowledge of the developers as being the main obstacles in order that their projects could be accessible. The lack of knowledge has a direct impact on the other difficulties raised by the authors of this work as research hypotheses. These results corroborate with those identified by Oliveira et al. [21] and indicate how accessibility is still a poorly understood resource for IT professionals and how difficult it is to think and empathize with each other, thus fostering sustainable behavior. Much is discussed by the academy on the subject, but in practice, what is observed is the non-compliance of guidelines.

The results also show that it is necessary to invest in the process of training these professionals still in the educational institutions, so that the technical knowledge is already acquired in this environment. However, if professionals come to companies without this knowledge, it should be the companies' role to provide specific training.

The lack of time to insert accessibility in projects, for example, reinforces the argument of lack of knowledge, since - once having acquired the knowledge and the habit of using accessible tags - the developer will become accustomed to the use of them, as well as will become accustomed to the use of other accessibility tools. This professional can easily enter these features at the time they are scheduling. This action would become part of the development practice, adding to that developer a differential.

About IT project managers and managers, responsible for selling and managing software production, we hope that - as well as usability and user experience requirements - they are now automatically incorporated into the project and no longer sold as an exclusive differential, it is expected that in the near future, accessibility requirements can also be incorporated into codes. There is, however, a need to raise awareness among stakeholders.

ICTs should not be a barrier to inclusion. It is the duty of technology producers, especially developers, to seek knowledge of accessibility guidelines, techniques and tools so that they can develop applications that include as many people as possible.

This paper reports an overview of the issue and contributes to the clarification of the market accessibility requirement, and as such a requirement can be incorporated into projects with no higher costs, both in terms of time and cost and effort.

Some limitations of this work include the non-generalization of the research context to other countries, as well as the non-coverage, especially in the second study, of guidelines other than WCAG.

Works currently carried out include a systematic review to evaluate similar accessibility initiatives in other countries. Initial research pointed out initiatives in Europe, such as Directive (EU) 2016/2102 of the European Parliament and of the Council of 26 October 2016 about accessibility of the websites and mobile applications of public sector bodies[8]. Similarly, European countries have had difficulty in applying the guidelines effectively, but we need to carry out a larger study, including about the other American countries.

Future works includes evaluating the impacts of adopting accessibility features in medium- and large-sized enterprises, as well as disseminating this material so that developers become aware of the importance of producing accessible technology and who can acquire a greater knowledge of the tools and techniques accessibility on the web and mobile.

References

1. Baranauskas, C.C., Souza, S., Pereira, R.: GranDIHC-BR: prospecção de grandes desafios de pesquisa em Interação Humano-Computador no Brasil. In: Companion Proceedings of the 11th Brazilian Symposium on Human Factors in Computing Systems (IHC 2012), pp. 63–64. Brazilian Computer Society, Porto Alegre, Brazil (2012)
2. Baranauskas, M.C.C., Souza, C.S.: Desafio no 4: Acesso Participativo e Universal do Cidadão Brasileiro ao Conhecimento. Computação Brasil, Ano VII, No. 23, p. 7 (2006)
3. BRASIL. Comitê Gestor da Internet. Dimensões e Características da Web brasileira: um estudo do.gov.br (2011). http://cetic.br/media/docs/publicacoes/4/cgibr-nicbr-w3c-censoweb-govbr-2011.pdf. Accessed 29 Mar 2019

---

[8] https://eur-lex.europa.eu/legal-content/EN/TXT/?uri=uriserv:OJ.L_.2016.327.01.0001.01.ENG.

4. BRASIL. Decreto 5.296/2004. Disponível em (2004). http://www.planalto.gov.br/ccivil_03/_ato2004-2006/2004/decreto/d5296.htm. Accessed 29 Mar 2019
5. BRASIL. Lei 13.146/2105 (Estatuto da Pessoa com Deficiência) (2015). http://www.planalto.gov.br/ccivil_03/_ato2015-2018/2015/lei/l13146.htm. Accessed 29 Mar 2019
6. Britto, T.C.P., Pizzolato, E.B.: Gaia: uma proposta de um guia de recomendações de acessibilidade de interfaces web com foco em aspectos do autismo. V Congresso Brasileiro de Informática na Educação (CBIE 2016) (2016)
7. Carter, J., Markel, M.: Web Accessibility for People With Disabilities: An Introduction for Web Developers. Marketron, Inc., EUA; Boise State University, Boise, EUA (2001). https://onlinelibrary.wiley.com/doi/10.1002/9781119134633.ch76. Accessed 29 Mar 2019 (2001)
8. Consortium. World Wide Web. Mobile Accessibility: How WCAG 2.0 and Other W3C/WAI Guidelines Apply to Mobile (2015). https://www.w3.org/TR/mobile-accessibility-mapping/. Accessed 29 Mar 2019
9. Dias, C.: Usabilidade na Web: criando portais mais acessíveis. Alta Books, Rio de Janeiro (2007)
10. Ferreira, S.B.L., et al.: Accessibility and Digital Inclusion: Utopia or a Great Challenge?. In: Proceedings of the XVI Brazilian Symposium on Human Factors in Computing Systems (IHC 2017), p. 6. ACM, New York, NY, USA (2017). Article 68. https://doi.org/10.1145/3160504.3160563
11. IBGE, Instituto Brasileiro de Geografia e Estatística. Censo Demográfico 2010: População residente por tipo de deficiência permanente. https://www.ibge.gov.br/estatisticas-novoportal/sociais/educacao/9662-censo-demografico-2010.html?edicao=9749&t=destaques. Accessed 29 Mar 2019
12. IBGE, Instituto Brasileiro de Geografia e Estatística. Censo Demográfico 2010: Características gerais da população, religião e pessoas com deficiência. Disponível em. https://ww2.ibge.gov.br/home/estatistica/populacao/censo2010/caracteristicas_religiao_deficiencia/caracteristicas_religiao_deficiencia_tab_xls.shtm. Accessed 29 Mar 2019
13. INTERNATIONAL ORGANIZATION FOR STANDARDIZATION. ISO/IEC 40500:2012 (W3C) (2018). https://www.iso.org/standard/58625.html. Acesso em: 20 mai. 2018
14. Kitchenham, B.: Procedures for Performing Systematic Reviews. Software Engineering Group, Keele University, Australia (2004). http://www.ifs.tuwien.ac.at/~weippl/systemicReviewsSoftwareEngineering.pdf. Accessed 29 Mar 2019
15. Lazar, J., Dudley-Sponaugle, A., Greenidge, K.D.: Improving web accessibility: a study of webmaster perceptions. Department of Computer and Information Sciences and Center for Applied Information Technology, Towson University, EUA (2004). https://www.sciencedirect.com/science/article/pii/S0747563203000906. Accessed 29 Mar 2019
16. Leitner, M.L; Strauss, C., Stummer, C.: Web accessibility implementation in private sector organizations: motivations and business impact. University of Vienna, Áustria; Bielefeld University, Alemanha (2016). https://link.springer.com/article/10.1007/s10209-014-0380-1. Accessed 29 Mar 2019
17. Maciel, M.R.C.: Portadores de deficiência: a questão da inclusão social. São Paulo Perspec., São Paulo, vol. 14, no. 2, pp. 51–56, Jun 2000. http://www.scielo.br/scielo.php?script=sci_arttext&pid=S0102-88392000000200008&lng=en&nrm=isso. Accessed 29 Mar 2019
18. Miñón, R; Moreno, L; Martínez, P; Abascal, J. An approach to the integration of accessibility requirements into a user interface development method. University of the Basque Country, Espanha; Universidad Carlos III de Madrid, Espanha (2014). https://www.sciencedirect.com/science/article/pii/S0167642313001032. Accessed 29 Mar 2019
19. Neris, V.P.A, Rodrigues, K.R.H., Silva, J.B:. Futuro, Cidades Inteligentes e Sustentabilidade. In: I GranDIHC-BR - Relatório Técnico. CEIHC-SBC (2014)
20. Nielsen, J.: Projetando Websites: Designing Web Usability. Campus, Rio de Janeiro (2000)

21. Oliveira, R.R., Neris, V.P.A., Galindo Júnior, N.A.: Perceptions of sustainability aspects in computing. In: Proceedings of the 15th Brazilian Symposium on Human Factors in Computing Systems (IHC 2016), p. 4. ACM, New York, NY, USA (2016). Article 55
22. Pressman, R.S., Maxim, B.R.: Engenharia de software: uma abordagem profissional, 8th edn. AMGH, Porto Alegre (2016)
23. Santos, L.P., Pequeno, R.: Novas tecnologias e pessoas com deficiências: a informática na construção da sociedade inclusiva? In. Sousa, R.P., Moita, F.M.C.S.C., Carvalho, A.B.G., orgs. Tecnologias digitais na educação [online]. Campina Grande: EDUEPB, 2011. 276 p. (2011). http://books.scielo.org/id/6pdyn/pdf/sousa-9788578791247-04.pdf. Accessed 29 Mar 2019
24. SBC Grandes Desafios da Pesquisa em Computação no Brasil – 2006–2016. Relatório sobre o Seminário realizado em 8 e 9 de maio de 2006 (2006). http://www.sbc.org.br/index.php?option=com_jdownloads&Itemid=195&task=view.download&catid=50&cid=11Ú&task=view.download&catid=50&cid=11Ú&catid=50&cid=11Ú&cid=11. Accessed 29 Mar 2019
25. Torres, E.F., Mazzoni, A.A, Alves, J. B. da M. A acessibilidade à informação no espaço digital. Ci. Inf., Brasília, vol. 31, no. 3, pp. 83–91, set. 2002 (2002). http://www.scielo.br/scielo.php?script=sci_arttext&pid=S0100-19652002000300009&lng=pt&nrm=iso. Accessed 29 Mar 2019
26. Velleman, E.M., Nahuis, I., Geest, T.V.D.: Factors explaining adoption and implementation processes for web accessibility standards within eGovernment systems and organizations. Accessibility Foundation, Holanda, University of Twente, Holanda (2017). https://link.springer.com/article/10.1007/s10209-015-0449-5. Accessed 29 Mar 2019
27. W3C BRASIL. Cartilha acessibilidade na Web [livro eletrônico]: fascículo 2: benefícios, legislação e diretrizes da acessibilidade na Web. – São Paulo: Comitê Gestor da Internet no Brasil, 2015 (2015). http://www.w3c.br/pub/Materiais/PublicacoesW3C/cartilha-w3cbr-acessibilidade-web-fasciculo-II.pdf. Accessed 29 Mar 2019
28. WAI-ARIA (2018). https://www.w3.org/WAI/intro/aria.php. Accessed 29 Mar 2019
29. Silva, B., Rodrigues, K.: Accessibility challenges in web systems implementation (in Portuguese). In: Proceedings of Workshop on Aspects of Human-Computer Interaction on the Social Web (WAIHCWS) (2018). http://portaldeconteudo.sbc.org.br/index.php/waihcws/issue/view/253. Accessed 29 Mar 2019
30. Granollers, T., Lorés, J.: Usability effort: a new concept to measure the usability of an interactive system based on UCD. In: Navarro-Prieto, R., Vidal, J. (eds.) HCI related papers of Interacción 2004. Springer, Dordrecht (2006). https://doi.org/10.1007/1-4020-4205-1_9

Author Index

Printed in the United States
By Bookmasters